Tip of t]

Tip of the Blade: Notes on Rowing

Marlene Royle

2008

Tip of the Blade: Notes on Rowing

TABLE OF CONTENTS

ACKNOWLEDGMENTS

I would like to express gratitude to Sasha Sokolov, Rebekah Royle, Gordon Hamilton, Holly Hatton, Gennady Sapozhnikov, Tom Boyer, the Florida Rowing Center, Craftsbury Sculling Center, Concept2, Van Dusen Racing Boats, Row2k.com, Tiberias Rowing Club, FISA, USRowing Association, Masters Rowing Association, Row As One, Boston Rowing Club, Boston University Crew, the West Side Rowing Club of Buffalo, my colleagues, and my students for their support.

With permission, many of the articles included in this collection have appeared in *Rowing News,* originally under the rubric of *Tip of the Blade* later, *Get Better.* Thank you to my editors and the staff of *Rowing News*: Chip Davis, Chris Milliman, Ed Winchester, Richard Branch, Chris Pratt, and Kathleen Oscadal for their professional guidance.

This book is to my native Niagara
I began on its waters
From the day I stepped into a shell
I knew that rowing was beautiful
Rowing became my culture and my home
A new dimension to live life in
My rowing notes started thirty years ago
After the first lesson.

CHAPTER 1

BASIC STUFF

*FLEXIBILITY. BREATHING. POSTURE. SKILLS.
TRAINING.*

FIRST STEPS TOWARDS OARSMANSHIP

Making the decision to row is the first step. Signing up for a program the next. Once you have joined a class for beginners you become part of a sport that is not only excellent for your physical fitness but is a rich culture of friendship, good sportsmanship, and fine tradition. Your coaches will be those who want to pass their enthusiasm on to you by teaching you the basics of oarhandling and moving a boat. The skill of a good oarsman takes years to develop but you can start to build up your proficiency right from your first day by practicing habits that will help you learn how to learn and be a valuable member of a crew. Here are some important points for newcomers.

Be at practice on time rested up and ready to go. Most adults and students have busy schedules so starting practice exactly when it is scheduled ensures that you get the full time designated for your training. If one person is late it holds up the entire crew and a 90-minute session can rapidly deteriorate into just an hour-long session; then no one gets as much coaching as they might have.

Give yourself time to warm up before exercising. Many learn-to-row programs operate on tight timetables. One crew may be coming into the dock to quickly exchange seats with the next group. This means you should arrive early enough to do a warm-up on land. Spend about 15 minutes doing light aerobic activity such as jogging, spinning on a stationary bike, or rowing on the erg. If you don't have any equipment or a place to run then do some basic sit ups, squats, or jumping jacks to get your blood flowing. Then a few minutes stretching before you go to your boat.

Dress appropriately for the day. Listen to the weather report to know if you are expecting rain, high winds, hot temperatures, or a cold front. It is quite possible to start your row in one type of situation and have dramatically different conditions by the end of it. I can recall a spring outing of seat racing on the Charles River that started out as a seemingly nice day then suddenly turned into a snow squall within an hour. The risks of hypothermia are high in such a situation unless you have adequate clothing. If you suspect the weather will get cooler make sure to have a long sleeve shirt or wind shirt with you in the boat so you do not catch cold especially in the spring and fall. Wear tights instead of shorts if the temperatures are bordering on cool. Have a hat. Always have more clothes than you think you will need. Play it on the safe side.

Be well fueled and hydrated for a training session. Make sure to have eaten a snack at least an hour before training. It need not be a lot of calories but you should not train on an empty stomach. If you row early in the morning, a bagel with peanut butter, a banana, and a sports drink or a quick bowl of oatmeal may be enough. It is important to drink fluids right after waking up after a night's sleep. If you tend to row in the evening have a bigger lunch then a quick snack before your row. Stay well hydrated all day long, that means drinking water regularly. As a habit, take a bottle of water or sports drink with you in the boat. If it is a hot day take an extra bottle with you. It is better to have too much water than not enough. Dehydration quickly leads to decreased performance capacity.

Pack your duffle bag with the kitchen sink. Designate a bag that you always take to practice with you. Keep in it: clean rowing clothes, a dry change of clothes, extra socks, a towel, a sweatshirt, tights, a wind jacket, water bottles, a hat, sunglasses, sunscreen, shower supplies, emergency snacks like chocolate or dried fruit, your butt pad, athletic tape, a lock for your locker, and any other items you regularly use.

Listen to your coach and coxswain. For a practice to run efficiency athletes need to pay attention to commands. If you are socializing you might miss important details. Know what your coach is instructing and the plan for the row. Know what you are supposed to be working on. Cooperate with and follow the directions of your coxswain at all times. The coxswain is the sole voice to get the boat off the dock in a timely fashion, communicate the workout to the crew, safely maneuver the shell, and return the crew to the dock.

Avoid talking in the boat. There is the voice of the coxswain and of the coach. All other conversation should be suspended during the row unless there is a critical situation. Chatter in the boat disrupts the concentration of the crew and others may not be able to hear what the coxswain or coach are saying. If there is something you do not understand ask the coxswain or discuss it with your coach on land. Enjoy yourself but do your socializing on land once the boat is stored away.

Focus on mastering the basics of the stroke. Learn to set the boat up, progressively row full strokes with proper bladework, and be receptive to the feedback of the coach. Understand that each seat in a boat has a particular purpose. Every seat is equally important to the overall functioning of the crew. Refrain from getting caught up with who is stroking or who is in the bow-seat; let the coach decide. As a novice, your skills will progress faster if you focus on what you need to do to improve your individual stroke. Steer clear of pointing fingers at other rowers; take responsibility for your own actions in the boat. If you have questions or issues speak with your coach individually.

Lastly, avoid calling your oars 'paddles' or spelling sculling with a 'k'. Do respect your crew, be helpful, and enjoy your time on the water.

LEARN TO ROW, LEARN TO STRETCH

Rowing has a high degree of sport-specific flexibility. As a novice rower, developing good technique, while increasing the length of your stroke, requires that you have enough flexibility in your legs, hips, and back to accommodate the positions required for rowing. Power, length, and rate are three factors that determine the speed of the boat. When fatigue sets in stroke length typically deteriorates first. Preparing for a stroke, your head is up to maintain posture, the chest comes against the thighs keeping the lower back firm, and your shins are vertical to create a strong position for the quads to work. The ability to set and maintain your body angle on the recovery, achieve full compression of the lower body at the entry, and hold the posture of your trunk throughout the stroke cycle means good hamstring and ankle flexibility are a must. Improving the ability of these muscle groups to lengthen as you compress helps you steady your body preparation, keeping the connection to the blade as you apply your legs. Lack of muscle length in the calf, hamstrings, quadriceps, or lower back is a limiting factor to your progress.

Stretching aids muscle elasticity, relief of soreness, range of motion, blood circulation, and injury prevention. Include stretching exercises in your warm-up as your body gets physiologically prepared to row. Stretching exercises should follow light aerobic activity such as a slow jog or light row on the erg. The intensity should be mild to moderate for five to ten minutes to increase the body's metabolic rate by increasing blood flow to the working muscles and raising the muscle's temperature prior to stretching. Increased body temperature allows nerve impulses to travel faster maximizing coordination. Stretching during the warm-down period is often neglected. It should be a component of your warm-down to accelerate the return of blood to the heart and lungs. The warm-down helps reduce the build up of waste products in the muscles and assists in waste removal by providing adequate blood flow away from the working muscles. Flexibility exercises aid in preventing muscle soreness and averts muscle fiber shortening. Additional flexibility is gained by stretching during the warm-down because you can concentrate on the muscles predominantly used in rowing. During the warm-down they can be elongated more intensively and specifically.

Passive stretching is characterized as low force, long duration exercises which produces good results with little muscle soreness. Passive stretching produces less tension and less resistance. When performed correctly, passive stretching increases range of motion and is a safe procedure. It involves a slow, gradual movement through the range of motion followed by holding a static position, placing the muscles at their greatest possible length for a period of time before relaxing. A passive stretching position is normally held for 10 to 30 seconds and is repeated three to four times for maximum effect. A normal breathing rate should be maintained during the stretch phase. When attention is paid to relaxation the muscles benefit more.

Here are five main stretches to include in your routine each time you row. They can be part of the warm-up and the warm-down. The *feet together groin stretch* develops flexibility in the groin, specifically the adductors. While sitting, slowly flex the knees bringing the feet towards the trunk. Keep the back straight while putting the soles of the feet together. Grasp the ankles and gently pull the heels towards the groin. Slowly let your knees fall towards the floor until a comfortable stretch is felt in the groin. The *hamstring hurdler stretch* develops general flexibility in the posterior trunk, hip, thigh, and calf. Specifically in the hamstrings, gluteals, erector spinae, quadratus lumborum, gastrocnemius, soleus, and tibialis posterior. Sit with one leg completely extended and the other tucked into the groin. Lean forward towards the extended leg by flexing at the hips reach towards the ankle of the extended leg. A comfortable stretch should be felt in the hamstrings. Caution, people with existing lower back injuries should be careful when performing this stretch. The *prone quadriceps stretch* improves general flexibility in the anterior hip and thigh, as well as, the shin by focusing on the quadriceps, iliopsoas, and tibialis anterior muscles. Lie facedown and bend at the knee. Reach back with the same side arm and grasp the ankle. Pull the ankle towards the buttocks until a gentle stretch is felt in the thigh. If you have existing knee injuries do not perform this stretch.

For flexibility in the anterior trunk to open your chest up, the *standing arm, shoulder, and chest stretch* targets the anterior deltoid, long head of the biceps brachii, corocobrachialis, and pectoral muscles. Interlace the fingers behind the back with the palms facing up. Slowly turn the elbows inward while straightening the arms, and then raise the arms behind the back until a gentle stretch is felt in the arm, shoulder, and chest. The *kneeling chest and lower back stretch* facilitates increased mobility in the back, posterior shoulder and arm by specifically addressing the latissimus dorsi, erector spinae, pectorals, and triceps muscles. Start on all fours with palms on the floor. Keeping the hips over the knees, slowly lower the chest towards the floor until a gentle stretch is felt in the shoulder, middle back, and lower back.

Additional effective exercises that can be added to your pre- or post-row program include the *supine hip flexor stretch*, the *seated hamstring and calf stretch* using a towel, the *cat stretch*, *spinal rotation with hands on hips*, and a *supine general stretch*. The *supine hip flexor stretch* improves mobility in the anterior hip and abdominals by targeting the iliopsoas, quadriceps, and rectus abdominus muscles. Lie facing up with knees flexed and the soles of the feet on the floor, shoulder width apart. Tighten the abdominal and buttock muscles to raise the lower back and hips off the floor. Raise the back as high as is comfortable while keeping the shoulders in contact. Avoid arching the lower back when performing this exercise.

The purpose of the *seated hamstring and calf stretch using a towel* is general flexibility in the posterior thigh and calf muscles. The hamstrings, gluteus maximas, erector spine, quadratus lumborum, gastrocnemius, soleus, and tibialis posterior are stretched. Sit with the legs extended in front. Grasp the ends of a towel in both hands. Bend the trunk forward by flexing at the hips, while wrapping the towel around the bottom of the feet. Pull the upper body closer to the legs by pulling the towel. A comfortable stretch should be felt in the buttock and hamstring areas. The *cat stretch* is for the lower back especially the erector spinae, rhomboids, and middle trapezius. Kneel on all fours with a flat back, the tops of the feet on the floor. Keep the shoulders and hips directly above the hands and knees respectively. Round the back while tightening the abdominal muscles then relax and return to the start position. *Spinal rotation with hands on hips* works the back and lower abdominals through the latissimus dorsi, rhomboids, and oblique abdominals. Stand with your hands on hips, slowly rotate your upper body in one direction as far as comfortable while keeping both feet flat on the ground.

A great way to conclude your routine is with the *supine general stretch* for flexibility in the front of your body including the serratus anterior, pectorals, latissimus dorsi, teres major, triceps, wrist flexors, finger flexors, rectus abdominus, iliopsoas, tibialis anterior, and toe extensors. Lie face up with both legs extended. Extend both arms directly over your head and interlace your fingers with your palms facing out. Point your toes down and gently elongate your body from tips to toes. A good stretching routine is based on frequency and consistency. On a daily basis, attention to stretching need not take more time than drinking a good cup of coffee does.

FLEXIBILITY: ACTIVE-ISOLATED STRETCHING: PART ONE

Power, length, and rate are three factors that determine the speed of the boat. Every crew and sculler needs to find the right technical balance to link how fast the boat travels, how far the boat runs, with the number of strokes rowed per minute to perform their best. Stroke length is often the first component to deteriorate in a racing situation due to shortening of the slide and missed entry timing. Preparing for a stroke, your head is up to maintain posture, the chest comes against the thighs keeping the lower back firm, and your shins are vertical to create a strong position for the quads to work. Achieving this poised position means good hamstring and ankle flexibility are a must. Improving the ability of these muscles to lengthen as you compress helps you hold your body preparation, keeping the connection to the blade as you apply your legs first. This is critical especially in races at higher stroke rates.

Indifference to stretching is rare. You love it, hate it, or know you should do it, but don't. Flexibility work gets pushed aside in a training program when time is tight. Every season I hear masters say, "Stretching is so uncomfortable, I avoid it," and juniors groan lazily, "Do we have to do it?" Inflexibility in our posterior muscles is a major limiting factor in technique. Reasons for lack of flexibility include: muscle imbalance, injury, overuse, aging, or periods of rapid growth. Today's lifestyle exacerbates the situation because sitting at a computer or driving long hours keeps these muscles shortened for extended periods. The rowing motion then demands them to be lengthened repeatedly every practice. Last summer, I was amazed to see such a high percentage of high school rowers already unable to touch their toes. Finding flexibility exercises for people who shy from stretching is one solution to the problem.

Active-Isolated Stretching employs the contracting muscles opposite to the muscles that are to be lengthened as the movement force. I have found this method, popularized by Sarasota-based kinesiotherapist, Aaron Mattes, to be excellent for targeting the posterior muscles we need for developing stroke length. They are very comfortable to do and not time consuming. In order to fully appreciate this system of exercise, we need to understand a bit about the mechanism of stretch.

The stretch reflex is a regulatory mechanism that assists the body to maintain muscle tone, posture, and protect muscle from overstretching. In his book, *Flexibility: Active and Assisted Stretching*, Mattes explains, "When someone does not posses adequate flexibility for a required movement, the stretch reflex contraction exerts force against the desired movement, thus requiring more energy to overcome the stretch reflex force and increasing the possibility of injury." There are two components of the stretch reflex that you need to know about: the muscle spindle and the Golgi tendon organ.

When muscle is stretched, the muscle spindle signals to contract, preventing overextension. If a stretch is hard, the contraction is proportionately strong and injury potential increases. The spindle is also responsible for the reciprocal innervation of the agonist and antagonist muscle groups that provide for smooth movement. Put simply, this means when one muscle works, the opposite muscle relaxes. For example, as the biceps contracts, the triceps relax to allow the biceps to flex the elbow joint. Without reciprocal innervation our movements would be jerky or cogwheel-like; Compression into the entry would certainly be very difficult.

The Golgi tendon organ is located where the muscle fibers and the tendons join. They are sensitive to changes in muscle length but cannot differentiate between muscle contraction and muscle stretch. They react to any tension in the muscle. When they discharge, they cause the working muscle to be inhibited so that it may not overstretch the opposite muscle. There is a window of time, approximately two seconds, when a muscle can be stretched before the Golgi tendon organs kick in to interrupt the increased tension. Active-Isolated Stretching utilizes this two-second window to perform, and then release, the motion without activating the stretch reflex. In part two, I will review specific exercises that you can easily incorporate into your routine to improve your flexibility and lower body compression into the entry.

EXERCISES TO IMPROVE FLEXIBILITY: ACTIVE-ISOLATED STRETCHING: PART TWO

Do you put your oars in the rack and dash out of the boathouse? No extra time? Don't like stretching? Or both? In my last article, I introduced Active-Isolated Stretching (AIS) to you promising a solution for painful stretching. Effective and comfortable, AIS improves your flexibility while targeting specific muscles. Based on preventing a muscle's internal stretch reflex from triggering during stretching, you first relax the muscle to be lengthened, by contracting the muscle opposite to it, and then you move through the controlled motion with no more than two seconds at the end range. By holding the position breifly, the stretch reflex does not have time to kick in and restrict the muscle. If the reflex activates when you are stretching, it will interfere with the lengthening of your muscle because it wants to protect your muscle from overstretching and tearing. Should an inner tug of war start during your flexibility exercises it negates exactly what you are trying to accomplish-more muscle length to improve leg compression on the slide.

This way of working on your flexibility is very relaxing. The exercises are best performed right after rowing or lifting when your muscles are still warm. If that is not possible, you may include them in your warm-up, do them at home, or even during your lifting session. The first exercises aim at improving hip flexibility so they address both the lower back and the hamstrings. Several muscles that flex and extend the hip are also part of the low back and knee. Restrictions in two-joint muscles such as the hip flexors or hamstrings limit the hip, pelvic girdle, and low back motions. This is a red-hot area for rowers. Put particular emphasis on these stretches in your workouts.

The *hamstring stretch-supine* is done lying down on your back. You will need a boat strap or piece of rope long enough to stirrup around your foot. Hold one rope end in your left hand and the other in your right. Using the contraction of your quadriceps (thigh) muscles will assist the stretching of your hamstrings. Your non-exercising leg should remain flat on the floor. If you have severe low back considerations, then you may flex your non-exercising leg slightly. Keep the exercising leg straight at all times. Lift your leg straight up off the floor by contracting your thigh muscles. Continue as high as you can without bending at the knee. Give brief, gentle overpressure with the rope at the end of the movement as the quadriceps muscles move your leg. Release and return your leg back down to the floor. Repeat a set of 10 repetitions twice on your right leg, then on your left leg. If you notice one leg is tighter than the other-common among sweep rowers-do an extra set of 10 repetitions for that leg until you feel balanced. In the event you don't have a rope you can use your hands behind your knee to apply overpressure. Be careful not to allow your knee to bend.

An advanced exercise for the hamstrings is the *hamstring stretch sitting-straight legs*. This is for rowers who are already quite flexible. The hamstrings are lengthened using the quadriceps muscles to lock the knees during the exercise. Start from a sitting position, draw you chin to your chest, exhale, and tighten your abdominals firmly as you lean forward. The knees are not allowed to bend. Use your hands near your ankles to give a light assistance at the end of the motion. Return to sitting and repeat 10 times. It is best to do this stretch after the *supine hamstring stretch* above.

In the gym or resting between pieces on the erg, you can use the *hamstring stretch-standing* if you feel the need to stretch the hamstrings and back during your workout. From standing, contract the abdominal muscles so the back muscles can be stretched without tension. Contract the front thigh muscles. Lean forward as for as you can as if you were bringing your nose to your knees. Use your hands around your calves for gentle assistance at the end of the movement. Then slowly return to standing. Repeat 10 times. Do not bounce; simply move into the end range of the motion and then out of it in a controlled way.

The final exercise is for your calf muscle to improve ankle flexibility. The purpose of the *gastrocnemius (calf) stretch* is to lengthen the two-joint gastrocnemius muscle improving your Achilles tendon extensibility. Adequate Achilles tendon length is important for the final one-quarter of the recovery as you approach the shins-vertical position and in the weight room for squats or leg presses. Sit on the floor with your legs flat. With your exercising leg, keep your knee locked using your thigh muscles. Using the shin muscles, pull your toes towards you. Using a strap or rope, as in our first exercise, apply gentle overpressure at the end of the motion. Make sure the shin muscles continue to be contracted when you apply assistance. Hold briefly then relax your foot letting your toes point away from you. Do two or three sets of 10 repetitions, first the left, then the right. Spend more time on one ankle if you feel an imbalance.

You will soon notice improvements in your flexibility when you begin to use these AIS exercises. To measure your gains or losses objectively you can do an easy test. Put a milk crate against the wall. Sit on the floor. Place your feet flat against the side of the crate. Lean forward as in the *hamstring stretch sitting-straight leg* and measure the distance between your fingertips and the edge of the crate. The edge is your reference of zero inches; if you cannot reach the edge you have a minus value. The distance you reach beyond the edge has a plus value. Values greater than five inches are good; more than 10 inches represents excellent low back and hamstring flexibility.

Good rowing technique requires adequate mobility for biomechanical reasons. Restrictions in the hips and ankles necessitate modifications be made through your rigging to achieve the right angle of entry. In extreme cases this can be quite difficult. Making your muscles more elastic will reduce the need for compensation through your equipment, reduce your risk of injury, and help you acquire better stroke length through the water.

MINDFUL BREATHING

At the 2006 World Rowing Championships in Eton, Ekaterina Karsten, two-time Olympic gold medalist in the women's single, rowed to her fourth title in the same event. Karsten's model sculling technique, combined with her excellent physical preparation, enabled her to dominant the field. One noticeable feature is her pronounced breathing pattern that is synchronized within each stroke cycle. Several sports, such as weight lifting or swimming, connect the breathing rhythm to the specific movement. In rowing, the correct breathing rhythm can particularly influence performance because the thorax muscles are also part of the muscle system involved in the motion and are an influencing factor of breathing.

Simply defined breathing is making sure that your body gets the oxygen it needs when it needs it. External and internal breathing subsystems are involved in the intake, transport, and processing of oxygen: the air you breathe in, the exchange of gases in your lungs, the binding of the oxygen to the erythrocytes (red blood cells), the transport of oxygen in the blood, followed by the delivery and use of the oxygen in the muscle tissues. In *Periodization: Theory and Methodology of Training,* Bompa writes, "Breathing plays an important role in endurance training. The athlete must perform it deeply and rhythmically, because active exhalation is critical for an adequate performance. Most athletes have to learn how to exhale to evacuate as much air as possible from the lungs, because the oxygen has already been extracted. Without proper exhalation, the concentration of oxygen in the freshly breathed in air will be diluted, which will adversely affect performance. A forceful exhalation is even more important during the critical phase of a race or game, when an adequate supply of oxygen can enable athletes to overcome the difficulty." *Rowing Rudern,* gives considerable attention to breathing in *Chapter Five, The Technique of Sculling and Sweep Oar Rowing,* "Technique in racing is contrary to the conditions required for deep breathing. If one is to breathe in freely, the upper body must be straight and the diaphragm unhindered. The oarsman, like the weight lifter, can only perform hard work with his breath held (under pressure). This work is done during the propulsion phase. He is obliged to breathe in fully in the period shortly before and during entry. These are unfavorable conditions, since the diaphragm is constricted in the lean-forward position and, in sweep rowing at least, the chest is also restricted by the position of the arms."

The importance of becoming very aware and accustomed to a short but very deep inhalation is stressed to make sure that the high demand for oxygen is met. Breathing out coincides with the timing of the blade being released. Through her entire race when Karsten exhales, her billowing cheeks are very evident when she completes every drive. *Rudern* continues, "Generally, this first expulsion of air is not sufficient, and a second exhalation occurs during the final third of the slide forward. This constitutes the commencement of inhalation... this breathing technique is practiced on the course at a steady state of the regatta tempo with slight variations."

I recently corresponded with a master sculler from California who wrote to me, "I have always complained about running out of air long before muscles begin to start burning. I have complained to coaches before, but Gordon Hamilton was the one who finally identified the problem as carbon dioxide build up. He explained that the body has no natural response to purging carbon dioxide, so it has to be done. Forcing all the air out of my lungs before inhaling during a hard sprint has given me greater endurance. The difference is immediate and noticeable. But you have to remember to do it, just like every other good technique." Then I contacted Hamilton who recommended reading the book, *"The Science of Breath- A Practical Guide"by Swami Rama, Rudolph Ballentine M.D., Alan Hymes.* Hamilton's work-in-progress *Notes on the Technique of Rowing: Sweep Rowing Compared with Sculling*, addresses the value of breathing and of rhythm in the stroke cycle. He writes, "While it seems almost ludicrous to even mention that breathing is extremely important for the supply of oxygen to your muscles and for the removal of carbon dioxide from the lungs, it is an element of the stroke cycle that is often overlooked. It is also very important for establishing and sustaining your rhythm. The basic pattern should be to inhale at the entry, hold your breath during the drive, and exhale at the release. However, I prefer a secondary exhale just before the inhale at the entry. This is accomplished by relaxing the belly just after rotating the pelvis as you begin the recovery body angle. At this point, you can take a small inhale and then a strong exhale is possible just before inhaling at the entry. This secondary exhale is, I believe, important because while your muscles make their need for oxygen more than apparent and your body naturally responds to this need, there is no internal mechanism which tells you to get rid of the resulting increased build-up of carbon dioxide in your lungs. This build-up can cause the sensation of being short of breath because there becomes less and less room in your lungs for fresh oxygen. Furthermore, the exchange of oxygen into the bloodstream is much more efficient in the lower regions of the lungs. You should take special care to get rid of as much carbon dioxide as possible; therefore I prefer the double exhale. I think that this should become your pattern no matter how hard you are rowing, even at steady state, when the demands are not so great that a second exhale is, perhaps, necessary. You want to establish a pattern that will meet all needs of a race and practice so that you are not forced to make a change in your pattern nor have to think about it."

Achieving a sense of flow in the boat is a feeling that we continually pursue in practice and in racing. We know we have it when we have the sense that time is stretched, that there is length in every stroke no matter the rating, the power is effortless, and there is ease in your motions. Most of us can name exactly when we have experienced this. The correct breathing pattern helps you center yourself in the boat and establish a consistent cycle. Regarding rhythm Hamilton concludes, "Many coaches talk of the importance of ratio during the recovery. What they are really after is this sense of flow. If a boat is moving with this sense of flow, the perception is that the recovery is taking twice or even three times the time of the drive, while the reality is that when racing at full speed the ratio is much closer to one to one. It is the sense of this flow that gives us this feeling. I believe that it begins by this effortless change of the direction of the oarhandle, which, as mentioned, is caused by releasing at the correct time, and bracing the trunk, and legs while you gently swing the handles away and then resting once you have achieved your body angle. The sense of ease continues with the sense that the seat is traveling at the same speed as the boat, that the next stroke is coming to you, creating this sense of stillness and as you flow toward the entry. It continues as the recovery seamlessly blends into the entry and then drive, which through attention to the point when the arms join the legs and back continues to be smooth. All this is held together by consistent pressure against the pin and contact with the shell from the feet and seat and by a rhythmic breathing pattern."

CORRECT POSTURE

Sound upright posture or to use the Fairbairnism, "freely erect" posture, is important for the proper application of body weight. Vertical orientation of posture allows the core trunk muscles to support the body weight through the release allowing the oarhandles to rebound lively through the turn. Keeping the head up with the chin held level, eyes focused above the horizon, and the rib cage lifted provide the stability the body needs to apply its weight on the oarhandles and into the riggers. Posture is of particular importance at the entry and release, transition points of the stroke, when the weight changes direction. Collapsing of posture at either of these points drives the boat down into the water and causes the collars to separate from the oarlocks. This vertical motion of the hull creates wakes slowing the boat, disrupting the run.

Posture can be practiced out of the boat throughout the day and be transferred into the boat during training sessions. Stand and sit tall; correcting slumping or forward-head posture while working on your computer or driving your car will improve your posture in the boat. Specific strengthening exercises can also be done using weights, calisthenics, or a therapy ball to develop strength in weak postural muscles.

THE STRAIGHT TRUTH ON POSTURE

The image of a slumping swan is not what you plan on when going to see the ballet *Swan Lake*; you expect the tall posture and sense of lightness that are part of the elegance of the dance. Most sports, from martial arts to show jumping horses use posture as an axis to support the limbs and execute correct technique. In sculling or rowing, our core strength and trunk stability serve to connect our leg power to the oarhandle. In a racing situation you need to stay composed when fatigue sets in to stay effective in the boat. Losing trunk control means that power is lost.

Volker Nolte's article, *Biomechanics of Rowing* in *Rowing Canada Aviron, Winter 2002*, describes posture as one of the three key principles of the stroke, "Good posture reduces the probability of losing any force through movable soft parts of the body and prevents injury at the same time. Good posture means a strong and solid body positioning but not stiff." The famous coach and inventor of modern rowing technique, Steve Fairbairn, called it "freely erect" posture-horizontal chain and keeping the head and shoulders moving on one level during the whole stroke are main indications when the rower does it correctly, "If this horizontal movement of the head and shoulders is achieved, the center of gravity of the rower moves minimally in the vertical direction, conserving energy, and maintaining the run of the boat." Nolte continues that rowers with good posture put themselves in a position to transform all their forces onto the handle, maintain a large force over the whole stroke, and produce a high peak force. Although good posture is necessary during the whole stroke, it is most important at the entry and at the release. In these positions, the rowers can gain the necessary length of the stroke arc and stabilize their bodies to avert injuries. The length of the stroke depends on several factors: the size of the athlete, the fitness of the athlete, the boat class, the length of the oar etc. The larger and stronger the athlete, the faster the boat; the shorter the oar, the longer the stroke must be! However, the athlete must always maintain good posture.

What is good posture? When you are standing correctly your ear, shoulder, and hip are in a straight line from a side view. Your head is directly on top of your shoulders without deviating in front of your spine. Your upper back is generally straight and is not slouched. Shoulder blades are lying flat against your back; shoulders are level and relaxed. Your pelvis is in neutral meaning the bony protrusions toward the top of the pelvic bones line up vertically with the pubic bones. The top of your pelvis does not tilt forward or backwards in any extreme way. When you sit in your boat, initially establish your posture by sitting with your ear, shoulder, and hip in a straight line. Make sure you head is centered over your shoulders and not dropping forward. Lift your rib cage and relax your shoulders. Settle your "sit bones" or ischial tuberosities in the holes or depressions of the seat so you feel you are sitting squarely and firm up your abdominal muscles. Although your upper body angle will change during the stroke, aim to feel that you maintain the firmness of your abdominal muscles, keep your rib cage elevated, and head up.

Modern life works against good posture. Driving cars and hours of computer work encourage a forward-head posture that is carried into the boat with you or can lead to nerve compression syndromes in the upper extremities. You can improve your rowing technique on land if you are aware of your posture throughout the day and make a point to do exercises to align your body when you take breaks from your work. In her book, *Posture, Get it Straight*, Janice Novak offers a simple routine to correct imbalances. Her sequence of movements starts with standing with your feet hip-width apart. Knees should be soft and neutral, not locked. Pull in your abdominal muscles like you are pulling your belly button towards your spine. Lift your rib cage and try to elongate your midsection by drawing your rib cage away from your hip bones. Unround your shoulders by rotating your arms until your thumbs are in a hitch hiking position. Press your shoulders down away from your ears. Move your shoulder blades towards your spine. Then relax your arms at your sides. Finally, stretch the top of your head toward the ceiling as if a string were pulling you upward. Hold the position for a few moments, relax into it, and breathe normally. Then walk around the room for a few minutes and repeat the movement series to reset your posture. With practice you will feel more comfortable and be able to find a natural position.

When you are behind the wheel of your car adjust your seat to keep your body aligned while driving. Set your seat close enough to the pedals so your pelvis is in neutral. Be able to rest your back against the seat and still sit up straight. Your seat should not incline more than 10 degrees. Adjust your headrest so you can sit with the back of your head resting on it. This will position your head over your spine and allow your neck muscles to relax. If you work extended hours on a computer make a point to ask your employer to provide a consultant who can position you correctly at your workstation. Taking the time to care for your body position during the day will carry over into your technique in a positive way.

ON LAND: DEVELOPING SITTING BALANCE

Balance in the boat develops as skill, rhythm, and speed improves. Body awareness and kinesthetic sense is important for learning better skill. Land exercises can be used to improve balance over the winter months.

This is an exercise performed using a 28- to 30-inch therapy ball, sometimes referred to as a Swiss Ball. Therapy balls are widely used in a physical therapy setting for core strengthening and balance training. The implications for use in developing rowing skills are very positive. For the following exercise you will need a therapy ball, available at many sporting goods stores or in medical catalogs, and a mirror.

- Keep all movements slow and controlled.
- Focus on keeping abdominal muscles and lower back firm.
- Sit on the ball with both feet placed on the ground, sit up tall as you would in the boat; Eyes looking straight ahead.
- Extend your arms out to the side at shoulder height, during the exercise keep the upper body quiet and shoulders level.
- Raise one foot off the floor and then straighten out your leg, keep balance for a count of 20. Balance with the lower body only. Keep the upper body still. Now try the other leg for a count of 20.
- Once you have mastered steady balance with one leg off the ground, it is time to balance with both legs up parallel to the floor-as you sit in the boat. Again, focus your center of gravity in your abdominal area to balance on the ball.

- • Work up to a count of 20. Repeat three times. Practice three to four times per week.

For sculling, learning good sitting balance is particularly useful for developing a stable platform in a single or double. For sweep rowing, balance exercises on the ball will help novice and experienced rowers learn more precise control over the balance of the hull and body awareness.

ON LAND: SWISS BALL STABILITY EXERCISES

In part one of this article, we addressed balance exercises on the ball to help develop stability and body awareness in the boat. The following exercises are to develop core postural strength in the muscles used in sculling and rowing. Use them as part of your warm-up for a weight session or do a separate 20 to 30 minutes strengthening session three or four times per week. Select four to five exercises to do each session. On another day select different exercises for variation. Swiss balls or physioballs are found in most fitness centers. They can also be purchased at sporting goods stores or can be ordered from medical catalogs. The ball diameter should be sized closest to the length of your armpit to fingertips.

Training Guidelines

- Keep all movements slow and controlled.
- In all exercises focus on maintaining tension in your abdominal muscles.
- In all exercises that call for you to be parallel to the ground, do not let your hips sag towards the floor.
- Work in an uncluttered area free of obstacles.

Stability Exercises

Praying Mantis

Start position: Kneel facing the ball, clasp hands. Lean forward and place bent elbows on the ball.

Movement: Roll ball forward with elbows and then back again keeping abs tight throughout.

Repetitions: 10 to 20

Prone Walk Out

Start position: Press up position, ball beneath thighs.
Movement: Walk arms out with small steps until feet are on the ball.
Repetitions: walk out and back 2 to 5 times.

Leg Raise Prone

Start position: Press up position, ball beneath feet.
Movement: Raise one leg off the ball by contracting your buttocks muscles. Do not allow your upper body to twist.
Repetition: 1 to 5 with leg holding top position 3 to 5 seconds.

Hamstring Curls-Two legs

Start position: Lie with shoulders on the floor, hips off the floor, and calves on the ball so your body is straight.
Movement: Draw the ball in towards your by contracting your hamstrings.
Repetitions: 8 to 30

Hamstring Curls-One leg

Start position: Lie with shoulders on the floor, hips off the floor, and one calf on the ball so that your body is straight and the other leg is outstretched above the ball.
Movement: Draw the ball in towards you by contracting your hamstring.
Repetitions: 6 to 20

Abdominal Crunch

Start position: Press-up position with shins on the ball.

Movement: Slowly draw ball in towards body by flexing abdominals.

Repetitions: 8 to 15

Push ups

Start position: Push up position with hands on ball and feet on the floor.

Movement: Lower your chest to the ball, push up.

Repetitions: Maximum

Back Extensions

Start position: Lying over the ball with ball beneath hips, arms out to side level with head. Legs straight with feet wide apart. Tip toe balance.

Movement: Extend upper back slowly by contracting low back, rising until your body is straight.

Repetitions: 12 to 30

Hip Extensions

Start position: Back against ball hips near floor.

Movement: Push hips to ceiling keeping abs tight.

Repetitions: 20 to 30

Progress to only one foot on the floor. The other leg is outstretched.

Repetitions: 20 to 30

Four-Point Dog

Balance: Both hands and knees on the ball.

Maximum time.

Balance: Go around in a circle and remove one limb at a time.

Hold each three-point position for 10 seconds.

Two-Point Dog

Balance: Extend right leg and left arm, hold for 5 to 10 seconds, then switch left leg and right arm for 5 to10 seconds.

Then try to extend right leg and right arm for 5 to 10 seconds, the switch to left leg and left arm for 5 to 10 seconds.

Extra Balance Exercises

- Seated on a ball with perfect posture and both feet on a second small ball.
- Seated on a ball with perfect posture and one foot on a second small ball and the other leg extended.
- Perform seated drills while passing a ball to a partner or bouncing it off the wall.
- Kneeling upright on the ball, no hands at all.
- Frog on a lily pad: sitting a squat on the ball with both hands and feet on the ball

GETTING STARTED IN THE SINGLE

I clearly remember the first time I fell out of a single more than the first time I rowed in one. It was in a pristine lagoon in Florianopolis, Brazil. I was training in a wide beam boat just for fun that day. In the middle of a five-minute piece, just as I approached the entry, the gate on my port oarlock broke and I was tossed out of the boat instantaneously swimming in water I hoped was not full of too many tropical animals. I had known all along that the day would come when I would fall out of the boat-I sculled for 17 years before paying my initiation rites. I spent half an hour standing on a rock scooping water out of the boat with my water bottle before getting back in, hoping another decade would pass before that happened again. Though I admit it was dramatic.

With few exceptions, most single scullers fall out of their boats during the course of their rowing careers. Collisions, breakage, catching crabs, or losing an oar are all causes. If you are just learning to row a single, tipping out of the shell can be a common event. The record number of times I've seen for one person is 16 flips in one day. Knowing how to get back into your boat from the water is important part of getting started in the single. First, if you tend to scull alone and do not have shores that you can swim to, knowing how to climb back in can be an important safety skill. Second, being able to handle yourself in the event that you do fall in builds confidence. That will help you become more comfortable in your boat so you can relax and learn technique better. Third, if you row in cold water, handling yourself and the boat quickly can prove critical in a dangerous situation.

Here are the steps to practice getting back into your boat from the water. First, hold onto the boat once you are in the water. Never leave your boat and try to swim. The boat and oars will float you. Come up near the rigger. Stay relaxed and catch your breath. Next, make sure that the boat is righted and the seat on track. If you rolled the boat over so it is upside down, press down on the rigger nearest you and begin to roll the boat. Then reach across and pull the other rigger down towards you so the boat will be sitting correctly.

The oar closest to you should be all the way into the oarlock and the blade feathered flat on the water so it can support you. Hold this handle down in the boat with your hand nearest the footstretchers. Next, you need to get the other oarhandle so you can hold both handles in the bottom of the boat. You may need to jump up or reach to get the other handle but you must get both handles together in one hand before you can continue. If the other oarhandle is out of reach, pull the handle that you have control of across the boat and put it through the opposite rigger to stabilize it. Swim around the boat and take the other oarhandle. Then you can get both handles together.

Push your seat towards the stern to give you more room to jump in. Hold both handles in your hand closest to the footstretchers, and with your other hand reach across to the gunnel. You will need to keep pressing down on the handles. Kick and jump into the boat as if you are getting out of a swimming pool onto the deck of the pool. You need to be concentrated on getting the weight of your hips over the boat and into the seat deck. Avoid trying to pull yourself into the boat because you will probably pull the boat over you rather than being able to hop in.

Once your hips are in the boat, you are stomach-down, kick again, turn and sit, letting your legs dangle over the side of the boat still. Do not let go of your oarhandles here. Raise your oarhandles up to right the boat and make sure both blades are completely flat on the water and you are stable. You can then swing your legs in the boat and scoot yourself back on the seat.

Put your feet back in the shoes and then practice it again. Be able to get in from both sides of the both with equal agility.

If you row a wing rigger boat or a boat without back stays this method will work well. If you have trouble getting your hips into the boat you may need to do some upper body strengthening and learn to kick stronger when you jump from the water. For boats with back stays, some scullers carry a terry cloth wrist band on their oars and can use it to hold the handles together in the event that they need to straddle the boat and get back into the seat deck from the bow. Whichever method you choose, assure yourself that you know what to do in case you go in the water. If you do not want to practice in your own boat use a training-type single or a more stable boat to learn how to get back in. When you start learning how to scull in a single, you need to know the basics of maneuvering your shell. Here are exercises to begin getting comfortable in a single:

First, spend time rowing in circles with one blade. Start from the release position, blades flat on the water, boat balanced. Row with one oar only, leaving the other oar feathered on the water for stability. The stabilizing oarhandle should be held against the body. Follow the blade with your eyes to see the effect of your actions through the water. Try placing the blade in the water, letting the handle go free to see the natural depth of the blade, and then placing your hand back on the handle to follow the movement of the oar. Row yourself in a full circle with one oar and then switch and row around in the other direction with the other oar. Use the light power and a loose grasp.

Practice how to stop rapidly. From a moving position, at the release, square the blades and press them into the water for a braking effect. Lean your body against the handles if needed. If you need to turn put more pressure on one side.

Master backing down. Backing is when you move the boat toward the stern. First begin by practicing gliding up and down the slide keeping the blades slightly tilted on the surface of the water. Then practice backing with one hand only, the other rests near your body. Start from the release position, square one blade in the water, letting the blade float; push your hands away from your body. At the end of the stroke, turn the blade feathered with the concave surface facing the water so the tip of the blade skims the water as you bring your hand back to your body. Go all the way around in a full circle with one hand and then switch to the other hand. Then progress to using both together. When you are comfortable with the backing motion you may add in slide length as you push away to make the stroke longer. Work up to backing for 50 consecutive strokes.

Once you are able to back the boat down, you are ready to learn a river turn. You move your hands together but alternate the position of the blades. Using arms-body only, push your hands away from you with the port blade squared and the starboard blade feathered on the water; port backs, starboard is feathered on the water. Then take a stroke with the starboard blade as the port blade is feathered and skims the water; starboard rows, port is feathered. When you have perfected this you can lengthen your slide to take longer strokes. This is a quicker, more efficient way to turn the boat than simply rowing yourself around with one oar, especially if the water is fast or there is strong wind.

HOW TO GET BACK INTO YOUR SHELL AFTER FLIPPING

With few exceptions, most single scullers fall out of their boats during the course of their rowing careers. Collisions, breakage, catching crabs, or losing an oar can all be reasons. If you are just learning to row a single, tipping out of the shell can be a common event. Knowing how to get back into your boat from the water is important. First, if you tend to scull alone, and do not have shores you can swim to; the skill of climbing back in is important for safety. Second, knowing you can handle yourself in the event that you do fall in builds confidence that will help you become more comfortable in your boat so you can relax and learn technique better. Third, if you row in cold water, being able to handle yourself and the boat quickly avoids a dangerous situation. Here are the steps to get back into your boat from the water:

- Hold onto the boat once you are in the water. Never leave your boat and try to swim. The boat and oars will float you. Come up near the rigger.
- Stay relaxed and catch your breath.
- Make sure that the boat is righted with the seat up. If you rolled the boat so it is upside down, press down on the rigger nearest you to begin to roll the boat, then reach across and pull the other rigger down towards you so the boat will be right.
- The oar closest to you should be all the way into the oarlock and the blade flat on the water so it can support you. Hold this handle down in the boat with your hand nearest the footstretchers.
- Next, you need to get the other oarhandle so you can hold both handles in the bottom of the boat. You may need to jump up or reach to get the other handle but

you must get both handles together in one hand before you can continue.

- Push your seat towards the bow.
- Hold both handles in your hand closest to the footstretchers, and with your other hand reach across to the gunnel. You will need to keep pressing on the handles.
- Kick and jump into the boat as if you are getting out of a swimming pool onto the deck of the pool. You need to be focused on getting the weight of your hips over the boat and into the seat deck. Avoid trying to pull yourself into the boat.
- Once your hips are in the boat, you are stomach-down, kick again, turn and sit, letting your legs dangle over the side of the boat still. Don't let go of your oarhandles here.
- Raise your oarhandles up to right the boat.
- Make sure both blades are flat on the water and you are stable.
- Swing your legs in the boat.
- Put one foot back on the seat deck and scoot back on the seat.
- Put your feet back in the shoes.
- Practice it again.

If you row a wing-rigger boat or a boat without back stays this method will work well. If you have trouble getting your hips into the boat you may need to do some upper body strengthening. For boats with back stays, some scullers carry a terry cloth wrist band on their oars and use it to hold the handles together in the event that they need to straddle the boat and get back into the seat deck from the bow. Whichever methods you choose feel confident knowing what to do in case you go in the water. If you do not want to practice in your own boat use a more durable single or a more stable boat to learn how to get back in.

ACQUIRE BETTER SKILLS

Building the skills to row well requires thousands of strokes. Mastery of performance is infinite. As a novice or an experienced competitor, the pursuit of technical expertise is a factor in furthering your ability. Thorndike's law of exercise states that, "without an immense number of repetitions, a skill cannot become automatized or reach a high level of technical stability." An understanding of the process of how the body learns skill helps a coach customize their approach to individual athletes, as well as, assists athletes to learn more about themselves and become aware of what methods help them learn best. This is important for comprehension of doing purposeful technical drills appreciating the stages of the skill the athlete is progressing through. But how do we develop skill over time? How do we learn to become better rowers and accomplish new tasks? Some important factors to consider are: what stage of motor learning you are in, how do you learn best, what is the learning environment, and what other barriers exist.

Skill acquisition takes place in stages. The initial stage of motor learning can answer the question; was the movement pattern effective or not? Trial and error strategies are usually used during this phase to help the learner develop a general idea of the desired movement. Consider learning the sculling stroke. You cognitively focus on the stroke by taking a sculling lesson, reading books, or watching other scullers train on a nearby river. Regardless of the time spent mentally rehearsing the stroke, the actual performance of the stroke means that now your body must do what you have been taught, read about, or watched. At this point in learning, success may be considered staying upright in the boat or keeping the blades in the water without going too deep. In this phase it is easy to become overwhelmed with details such as correct hand placement on the oars, proper posture, eye focus, consistent pressure on the drive, or body control on the recovery. This phase of learning is cognitively demanding for the novice sculler and the complexity of the task will directly influence the length of time it takes to become comfortable with the new skill on a basic level.

The trial and error nature of this initial phase is largely due to poor neuromuscular coordination and extra movements occurring. It is normal to experience a heightened distribution of nervous impulses, stimulating extra muscles, when old habits are being interrupted and new habits are being formed. I call this state, "neurological chaos" when one habit has been let go but the new habit has not developed yet. Once the motor skill is established and adequate coordination is present the basic stereotype of the skill is formed. This can often be a frustrating stage for the athlete but as they continue to work at a technical element a new habit will form to replace the old habit.

Late stages of learning correspond with an automatic phase leading to mastery. During this stage the athlete learns fine movements, subtleties, efficiency, as well as the ability to perform the skill in various environmental conditions. Through experience, an athlete develops resources and a repertoire of responses relating to both self and environment. For example, a sculler may release the blades from the water symmetrically seven of 10 times. Error detection for an unbalanced release would include visual feedback-seeing one blade come out ahead of the other, and tactile feedback- feeling one oar out of the water and the other still under the water. This sensory feedback combined with the actual outcome of the motion and memory of previous successful experiences can all help the sculler further execute clean releases from the water so a higher ratio of success is achieved.

Eventually, when a skill requires less cognitive demand or awareness of how to move than previously required, an automatic stage of movement is reached. During this period, the sculler may not have to think about each element of the stroke but will be able to execute the stroke as a whole. The degree of skill achieved by an athlete depends on the athlete's ability to analyze and solve movement problems, use resources, and remain motivated in a variety of situations. Practice in diverse conditions develops skills in diverse conditions. Perfecting skill is an ongoing athletic focus and is aimed at fine-tuning technique and then adapting the technique for competitions or maximal performance. This final phase of refinement is dependent on earlier learning, which emphasized perfecting the separate elements, integrating the elements into a whole, and developing the physical musculoskeletal requirements to support the technique being learned.

Improving your skill comes from progressive pictures, step-by-step modeling, and repetition. If you respond well to visual input then demonstration, modeling an instructor, watching videotapes, or rowing in a team boat with other scullers will help you create the visual image you need to improve your stroke. Kinesthetic input would include learning how the motion feels by practice or by having a coach guide you through the movements. When you envision yourself rowing you can note whether you *see yourself* (visual imaging) rowing or rather *you sense* (kinesthetic imaging) what the stroke feels like without having an actual picture in your mind. One way will usually be dominant but you may discover that you have a combination of images too.

You and your coach must be aware of what stage you are at in rowing to progress your skills at a reasonable pace; one that agrees with your current level of understanding and ability to concentrate on the task at hand. A coach needs to know what you want to do *or can do* and needs to grade the demands of the training session accordingly. If the level of difficulty of a given task is too complex or challenging, frustrations, anxiety, worry, and often failure results with a decline in performance and motivation. One the other hand, when your skill level is higher than the task requires then boredom can result. The correct balance between demands of the exercise and existing skill level creates the conditions for a flow experience, ultimately resulting in creativity, mastery, competency, and fun. In sport, experiencing success is critical. Your training regime must be designed to offer success plus challenge to spur you on to the next level of competence.

LEARNING AND PERFECTING SKILL: PART ONE

Developing your technique and acquiring the skills to row effectively requires thousands of repetitions of the stroke cycle. Thorndike's law of exercise states that, "without an immense number of repetitions, a skill cannot become automatized or reach a high level of technical stability." Whether you are new to sculling or have several years of experience, the pursuit of technical proficiency will play a role in your athletic career. The mastery of technique is limitless. A main objective of training for the duration of one's sculling life, good technique contributes to reaching competitive results, as well as, enjoying of the aesthetics of the movement itself. But how do we actually learn new motor skills and patterns? How is skilled movement achieved and how do we create new habits? This series of articles addresses the concepts of how movement is generated and learned. Also considered will be the learning styles of the athlete, the art of practice, and using feedback. Part one is a brief review of neuroscience will serve as a starting point for understanding the basics of controlling movement.

The Role of the Central Nervous System

The central nervous system (CNS) is responsible for controlling behavior. It is comprised of the brain and the spinal cord, which receive sensory information, process it, and then initiate adaptive responses to produce a desired outcome. The central nervous system consists of seven main parts: the spinal cord, medulla, pons, cerebellum, midbrain, diencephalons, and cerebral hemispheres. The spinal cord is directly responsible for controlling the sensory and motor functions of the head and body. The medulla controls life support functions including breathing, heart rate, digestion, and arousal. The pons influences the cerebellum, which is involved in motor control and motor learning. The midbrain coordinates eye movement. The diencephalon is the main subcortical sensory integration center. The cerebral hemispheres are the highest level of the central nervous system controlling cognition, memory, language, motor control, and sensory perception.

CNS control of movement is complex and a complete review is beyond the scope of this text, but an introduction to the major neural mechanisms involved in the planning and execution of movement will help you appreciate not only the factors involved in skill acquisition but ways that you can help yourself learn and utilize coaching better.

The Sensory Systems

Sensory systems play a large part in influencing movement patterns. Movement depends on sensory input coming into the CNS so that systems such as the proprioceptive, vestibular, and visual can plan the movement before it happens in a feed forward manner, as well as, use feedback mechanisms to guide movement as it occurs. At the level of the spinal cord, sensory information is received from skin, muscles, and joint proprioceptors (which are responsible for providing us with a sense of body and joint position in space). The body then uses this input for both the reflexive and volitional control of movement. The information travels up the spinal cord towards the brain being processed at several levels. Once processed, the body uses the information to elicit an appropriate response. The cerebellum is a key player. Receiving information from all sensory systems, the cerebellum plans, executes, and learns movements. Part of the cerebellum is even dedicated solely to input from the vestibular system so it may influence muscle tone, posture, and reflexes.

The Spinal Cord

The spinal cord integrates sensory, motor, and interneurons

(nerve cells that act as communicators between incoming and outgoing impulses) in order to organize both voluntary and reflex movement. Nerve tracts traveling and carrying information up and down the cord accomplish this. The spinal cord relies heavily on proprioceptive feedback and sensations from the skin so that it may read the state of the body. Its interaction with the environment, determine the task to be accomplished, and then execute the commands coming from higher centers of the brain to make movement occur. Whether the act is simple (wiping your brow with a towel) or complex (executing a racing start at high cadence), the resulting musculoskeletal action is a complex interplay between higher and lower CNS centers coordinating multiple motor neurons.

The Vestibular System

Functions such as balance, equilibrium, maintaining eye fixation during head movement, and conscious awareness of head motion are modulated through the vestibular system. Vestibular system activation affects levels of arousal, which can include fight-flight reactions. Partly located in the fluid-filled semicircular canals of the inner ear, this system's functioning has a great influence on technical performance in sculling. Eye fixation prevents sight from blurring when the head is turned to the side and restores the eyes to the direction the head is facing. Automatic balance mechanisms (equilibrium reactions) work if you begin to lose balance by activating the muscles necessary to keep the body upright. Although balance is normally automatic, it can to some extent be consciously controlled because of vestibular influences and interaction with other areas of the brain. The inner ear structures also provide information to the vestibular system regarding vertical and horizontal acceleration of the head, which then coordinates with the cerebellum to then correct any disruption to balance.

The Cerebellum

The cerebellum plays a chief role in the initiation and planning of volitional (voluntary) movement. This part of the CNS has direct access to the state of the person relative to the environment and the nature of the task to be completed. It acts as a guidance system to keep movement on target and in time with the needs of the task. For example, When preparing to make the entry of the sculling stroke, the cerebellum analyzes the task requirements by drawing on past experiences such as the distance, speed of incoming stimulus, balance, weight shift, and the total body movement pattern required to complete the recovery and put the blade in the water. It then communicates with the cerebral cortex for motor planning. After receiving a response, the cerebellum directs the movement, including posture, balance, and timing until the entry is taken. By comparing the intent of the motor act with the result of the motor command, the cerebellum plans and coordinates the actual movement. The cerebellum also has strong connections with the vestibular system and therefore influences balance and equilibrium reactions as well.

The Basal Ganglia

Another CNS structure that is critical for planning and executing movement is the basal ganglia. The six main duties of the basal ganglia are: influencing high-order cognitive aspects of motor behavior, initiation and planning of movement, control of movement to completion including the cessation of motor activity, regulation of muscle tone and posture, processing the context of task requirements, and control of the amount of effort and direction need for a task. Basal ganglia activity begins with a request for planning from the cerebral cortex and then interacts with the cerebral cortex in a variety of relay loops to then create well-planned motions.

The Cerebral Cortex

The functional control of the planning and initiation of movement is orchestrated in the cerebral cortex. This high center of the CNS solves the problems presented by each task and plans the solution to that task. This requires smooth coordination with the cerebellum and basal ganglia but also incorporates our sensations, emotions, motivations, perceptions, and memories. Various areas of the cerebral cortex are organized to perform specific functions. Many of these functions overlap each other and may vary slightly from individual to individual. This may in part be an explanation as to why a person may use different strategies to solve the same motor problem. In sculling, this could account for the determining factors of one's style.

The Limbic System

The final area of central nervous system review is the limbic system. Located within the cerebral cortex, the limbic system was originally considered to be the seat of emotions with little connection to actual movement. It was thought to have more influence on instinctual drives than human interaction with the environment. It is now apparent that the limbic system permeates all aspects of human behavior but for the most part those with an emotional or motivational context. Although the system is extremely intricate in nature, its main relevance is that there are few things that we do that do not have such an aspect to it-especially in sports. The amount to which the limbic system contributes to motor behavior depends upon the degree of motivation toward the task or activity. So the next time you put on a charging sprint to the finish line, your sculling is being boosted by elevated limbic activity influencing your actual movements.

LEARNING AND PERFECTING SKILL: PART TWO

In the first part of this series, *Learning and Perfecting Skill*, a brief review of the central nervous system's role in movement was given. Now that you have a general idea of how movement is controlled, attention can be turned to a discussion of how we develop skill over time. How do we learn to become better scullers or rowers and accomplish new tasks? Some of the factors to consider are what stage of motor learning you are currently in, how do you learn best, what is the learning environment, and what other barriers exist?

The Stages of Motor Learning

Skill acquisition takes place in stages. The initial stage of motor learning can often answer the question: was the movement pattern effective or not? Trial and error strategies are used during this phase the help the learner develop a general idea of the desired movement. Consider learning the sculling stroke. You cognitively focus on the stroke by taking a sculling lesson, reading books, or watching other scullers train on a nearby river. Regardless of the time spent mentally rehearsing the stroke, the actual performance of the stroke means that now your body must do what you have been taught, read about, or watched. At this point in learning, success may be considered staying upright in the boat or keeping the oars in the water without going too deep. At this stage it is easy to become overwhelmed with details such as correct hand placement on the oars, proper posture, eye focus, correct pressure on the drive, or recovery speed. This phase of learning is cognitively demanding for the novice sculler and the complexity of the task will directly influence the length of time it takes to become comfortable with the new skill on a basic level.

The trial and error nature of this initial phase is largely due to poor neuromuscular coordination and extra movements occurring. It is normal to experience a heightened distribution of nervous impulses, stimulating extra muscles, when old habits are being interrupted and new habits are being formed. Once the motor skill is established and adequate coordination is present the basic stereotype of the skill is formed.

Late stages of learning correspond with an automatic phase leading to mastery. During this stage the athlete learns fine movements, subtleties, efficiency, as well as the ability to perform the skill in various environmental conditions. Through experience, an athlete develops resources and a repertoire of responses relating to both self and environment. For example, a sculler may release the blades from the water symmetrically seven of 10 times. Error detection for an unbalanced release would include visual feedback (seeing one blade come out ahead of the other), and tactile feedback (feeling one oar in the air and the other still underwater). This sensory feedback combined with the actual outcome of the motion and memory of previous successful experiences can all help the sculler further execute clean releases from the water so a higher ratio of success is achieved.

Eventually, when a skill requires less cognitive demand or awareness of how to move than previously required, an automatic stage of movement is reached. During this period, the sculler may not have to think about each element of the stroke but will be able to execute the stroke as a whole. The degree of skill achieved by an athlete depends on the athlete's ability to analyze and solve movement problems, use resources and remain motivated in a variety of situations. Practice in diverse conditions develops skills in diverse conditions.

Perfecting skill is an ongoing athletic focus and is aimed at fine-tuning technique and then adapting the technique for competitions or maximal performance. This final phase of refinement is dependent on earlier learning, which emphasized perfecting the separate elements, integrating the elements into a whole, and developing the physical musculoskeletal requirements to support the technique being learned.

LEARNING AND PERFECTING SKILL: PART THREE

Individual learning style has an effect on the ability to acquire new skills. Using your naturally preferred style or being aware of your own learning style can optimize how you integrate new information into your rowing skills.

Learning Styles

Motor skills benefit from progressive pictures, step-by-step modeling, and repetition. If you respond well to visual input then demonstration, modeling an instructor, watching videotapes, or rowing in a team boat with other scullers, will help you create the visual image you need to improve your stroke. Kinesthetic input includes learning from how the motion feels in practice or by having a coach guide you through the movements. When you envision yourself rowing you can note whether you *see yourself* (visual imaging) rowing or rather *you sense* (kinesthetic imaging) what the stroke feels like without having an actual picture in your mind. One way will usually be dominant but you may discover that you have a combination of images too.

It is important for you and your coach to be aware of what stage you are at in rowing in order to progress your skills at a reasonable pace; one that agrees with your current level of understanding and ability to concentrate on the task at hand. A coach needs to know what you want to do *or can do* and needs to grade the demands of the training session accordingly. If the level of difficulty of a given task is too complex or challenging, frustrations, anxiety, worry, and often failure results with a decline in performance and motivation. One the other hand, when your skill level is higher than the task requires then boredom can result. The correct balance between demands of the exercise and existing skill level creates the conditions for a flow experience, which ultimately results in creativity, mastery, and competence. In sport, experiencing success is critical. Your training regime must be designed to offer success plus challenge to spur you on to the next level of competence.

Environmental Influences

A favorable learning environment can support better acquisition of motor skills. In sculling or rowing this could include: the type of water to be rowed on, air temperature, wind speed, amount of boat traffic on the water, quality of equipment, stability of the boat, weight of the boat, access to indoor training facilities, a boathouse or tanks, docking facilities, access to videotaping, or supervision of a coach. As a novice sculler, you will benefit from learning in a more stable environment-flat water, no wind, and a wide beam boat-for the simple reason that the initial learning of the exercise accounts for some rigidity of movement, improper use of the body, and inappropriate pauses in the continuity of the motion making the stroke rough. The strategy of using a more stable boat allows you to break the stroke into steps and go slow in order to facilitate the correct information processing and make modifications in the movement by simplifying and stabilizing the environment. Such learning can also take place in indoor rowing tanks or on indoor rowing machines but then must transfer to the natural setting where the rower learns how to row on the water. Competitive and highly skilled scullers can also benefit from periodic outings in a stable boat when a precise detail of the stroke is being refined and can then transfer the learning to their performance boat. The perfection of skill continually challenges the sculler to apply their skills in multiple situations both environmental and competitive. The right setting and equipment for learning can help you improve faster and pattern movements correctly from the beginning.

LEARNING AND PERFECTING SKILL: PART FOUR

What is practice? We know that practice is necessary for motor learning to occur, so we can learn to row better. Many of us row daily or twice per day to improve. There are many different ways of practicing and subsequently learning to be a better rower. Here are some types of practice that are common elements of a coach's repertoire and why they can contribute to better acquisition of skill.

Type of Practice: Active and Discovery

Learning by doing stresses the active participation of the athlete in performing new skills. Practice is more than just the repetition of a movement and should engage the athlete in solving specific problems or requirements based on the situation at hand.

Discovery learning is when the athlete learns actively through trial and error and through experience. Learners have been found to acquire skills better when they discover their own solutions versus being shielded from error through guidance. Physical and verbal guidance is an important part of coaching an athlete to improve their skills and certainly plays an appropriate role when learning new elements helping to understand the motion, reduce fear, or promote safety. There is, however, great value in a crew or sculler putting in miles on his or her own to work out technical elements. A goal of training may be to reduce the level of guidance a sculler or crew needs to perform a particular task.

Although practice is commonly considered to be a physical act, it includes mental practice as well. Both are an effective part of a training regime. It is well documented that imagining oneself *doing* something (mental imagery) activates some of the same nervous activity as does performing the actual movement; tendon reflexes increase and motor control areas of the basal ganglia are heightened. Three to five minutes of mental training sessions can be very beneficial if an athlete is unable to attend practice, is injured and cannot row, needs to conserve energy prior to racing, or needs to rehearse the race plan.

Type of Practice: Blocked versus Random

Practicing a movement repetitively or working on one skill at a time is termed *blocked practice*. In early stages of learning *blocked practice* is slightly more effective than *random practice* because the athlete can concentrate on one thing at a time. However, once a movement or skill has been performed successfully *random practice*, which introduces variety and mixed skills to the training situation, has been shown to improve motor learning retention more so than *blocked practice* over time. One can practice racing starts by repeating the first stroke several times then progressing to the first two strokes up to the first five strokes. This would be *blocked practice*. *Random practice* would include practicing the racing starts in different wind and water conditions, combined with transitions to base race pace, or from a moving position (flying starts) during a steady state row intermittently on the coach's command. The nature of *random practice* requires more integration of movement patterns because a second pattern is superimposed on the first one. The athlete must, in essence forget the first pattern when the second pattern is introduced and then regenerate the primary pattern again when returning to the first pattern. The process of returning to and recreating the movement pattern speeds up the learning process.

In clarification, the rowing stroke is a continuous skill, which has no distinct beginning or end. An example of *blocked practice* of a rowing skill would be performing blade placement drills; starting from the release, moving on the recovery, and placing the blade in the water as the conclusion of the recovery. Introducing *random practice* could include full-stroke steady state rowing and combining attention to both a clean release and then proper entry timing. By rowing full strokes and shifting attention to different movements within the stroke, you are allowed to forget within the context of the entire stroke and the bring attention back to the entry during the recovery. The technical goal would be to execute the entry dynamically with the precision it was learned in an isolated manner during the drill.

Type of Practice: Part-task versus Whole-task

In rowing, the translation is part-stroke versus whole-stroke practice. The stroke can be broken down into steps (entry, drive, release, recovery) or phases (acceleration, deceleration) and be taught as separate tasks when we do drills such as pausing arms-body away or time-on-the-slide. The stroke can also be practiced as a whole; rowing steady and focusing on an element within the context of the stroke cycle, i.e. releasing the blade. The goal of *part-task practice* is to transfer the skills learned to the performance of the whole skill and is very effective if the steps are progressive and integrate with the practice of the whole-task. In a continuous skill as rowing it is reasonable and beneficial to practice component parts (drills) and the whole cycle (full strokes) during the same session. Therein lies the benefit of drills.

LEARNING AND PERFECTING SKILL: PART FIVE

This is the final article in this series about skill acquisition. The principles and systems we have addressed can help both the coach who is seeking the best way to coach and the athlete who is looking for the best way to learn to row. Here we will take a look at feedback, when to practice technique, and reasons for errors.

Feedback

To perfect your rowing stroke, feedback is needed during all stages of learning and mastery. Feedback is categorized as either *intrinsic* or *extrinsic*: *Intrinsic feedback* is the information we receive from our sensory systems such as vision (you can see your blade is washing out at the end of the drive), proprioception (you can sense that you are dropping your wrists at the release), and cognition (you can judge how you need to adjust your handle height at the entry). Kinesthetic feedback is internal information that your body gives about its position in space and motion. This type of feedback and feedback about balance is generated by the vestibular system, visual system, as well as, special stretch sensors called muscle spindles located within the muscle fibers and golgi tendon organs which are found near the junctions of tendons with muscles. *Intrinsic feedback* is highly significant for learning the rowing stroke due to the need for balance combined with the accurate timing of bladework that is mandatory for good performance.

Extrinsic feedback is information that comes to you from external sources. This could be from a human (coach) or non-human environment (water or boat). Generally, frequent extrinsic feedback is needed for learning new skills but should gradually become intermittent in order to enhance performance. The feedback you receive may focus on information regarding the result or outcome of the movement, "You came off the starting line at 45 strokes per minute." This type of information is termed *knowledge of result*. Verbal or non-verbal feedback that focuses on the position or movement pattern used is termed *knowledge of performance*, "Your hands were too high at the entry; keep your wrists level at the release." *Knowledge of performance* is a more beneficial form of feedback for motor learning and motor teaching, but the combination of *knowledge of result* and *knowledge of performance* is better than one or the other in isolation. Proper and frequent feedback can have a highly motivating effect on an athlete, supplying the information required to detect and correct errors, as well as, providing positive reinforcement for good execution of the stroke.

When to Practice Technique

After physical preparation, the primary training factor, technical training is next on the list of priorities. Devoting attention to technical training can reap greater benefits if done at the correct time of the year and at the proper time in a training session. Technical work should be done in a rested, unstressed state because of the concentration needed to develop confidence in the technique. Technique is best changed when you are not fatigued. Once changed you must learn to perform correctly at race speed. This is also learned best when not fatigued. Finally, you must be able to make the transition to maintain correct technique when under race stress. This preparation requires a great deal of time and is an ongoing part of training in our sport.

Within the annual cycle of training much of the improvement in technical training is done during the preparation phase, which emphasizes general and specific endurance. Next, during the following pre-competitive phase, technical changes need to be maintained. This period of training produces high levels of fatigue and technical training is not optimum at this time. The later competitive phase, which includes sharpening and peaking, again calls for a return to technical training to perfect skill and apply it to racing situations.

On a daily level, technical work should be done at the beginning of the training session and may be included as part of the warm-up. Again, technical changes are best produced in a rested, concentrated state. Perform the elements or drills that you acquired in the previous training session, continue to perfect the skills that you are working on, and gradually apply those skills in identical conditions to competition. Designating an entire session to technique is a necessary part of the weekly training cycle and should be limited to a maximum of one hour. Because of the high degree of concentration required it is easy to become quite fatigued by the end of such a session. Rest days should be scheduled separately.

Causes of Technical Error

Technical improvement can often be delayed because of incorrect learning. The quicker an error can be corrected the faster the rate of progress. Mistakes have causes and identifying the grounds for the fault help direct the corrective route to take. An athlete may be responsible for faulty technique due to psychological limitation (satisfaction with a low level of skill), poor physical preparation (strength, coordination), misunderstanding of the correct movement pattern, fatigue, incorrect grasp of the handles, or morale (lack of confidence or fear). The approach of a coach can also cause technical problems due to an inadequate or incorrect teaching style, an inability to individualize teaching based on an athlete's needs, or a coaching style that is characterized by lack of patience. On the non-human level, the use of poor quality equipment, adverse weather conditions (cold, wind, waves), and an unorganized training program can contribute heavily to your technical troubles and insufficiencies. Investing in good coaching and becoming a member of a well-organized rowing program right from the beginning of your rowing career is well worth it to set you on the right technical track from the start.

COORDINATION TRAINING

When your exercise physiologist tells you that you are like a Clydesdale you're apt to be better at a sport that emphasizes strength-endurance than one that is more cheetah-like such as sprinting. In the case of rowing, physiologically you'll have more likelihood of success in head races or marathons than 500-meter dashes because your biomotor abilities just aren't up to par to tackle short, fast distances better than the next guy loaded with rapid reaction muscle fibers. Biomotor abilities are the physiological components and the capacity to perform a range of activities such as strength, endurance speed, coordination, and flexibility. They are to a great extent inherited but can improve with training. Each sport has its dominant ability but is also dependent on an assortment of other features. To reach high performance in a sport, the correct ratio of biomotor abilities needs to be trained adequately. For example, rowing is predominantly an endurance sport that also requires strength and speed though with a lesser emphasis than the endurance aspect. A discus thrower needs strength and speed but very little endurance and a wrestler equally works on strength, speed, and endurance. Flexibility and coordination are additionally important to overall training. In rowing, we must devote some effort towards improving the coordination of body motions and fine blade-handling to support higher performance.

In his book *Periodization: Theory and Methodology of Training,* Tudor Bompa writes, "Coordination is a complex biomotor ability closely interrelated with speed, strength, endurance, and flexibility. It is of determinant importance for acquiring and perfecting technique and tactics, as well as for applying them in unfamiliar circumstances. Such circumstances can include the alteration of terrain, equipment and apparatus, light, climate and meteorological conditions, and opponents. Coordination is also solicited in space orientation, either when the body is in unfamiliar conditions (vaulting, various jumps, trampolining) or when there is a loss of balance (slippery conditions, landing quick stops, contact sports). Bompa continues, "The level of coordination reflects and ability to perform movements of various degrees of difficulty quickly, with great precision and efficiency, and according to specific training objectives. It is considered that an athlete with good coordination is capable of performing a skill perfectly, as well as rapidly solving a training task to which he or she is exposed."

Coordination is based in the integration of the central nervous system's processes. The central nervous system is constantly regulating organs and systems to inhibit or excite. One main function is determining and executing a fast, accurate response to an outside stimulus. When movements are not yet automatic you will see the effects of uncoordinated nervous system excitation in the uncontrolled movements of the body or the blade. As many repetitions of a skill or stroke elements are practiced you will see the nervous processes of excitation and inhibition get properly coordinated, stabilize, and then finer motor skills that can be applied to different conditions (wind, water, higher stroke rates) will develop.

General coordination should be developed from the start of your sport life and is not dependent on your specific sport, in our case rowing. Sports such as soccer, basketball, and ultimate Frisbee are very good for developing general endurance and serves as a basis to build specific coordination. To improve rowing you must learn to perform the stroke flawlessly with ease and precision. Grooving in a specific rhythm, adapting to higher stroke rates, and being able to make quick adjustments in your stroke due to balance or bladework problems can all get better with defined exercises.

There are several methods to develop coordination. Performing a skill with the opposite limb or in an unusual position is one way. Applied to sweep rowing this could mean having athlete's regularly switch sides so they become competent on port and starboard, including drills that alternate hands on the sweep oar such as outside hand only, inside hand only, or outside hand on the drive/inside hand on the recovery. For scullers, the drill I call the *Swinford Switch* is excellent. Scull with the port blade squared and the starboard blade feathered for 10 strokes and then in one stroke, switch to the port blade feathered and the starboard blade squared for 10 strokes. This is a first-rate drill for right-left assimilation.

Altering the speed or tempo of performing a movement is another way to get more synchronized. Exercises that increase the stroke rate progressively or variations of stroke rate help accomplish this. For example, 40-stroke pieces where you row full pressure for 20 strokes at a base rate then raise the rate two strokes per minute every two strokes for 20 strokes. If your base rate is 30 strokes per minute, in the second 20 strokes your will increase to 32-34-36-38-40 strokes per minute. Many other combinations can be included in longer training sessions such as varying the rate every five minutes, 18-20-22 strokes per minute, or rowing four minutes at one rate plus one minute at a higher rate such as four minutes at 20 strokes per minute and one minute at 24 strokes per minute. Another excellent drill for high-speed reactions is rowing half slide at maximum tempo, increasing the pace until bladework deteriorates and the drill needs to stop.

Changing technical elements or skills in combination with unusual performance conditions better a rower's ability to cope and react in an efficient way. Examples here are frequently changing boat classes such from an eight to a pair, from a sweep boat to a single or double and having designated practices or parts of a season in each. Then go on to exposing the different boats to wavy water, windy conditions, and currents.

Finally, on the lighter side, games of all sorts or practicing some unrelated sports will help you develop a repertoire of movements and body knowledge that will be incorporated into your stroke in subtle ways. Horse riding, cross-country skiing, basketball, tennis, or rock climbing can all potentially take their place in your training plan.

A BIT ABOUT MUSCLE

Wanting to go as fast as you can requires that you have some basic understanding of your physiological characteristics and what rowing demands of your body. The training process changes our muscle's structure, metabolism, cellular activity, and ability to produce energy. Aerobic and anaerobic metabolic processes take time to develop and can continue to improve for many years with proper training. Next time you are getting ready to train, devote a moment to appreciating the processes that go on inside your body that create your movements as you row. Learn to listen to how your body feels with a fine tuned intensity that comes with attending to its details and subtle signals. As you become a more knowledgeable about your body, your experience will guide you to being a more successful athlete.

Our neuromuscular system is responsible for all movement from finely controlled movements to forceful actions. Reviewing some components of our neuromuscular structures will help you gain a better understand of how this system works. Comprised of more than 600 skeletal muscles and the nerves that control them, this system responds and adapts according to the demands of our exercise. The muscular system shapes and supports the skeleton. Our skeletal muscles are capable of developing a great deal of force. Metabolically, muscles use the majority of food and oxygen we consume to produce energy for movement and the heat that our body uses for regulation.

There are three types of muscular tissue: smooth, cardiac and skeletal. Smooth visceral or involuntary muscles function without will and are controlled by the autonomic nervous system. Smooth muscle is found in the walls of the stomach, intestines, and blood vessels; it does not attach to bone, can maintain a contraction for a long time, and doesn't fatigue easily. Cardiac muscle is found in the heart and is distinctly striated as the cells of skeletal muscle. Skeletal (striated) or voluntary muscles are controlled by will and by the central nervous system. They make up the fleshy areas of the body and attach to the skeleton.

There are a number of characteristics that enable muscles to perform their functions. Irritability or excitability is the capacity of muscles to receive and react to stimuli that can be mechanical, electrical, thermal, chemical, or impulses from the nervous system. Contractility is the ability to contract or shorten generating force. If a skeletal muscle is attached to a pair of articulating bones, when the muscle contracts the attachments are drawn closer together resulting in the movement of the bones. Muscle has elasticity, the ability to return to its original shape after being stretched, and extensibility, which is the ability of the muscle to stretch.

Skeletal muscles have several tissues including muscle tissue, blood, other fluids, nerve tissue, and connective tissue. Though we often visualize a muscle as a single entity, it is made up of a complex fiber arrangement of smaller units. A layer of connective tissue called the epimysium covers an individual muscle. Muscle tissue consists of contractile fibrous tissue arranged in bundles called fascicles where parallel muscle fibers are held into place by a connective tissue called the perimysium. The connective tissue supports the muscle in such a way that when the fibers contract, a force is exerted to the structure the muscle is attached to causing movement. Each fascicle or fasciculus is composed of smaller groups of muscle cells. An individual muscle cell is called a muscle fiber. This is the contractile unit of muscle tissue. The cells are long, cylindrical structures that generally extend the entire length of a muscle. Each muscle cell has a connective tissue covering called the endomysium that keeps its parallel position with other cells. Within the cells the sarcolemma is highly organized with myofibrils containing actin and myosin filaments. It is their interaction that gives muscle its contractile ability.

Most muscle fibers are connected to a branch of a motor neuron. Where the muscle fiber and nerve fiber meet is called the neuromuscular junction or the myoneural junction. Some specialized cells are called spindle cells that have both sensory and motor functions essential for muscle control and coordination. Although a muscle fiber has only one nerve fiber connection, a motor nerve may have many branches and connect to several muscle fibers. A motor neuron and all the muscle fibers it supplies make up a motor unit. When a motor nerve transmits a stimulus, all the muscle fibers connected to it contract simultaneously. In small muscles that perform intricate movements the motor units may be as few as two or three muscle fibers, whereas larger muscles that provide bigger movements may have several hundred fibers in a single motor unit. Motor units also tend to overlap with the muscle fibers of adjacent motor units.

Skeletal muscle fibers are not all alike but are classified by metabolic capacity, size, and contraction speed or force. Slow-twitch (ST) fibers have a small fiber size, small motorneuron size, 10 to 180 muscle fibers per motor unit, slow contraction speed, low force, low glycolytic capacity, high oxidative capacity, high capillary density, and a high resistance to fatigue. Fast-twitch 'a' (FTa) fibers have a large fiber size, large motorneuron size, 300 to 800 muscle fibers per motor unit, fast contraction speed, high force, high glycolytic capacity, moderate oxidative capacity, moderate capillary supply, and moderate resistance to fatigue. Fast-twitch 'b' (FTb) fibers have similar qualities as FTa except they have a low oxidative capacity, low capillary supply, and low resistance to fatigue. All three types of muscle fibers are capable of producing ATP through the anaerobic-glycolytic and oxidative pathways, however, slow-twitch fibers have a better capacity for oxidative metabolism giving them good endurance and fast-twitch rely more on phosphocreatine and anaerobic glycolosis for ATP production fatiguing faster because they produce lactate and do not have good endurance.

Because of their high-oxidative metabolic capacity, the slow-twitch fibers contain many mitochondria and have good blood supply through the surrounding capillaries. Mitochondria are the main source of cell energy. The fast-twitch 'b' fibers have fewer mitochondria and capillaries but high levels of stored glycogen. The fast-twitch 'a' fibers are between, having a moderate number of mitochondria, capillaries, and high glycogen storage. Long, low rows that develop oxidative metabolism help you grow more mitochondria in your cells to generate more energy thus giving you more energy and recovery ability.

Comprised of the brain and the spinal cord, central nervous system control of muscular movement is complex. The spinal cord is directly responsible for controlling the sensory and motor functions of the head and body. Sensory systems play a large part in influencing movement patterns that depend on sensory input coming into the central nervous system so that the proprioceptive, vestibular, and visual systems can plan the motion before it happens in a feed-forward way using feedback mechanisms to guide motions while they are happening. At the level of the spinal cord, sensory information is received from skin, muscles, and joint proprioceptors. Joint proprioceptors are responsible for providing a sense of body and joint position in space; for example, you know that your wrists are bent and you are dropping your elbows at the release. The body then uses this input for both the reflexive and volitional control of movement. The information travels up the spinal cord towards the brain being read at several levels. Once processed, the body uses the information to elicit an appropriate response or correction.

The spinal cord integrates sensory, motor, and interneurons-nerve cells that act as communicators between incoming and outgoing impulses-organizing voluntary and reflex movement via nerve tracts carrying information up and down the cord. The spinal cord relies heavily on proprioceptive feedback and sensations from the skin so that it may read the state of the body. Interaction with the environment determines what is to be accomplished. Then commands coming from higher centers of the brain travel the spinal tracts to make movement occur. Whether the act is small like wiping your brow with a towel or complex such as executing a racing start at high cadence, the resulting musculoskeletal action is an intricate interplay between central nervous system centers that coordinate multiple motor neurons resulting in helping you move your boat.

AEROBIC DISCIPLINE

Today, an e-mail message from a master rower read, "Marlene, I have done that 90-minute piece on the erg three times now. I have to confess that during the last 10 minutes or so I feel like I have to get a life. Does one really have to do this? I know the answer to that. Anyway, I will persevere. Please refresh my memory on the benefits of low and long pieces." Curiously, I get more of these e-mails than those bemoaning workouts that can raise enough lactic acid in the blood stream to strip the varnish off your vintage Stampfli single. It is a more formidable task to get masters or juniors to relax and do their base aerobic work correctly than to get them to charge into racing oblivion. But without the slow rowing there will be no fast rowing later on. In fact, to do your low intensity work with too much speed is one of the biggest training mistakes made on the market because you deny yourself the true benefits that oxygen utilization contributes to your fitness.

So I do my best to respond to the message of distress explaining why long, slow distance plays such an important part in getting ready for our events. The majority of your annual training time falls into this category during your preparation phases. In season these practices are sandwiched by oxygen transport and anaerobic work. It builds our capacity to recover from hard efforts; ultimately, how much we can safely do, without overtraining, is limited by our ability to recover. You might have 20 available exercise hours per week but if it takes you three days to recover from a difficult session your volume must then be reduced compared to taking one day to recover from the same session. When intervals are on the agenda, the amount of recovery time one requires must be factored into the weekly cycle. More significantly, if you are racing several times in one day or over multiple days, the athletes with the best ability to recovery between events will fare better in the final stages of a regatta.

I go on, understand that it teaches your body to utilize fat as a fuel. It boosts blood capillary density in the working muscles for greater oxygen delivery because you are requesting a constant supply of oxygen for a long period of time. It increases the number of the energy-producing mitochondria in the cells. It allows one to maintain longer peak conditioning and creates the conditions to develop technique under concentrated conditions. What could be better? Old timers say, "If you can't do it slow, you can't do it at all" and "mileage makes champions." Yes, if you are not careful, boredom can set in while you are putting in lengthy sessions, so for motivation keep your list of advantages taped to the refrigerator door because you will be getting hungry.

The level of aerobic base training can be measured in a few ways depending on your access to lab testing or personal preferences. Ways to define your low intensity rowing or cross-training includes: a blood lactate measurement of two Mmol/liter and the athlete's corresponding speed as determined by lab testing, a heart rate range of 65 to 75 percent of maximum, stroke rates between 16 and 22 strokes per minute, boat/erg speed that is approximately 70 to 75 percent of race pace for 2,000 meters, a 500-meter average speed that is 13 to 18 seconds slower than your 20-minute trial average 500-meter pace, or a comfortable speed that can be sustained for a one to two hours during which you are able to sing. You can manipulate your variables by distance, time, set stroke rate, or pattern of changing stroke rate. The volume you choose to do in one session depends on your current fitness level; for one athlete it may mean reaching the 60-minute mark, for another 180 minutes. Here are some variations for extended rows: 10 to 20 kilometers or up to 120 minutes at 18 strokes per minute stopping only to turn the boat around and hydrate; 10 to 15 kilometers with stroke rate changes every five minutes at 16, 18, and 20 or including one minute of a drill every five minutes; three sets of 20 or 30 minutes with three minutes rest between at a constant rating of 20 strokes per minute. All these kilometers solidify your technique so remember to concentrate on rhythm, ratio, and stroke efficiency to improve your boat run.

A blend of activities is good for the mind and for developing metabolic qualities in your non-rowing muscles. This is where cross training can fit nicely into a program. But save your upscale workouts, anaerobic threshold or faster, for on the erg or in the boat so they are sport-specific. On days when you want to get outside to do something with friends or just need a change of scenery, you can go for a bike ride, cross-country ski, run, hike, power walk, swim, or play a team sport. If you plan to do your longest session in the gym you can do what I call the aerobic medley. Check out what cardio machines you have available. It could include indoor rowers, treadmills, steppers, elliptical machines, spinning bikes, recumbent bikes, or climbers. If you were planning a total of 80 minutes of aerobic work you could do a steady piece on one apparatus but you have several choices to make the time go by fast and keep things interesting such as: alternating 20 minutes rowing with 20 minutes running on the treadmill; alternating 10 minutes each of rowing, running, elliptical, and spinning; alternating 10 minutes each of the stepper and spinning; or 20 minutes rowing then 40 minutes running then 20 minutes rowing; or include 10-minute segments of mixed calisthenics such as sit-ups, squats, push-ups, or jumpies in your routine. Variety and purpose makes it easier to comply with these valuable though time-consuming exercise bouts.

PERFORMANCE-BASED TRAINING PACES: HOW FAST OR SLOW TO ROW?

There are five different training categories within the aerobic system and one anaerobic category. Each classification produces specific physiological adaptations within the cell. An annual plan includes all of these training intensities utilized progressively during the year moving from low to high intensity. Speed, stroke rate and heart rate generally coincide.

The speeds that you train at for each category are determined by a performance test of 20 minutes on the ergometer or on the water. A performance-based method of determining your training paces is a very specific way to gauge your training and is used widely internationally. It is more accurate than heart rate in well-trained individuals and is the next best method of determining aerobic paces other than in a physiology lab. By regularly monitoring performance you can adjust training paces accordingly. If your performance improves-your training paces improve. If your fitness falls due to injury or lack of training-you establish an accurate baseline for resuming training.

The Training Categories Summarized

Category VI (Cat VI) is what is low intensity rowing. It can comprise up to 85 percent of a rower's annual volume. Cat VI rowing increases capillary density in muscles, improves the development of aerobic base, and trains better recovery ability during high intensity work. Compared to your 20-minute test's average pace per 500 meters, target pace is 13 to18 seconds slower per 500 meters in well-trained athletes and 18 to 23 seconds slower per 500 meters in club-level or novice athletes. Stroke rates usually fall between 16 to 20 strokes per minute and the perceived effort is conversational pace. A workout can last 40 to 120 minutes with only brief stops to rehydrate.

Category V (Cat V) also falls within the low intensity realm but it is a slightly faster pace. Cat V provides many benefits of Cat VI rowing except it utilizes an increased number of endurance fast twitch (FOG) fibers. Cat V target pace is 8 to 12 seconds slower per 500 meters compared to your 20-minute test's average pace per 500 meters. Stroke rates fall between 22 to 24 strokes per minute. The effort is comfortable and can be sustained for a long time. You may mix paces with Cat VI in one workout or do one out of 10 steady workouts at Cat V. An example workout is 2 x 30 minutes with 5 minutes rest at stroke rate 22.

Category IV (Cat IV) is anaerobic threshold pace. Anaerobic threshold work raises the level of your endurance capacity. This is the intensity where lactic acid begins to be produced in the muscles faster than it can be cleared. The pace is two seconds per 500 meters slower than your 20-minute test's average pace per 500 meters. The effort is comfortably hard and stroke rates are typically 24 to 26 strokes per minute. Within annual training volume Cat IV rowing represents approximately 15 percent. Improvement of your anaerobic threshold is one of the best predictors for improving your 2k or 5k time. A Cat IV workout example would be 3 x 20 minutes with 7 minutes rest between at stroke rate 24.

Category III (Cat III) trains you to perform at higher levels of lactate production and to promote the lactate recovery needed for racing. Cat III rowing increases VO2 max and accounts for about five percent of the total annual volume of training. These are intense intervals at 90 to 100 percent effort paced at two seconds per 500 meters faster than your 20-minute test's average pace per 500 meters. Stroke rates may range from 26 to 32. A typical workout is 5 x 5 minutes with 5 minutes rest between at stroke rate 30.

Category II (Cat II) is racing pace. This intensity increases VO2 max and specific endurance for racing. The pace is five percent faster than your 20-minute test's average pace per 500 meters. Stroke rates may range from 30 to 38 strokes per minute and lactic acid levels are high. A typical workout would be 4 x 1000 meters with 5 minutes rest between at stroke rates 32.

Category I (Cat I) is an anaerobic training category for speed development. Speed-bursts are typically 20 to 30 seconds in duration and lactic acid levels remain low. Stroke rates may reach high rates such as 40+ strokes per minute. Practicing starts or including 15-stroke accelerations during your Cat VI rows would be typical sessions.

Testing Yourself

Your 20-minute trial should be your best effort. You should go into it rested and mentally prepared to do your best at that given time. Attempt to maintain an even pace avoiding going out too hard and then dropping speed in the second half. When you have finished record your total time, average 500-meter split, average stroke rate, and maximum heart rate if you have a monitor on. Your paces are then based on your average 500-meter split plus or minus a certain number of seconds. You can correlate water times to paces on the water or erg times to paces on the erg. Recommended drag factors if you are on the Concept2 Indoor Rower are: men: 130, women: 120, lightweight men: 120, lightweight women: 110. You should retest yourself every four to six weeks throughout the year to reset your training paces.

WORKOUTS: CATEGORY VI: AEROBIC BASE TRAINING

This article is the first of a series to give you workouts suggestions for each of the six training paces that we use in our preparation for racing or for improving our fitness. For a complete overview of performance-based training paces see *Performance-Based Training Paces: How Fast or Slow to Row?* and *Testing for Improved Training.*

The Category VI Training Pace

Category VI (Cat VI) is consists of predominantly low intensity rowing. It can comprise up to 85 percent of a rower's annual volume. Cat VI rowing increases capillary density in muscles to improve blood and oxygen supply to the working muscles, increases mitochondria in the muscles cells, improves the development of aerobic base, and develops your recovery ability especially during high intensity work and racing. It is also when you work on solidifying technical changes before increasing the intensity. Psychologically, Cat VI training requires sustained concentration.

Compared to your 20-minute test's average pace per 500 meters, your target pace is 13 to 18 seconds slower per 500 meters if you are a well-trained athletes and 18 to 23 seconds slower per 500 meters if you are a club-level or novice athlete. Stroke rates usually fall between 16 to 22 strokes per minutes and the effort is a conversational pace.

Workouts for Cat VI Training Effect

- Row: Cat VI: 60' steady for technique. SR 18-20.

- Row: Cat VI: 3 x 25' with 3' rest between. Alternate stroke rate every 5' @ 20-22-20.
- Row: Cat VI: 4 x 20' (4'on/1'paddle), 7' rest between. Alternate stroke rates each piece: #1 @ SR 20, #2 @ SR 22, #3 @ SR 20, #4 @ SR 22.
- Row: Cat VI: Technique row: 15 km. Include a variety of drills.
- Row: Cat VI: 4 x 15' with 3' between, SR 22.
- Row: Cat VI: 2 x 30' with 5' rest between. SR 20. This technique row is focused on improving the entry, direct release, and stability of the boat.
- Row: Cat VI: 3 x 25' with 3' rest between. #1 & #3: alternate 4'@ SR 22 +1' @ SR 16.
- #2: Include technical drills: pause drills and square blade rowing for 1 minute every 5 minutes.
- Row: Cat VI: 60' changing the stroke rate every 6' @ (16-18-20-22-24-16-18-20-22-24)

WORKOUTS: CATEGORY V: AEROBIC BASE TRAINING

This article is the second of a series of workouts suggestions for each of the six training paces that we use in our preparation for racing and improving our fitness.

The Category V Training Pace

Category V (Cat V) pace is for training technique and developing basic aerobic endurance. Along with Cat VI training, Cat V is still in the realm of low intensity and low lactate level training. Combined Cat VI and Cat V training can comprise up to 85 percent of a rower's annual volume, of that approximately 10 percent will be at Cat V pace.

Done correctly, Cat V provides all of the benefits of Cat VI rowing (increases capillary density in muscles to improve blood and oxygen supply to the working muscles, increases mitochondria in the muscles cells, improves the development of aerobic base, and develops your recovery ability especially during high intensity work and racing), plus has the added benefit of utilizing an increased number of endurance fast twitch (FOG) fibers. The notch up in speed calls into action muscle fibers that are not generally recruited during Cat VI rowing. If Cat VI is 65 to 75 percent on an intensity scale, Cat V is 75 to 80 percent. It is during this type of training that you continue to groove in technical changes before increasing the intensity further. Psychologically, Cat V training has slightly greater concentration requirements than Cat VI.

Avoid Making Big Mistakes

Keeping Cat VI and Cat V at the correct slow pace is

critical to getting the benefit of these levels of training. One of the biggest mistakes that rowers make in training is doing Cat VI and Cat V faster than indicated. Going too fast at the lower rates denies your body the opportunity to develop optimum capillary and mitochondria density and this, in turn, does not develop your ability to recovery well from higher intensity work. If you think these speeds are too easy, add more time to your workout or take the stroke rates down but do not let the speed creep up. Don't worry about not doing enough work in training; the higher intensities will take care of that later.

In a nutshell, go slow when training calls to go slow, go fast when training calls to go fast. Avoid what I call the garbage zones the speeds that are neither fish nor meat so to speak. I cannot reiterate this strongly enough so please do take it seriously.

How Slow to Go

Compared to your 20-minute test's average pace per 500 meters, your target pace is 8 to 12 seconds slower per 500 meters; if your average pace from your test is 2:00, your Cat V is done at 2:08 to 2:12 per 500 meters. Target stroke rates are between 22 to 23 strokes per minute. Your effort has accelerated breathing but brief speech should be possible.

Workouts for Cat V Training Effect

- Row: Cat V: 60' alternate (12'@ Cat V pace/3' easy paddle). Continuous row.
- Row: Cat VI: 2-3 x 30' alternate (5'@ Cat VI pace/10' @ Cat V pace). 3' rest between each 30', Stroke rate range 18-22.
- Row: Cat V: 4 x 20' (4'@ Cat V pace/1' easy paddle), 3' rest between.
- Row: Cat V: Technique row: 10 km.
- Row: Cat V: 4 x 15' with 3' between, SR 22-23.

- Row: Cat V: 2-3 x 6,000 meters with 5' rest between. SR 22-23. This technique row is focused on improving the entry, direct release, and balance of the boat.

WORKOUTS: CATEGORY IV: ANAEROBIC THRESHOLD TRAINING

This article is the third of our series of workouts suggestions for each of the six training paces that we use in our preparation for racing and improving our fitness.

The Category IV Training Pace

Category IV (Cat IV) pace is for training your anaerobic threshold and your ability to hold a higher base speed over your racing distance, whether it is 1,000 meters or 5,000 meters. Anaerobic threshold is the point where lactic acid is produced faster than it can be rid of from the muscles. When lactic acid begins to accumulate it can cause you to slow down, so you want to improve how fast you can go until you reach this barrier. Cat IV training is done at a level best described as comfortably hard. It is not an all-out effort but one that represents a substantial workout and the pace should be able to be sustained for 30 to 40 minutes of total work time. A rower's annual volume will have about 10 to 15 percent Cat IV intensity training. The increased level of endurance capacity is often expressed as a percentage of maximum heart rate. Too much of Cat IV training can easily lead to overtraining so it should be used with respect.

If Cat VI is 65 to 75 percent on a subjective intensity scale and Cat V is 75 to 80 percent; Cat IV is 80 to 90 percent. This intensive level of endurance training requires will power and builds strength-endurance while improving oxygen uptake. There is a higher degree of load, breathing is more difficult, conversation is reduced, and the workout requires concentration.

How to Pace It

Compared to your 20-minute test's average pace per 500 meters, your target pace is two seconds slower per 500 meters; if your average pace from your test is 2:00, your Cat IV is done at 2:02 per 500 meters. Target stroke rates are between 24 to 26 strokes per minute.

Workouts for Cat IV Training Effect

- Do once or twice per week:
- Row: 4 x 10' @ Cat IV pace with 5' rest between.
- Row: 3 x 20' @ Cat IV pace with 7' rest between.
- Row: 1 x 30' @ set SR 24. Aim to improve your meters each time you do this workout.
- Row: 4 x 3,000 meters @ Cat IV pace, with set SR 22. This workout introduces a power element.

WORKOUTS: CATEGORY III: BUILDING VO2 MAX

This article is the fourth of our series of workouts suggestions for each of the six training paces that we use in our preparation for racing and improving our fitness.

The Category III Training Pace

Category III (Cat III) pace increases your VO2 max and is for training to perform at higher levels of lactate, as well as, promoting lactate recovery. In a rower's annual plan, this level of training comprises only five to 10 percent. If you are a racer, it is a must to do some Cat III training to raise your physiological abilities.

If Cat VI is 65 to 75 percent on a subjective intensity scale, Cat V is 75 to 80 percent, Cat IV is 80 to 90 percent, and Cat III is 90 to 95 percent. This intensive level of training requires a great deal of will and concentration to tolerate the high lactic acid levels that the pace demands. Conversation is not possible.

How to Make Sure You Go Fast Enough

Compared to your 20-minute test's average pace per 500 meters, your target pace is two seconds faster per 500 meters; if your average pace from your test is 2:00, your Cat III is done at 1:58 per 500 meters. Target stroke rates are 28+ strokes per minute. You must focus on maintaining the correct pace or you will not get the intended training effect.

Workouts for Cat III Training Effect

- Done once or twice a week for eight weeks prior to racing.
- Row: 3 x 2,000 meters @ Cat III pace with 10' rest.
- Row: 8 x 4' @ Cat III pace with 8' rest.
- Row: 5 x 5' @ Cat III pace with 5' rest
- Row: 5 x 1,000 meters @ Cat III pace with 5' rest

Cat II workouts are for improving your racing ability and Cat I is anaerobic speed work.

A Quick Review of Performance-based Training Paces

There are five training categories within the aerobic system and one anaerobic category. Each classification produces specific physiological adaptations within the cell. An annual plan includes all of these training intensities utilized progressively during the year, moving from low to high intensity. Speed, stroke rate and heart rate generally coincide.

The speeds that you train at for each category are determined by a performance test of 20 minutes on the ergometer or on the water. A performance-based method of determining your training paces is a very specific way to gauge your training and is used widely internationally. It is more accurate than heart rate in well-trained individuals and is the next best method of determining aerobic paces other than in a physiology lab. By regularly monitoring performance you can adjust training paces accordingly. If your performance improves your training paces improve. If your fitness falls due to injury or lack of training, you are able to establish an accurate baseline for resuming training.

REVIEW OF THE TRAINING CATEGORIES: OBJECTIVES, PACE, AND AVERAGE STROKE RATES

Cat VI

Purpose: Training of technique, will power, basic endurance, improved fat metabolism, increases capillary density, and recovery ability. Should feel pleasant and conversational, breathing and heart rate hardly noticeable.

- Target pace: 20-minute average 500-meter split plus 13 to 18 seconds if you are well trained; 18 to 22 seconds if you are at a club-level or novice level. The well-trained level should not be more strenuous than conversational pace.
- Subjective effort: 65 to 75 percent
- Target stroke rate: 18-22

Cat V

Purpose: Training of technique and aerobic endurance. Requires greater concentration than Cat VI, accelerated breathing, and brief speech is possible.

- Target pace: 20-minute average 500-meter split plus 8 to 12 seconds.
- Subjective effort: 75 to 80 percent
- Target stroke rate: 22-23

Cat IV

Purpose: Training will power, strength-endurance, intensive endurance training, and improving oxygen intake. There is a higher degree of load, breathing is more difficult, conversation is reduced and the workout requires more concentration.

- Target pace: 20-minute average 500-meter split plus 2 seconds.
- Subjective effort: 85 to 90 percent
- Target stroke rate: 24-26

Cat III

Purpose: Improves specific strength-endurance, race tactics, will power training, and improving oxygen intake. Requires a great deal of will and concentration to tolerate high lactic acid levels.

- Target pace: 20-minute average 500-meter split minus 2 seconds.
- Subjective effort: 90 to 95 percent
- Target stroke rate: 28+

Cat II

Purpose: Develops the feeling for racing speed, tactical skills, speed endurance, and technical efficiency at high level of exertion. Maximum individual speed over the course requires strong will. High motivation is needed.

- Target pace: 20-minute average 500-meter split minus 5 percent.
- Subjective effort: 95 to 100 percent
- Target stroke rate: 30+

Cat I

Purpose: Improve starts, accelerations, speed, and racing tactics at high stroke rates. Maximum exertion needed with extreme concentration.

- Target Pace: Maximum speed.
- Subjective effort: 110 percent
- Target stroke rate: 30-40

Note: To achieve a specific training effect in a workout you may have variations in the categories you use. For example, a workout that alternates Cat III and Cat VI speeds within the workout may produce a training effect of Cat IV.

KEEPING A LOGBOOK

Coaches and athletes need to monitor their training and track progress. Keeping a logbook is a must to follow your own or your team's response to training. Without a written record it is difficult to determine what worked in training and what didn't work. Being able to record the conditions of your row, what you learned, how you felt, what drills you did, or how you mentally handled your session give you a valuable ongoing reference. Your logbook can become very important if you are frequently injured or ill. You can go back and look for patterns that may have led to your illness. If you are an athlete prone to overtraining, your journal can give you a place to track the appearance of symptoms and identify conditions that push your training balance over the edge. Your log is a most importantly a private place where you can be honest with yourself, look at your performance, or work through intense aspects of training camp or team selection when you want to reach a goal. You should make an entry everyday while your training is fresh in your mind. Some days your entries may brief on others days you may have more time for writing.

In your entries record the date, day of the week, resting heart rate, planned workout, actual workout done, drills, boating, total distance or time, injuries, subjective feelings, and any other important notes you want to track. If you have just raced write down the good points and the weak points of your race.

Sample

01 October 2006
HR 48

AM) Row 1x: Cat. III: 3k warm up + 5 x 5' with 5' rest between.
HR: 172-174, SR: 27-28, 12k total, rainy & cold, good row.
Planned 6 pieces but started to lightening.

PM) Row 2x: Cat. VI: 10k with drills mixed in..
Worked on cleaner releases, better by the end.

02 October 2006
HR 50
AM) Row 4x: Cat. IV: 3k warm up + 3 x 3k with 6-7' rest.
HR: 166, SR: 23-24. 2-seat.

PM) Off, planned rest. Full sauna in evening (3 sessions of 15').

Tracking Volume

Make a table to track your volume of training. This should be in total minutes but write down your distance too. You can use an excel spreadsheet so you can easily add up monthly totals or you can keep a simple chart. At the end of each month you should add up your total time and distance. Comparing month-to-month and year-to-year will give you a guide for appropriately increasing training volume and avoiding the common pitfall of trying to do more than your body can adapt to and remain healthy.

CHAPTER 2

KEEPING ON

*HEALTH. GOOD HABITS. MOTIVATION. SPORTS
MASSAGE. DAILY LIVING.*

DEVELOPING GOOD HABITS

As competitive athletes and coaches most of our time is spent preparing for things: practice, time trials, and races. To be able to do your best on a daily basis and during your events you need to pay attention to the details of how you get ready to perform. This includes how you approach your training session every day. Here are some tips to practice and race better.

Daily Sessions

When you go to practice be on time. It helps you get into the right mindset for training and it shows respect to your crew. Arrive 10 to 15 minutes before you need to start practice so you have time to get dressed and begin to warm up on land. Dress neatly and according to the weather. Wear technical fabrics that wick away water and sweat so you stay dry. Loose baggy clothes can get caught in your equipment and are awkward when wet. Longer shirts keep your lower back covered and warm. When the weather is cold make sure to wear a knitted hat and a windshirt to keep your chest and back protected.

After your training sessions ends get dry and clean right away. Avoid standing around on the dock or in the boat bays when you are wet. It is easy to get chilled and catch cold. Go to the shower as soon as possible to clean your skin from salt and sweat. If you are unable to shower immediately have a full change of dry clothing to put on. It is especially important for scholastic coaches to keep an eye on their crews making sure they change right away. If you plan to work on flexibility after rowing, change your clothes first and then stretch taking care not to sit on cold floors or in drafty places.

During your row always carry your own water bottle. When training, rinse your mouth with a bit of water to clean impurities from your mouth before swallowing water directly from your bottle. Prevent the top of your water bottle from floating in water on the bottom of the boat. Keep it clean and rinsed on a daily basis.

Race Days

In addition to your physical and mental training for race day, there are many logistics that need to be taken care of when you compete. Being organized before the day of the race will decrease stress and make sure you have everything you need to concentrate and row your best. Here are some important points to help you develop your own system:

- Submit your entry form and entry fee on time.
- Make hotel reservations in advance, if needed.
- Plan adequate travel time so you have a chance to rest and relax before you race. If you need to fly and change time zones, allow one day at the site for every hour of change.
- Collect any information you need about the race site ahead of time.
- Make any boat repairs or rigging adjustments at home so you have a chance to row it before race day.
- Have a supply of healthy snacks and water with you in the event that there is a poor choice of food at the regatta site.

Before traveling to a race it is easy to forget important items, make sure you have everything you need.

Race Day Travel List

Equipment:
- Car rack
- Boat rack
- Boat cover
- Boat
- Seat
- Footstretchers
- Riggers
- Oars
- Boat slings
- Tie down straps
- SpeedCoach
- Bow markers
- Toolbox
- Water bottle
- Seat pad
- Spare fin
- Spare collars and oarlocks
- Duct tape

Clothing:
- Racing suit and shorts
- Tights
- Windshirt and pants
- Rain gear
- Sweatshirt and pants
- Dry clothes
- Change of shoes
- Jacket
- Hat or bandana

Miscellaneous:
- Road map
- Hotel information
- Entry confirmation

- Directions to race site
- Food and snacks
- Water and juices
- Sunscreen
- Sunglasses
- Blanket or lawn chair

THE HIGHLY MOTIVATED INDIVIDUAL

Motivation levels are high during racing season. Going to an event is usually in the forefront of your mind as you put your boat in the water well before the sun rises. Besides being competitive outlets, regattas are great social events and places to have fun with your teammates or fellow scullers. Once the fall season concludes and winter training enters the scene it can be a bit tougher to stay focused on daily training especially if you live in the northern climates and the days get short.

Strategies to keep training consistent may be a challenge especially if you train alone or have a demanding work and travel schedule. Being part of a group or a team can give you a structure so you have training partners. This could vary from a serious competitive setting to simply having a friend that you meet with a couple of times with to row or do weights. Having short-term goals for each week and month can keep you focused on your tasks at hand and build towards your long-term goals for next season. Doing time trials or regular set workouts will keep you accountable to yourself and your partners. Design your training schedule based on the amount of time that you know you can devote to exercise. Be conservative and plan what is realistically achievable then if you have one or two optional workouts you will feel more positive about doing them when you have extra time. Avoid getting yourself behind the eight ball by over booking your erg or gym time and feeling like you are never quite following the plan you want. You'll stick with a workout schedule if it works in the overall scheme of your family, school, or work life and allows you to be consistent.

Taking into account the facilities you have available in the off-season can help you to adjust your program to one that is doable given the constraints of time and daylight. A gym close to work or home can save you commuting time that you could better spend working out. Getting accustomed to different pieces of cardio equipment such as steppers, treadmills, and stationary bikes can give you some cross training options, provide variety, and use muscle groups in a way slightly different from rowing. Have a trainer instruct you in strengthening exercises such as Pilates, stability ball exercises, or weights. Taking a class in yoga or dance can give you skilled movement instruction that will transfer into qualities you can use in the boat plus you won't have to train alone. A small home gym can also be an excellent way to maximize your exercise time. With a few pieces of equipment such as an erg, Concept2 Dyno, stability ball, yoga mat, and a selection of free weights you can do substantial work in your own home listening to music that you like to play. The key is to look for opportunities that are convenient and easy to take advantage of. When traveling have a jump rope, a calisthenics circuit, or a core strengthening routine handy in the event that you do not have access to a boat, erg, or a place to run.

Training plans frequently change due to unforeseen circumstances so designate your priority workouts of the week ahead of time. In the event that you need to miss a session or two you know the ones that are the most important for you to do. This can be a very helpful approach if you travel a lot. When your motivation wanes a bit give yourself a chance to enjoy other aspects of rowing to get some inspiration. Watching racing videos, reading sports books, visiting a boatbuilders shop, or having a party for your rowing club friends can also boost your excitement for getting back on the water especially when training has to move indoors and the holidays edge closer.

LISTENING TO YOUR BODY

Staying healthy is the first requirement for consistent training. You need to be careful anytime you add new exercises to your routine. You need to practice regularly to improve your fitness and results but reaching peak fitness is like walking a fine line; there is a delicate balance between pushing yourself to the limits of health and that of overtraining.

As you develop your athletic abilities you will get to know your body better. You will feel how long it takes you to recovery from a steady distance row or an interval workout. You will sense when your muscles feel sluggish, your attention span waivers or your hamstring is aching. You will also know when you can work a little harder. Tuning into your body is a skill. It needs to be formed just as the skills of a racing start do. You will learn to become more sensitive if you take the time to listen to what your body and feelings are telling you. Be conservative. If you feel you need extra recovery time between workouts, take it. If you feel an injury coming on it is better to back off for two days than to lose a month of training later on. If you need a mental health day away from work and exercise take one to relax, especially on a sunny day. An ounce of prevention is truly worth a pound of cure when it comes to regular training, especially when you consider most soft tissue injuries require six to eight weeks to completely heal and overtraining syndrome in older athletes can take months.

Rowing is a sport that does pose some injury risks although it is generally much lower than impact or contact sports. Rowing overuse injuries can manifest as rib stress fractures, tendonitis in the elbow region, or lower back pain. For the most part, tuning into your body, improving your posture, and increasing your training load at a reasonable pace will help you to avoid common pitfalls. Most rowers get injured off the water during cross training in the weight room or running. When you lift weights, extreme care needs to be taken to use proper technique, this may mean hiring a trainer to teach you to lift correctly but the investment is well worth it.

Letting pain be your guide is not always be the best approach to injury prevention as each person has a different pain tolerance. A slight twinge to you could be excruciatingly painful to another. When in doubt be conservative; take an extra day off or revise your training to be an easier session. If you feel a trouble area is not improving you may need to have it evaluated by a sports medicine professional.

Maintaining flexibility in your major muscle groups is a key component of injury reduction. Flexibility will help you to achieve better technique and allow you to row more efficiently. Increased elasticity of your muscles and tendons allow the tissue to work without tearing; consider the difference between stretching a fresh rubber band and a brittle one. Hydration is another factor that contributes to your flexibility in addition to the recovery benefits.

A regular stretching routine need not be time intensive. It is better to spend five to 10 minutes addressing major muscle groups after each row than to stretch once a week for 45 minutes. If you are pressed for time stretch only the areas where you sense stiffness or resistance. Never force a stretch, just go to the point of feeling a barrier. If you have access to a yoga class, this a great way to work on balance and flexibility, otherwise include a good 30-minute stretching session once a week in addition to your daily stretches. Attentiveness to the beginning and end of your training session both prepares your muscles for work during the exercise time and initiates recovery after exercise has stopped. Include warm-up and cool-down time in your total workout time. Do not neglect these parts of your workout.

Be proactive when it comes to having a suspected injury evaluated. The earlier you identify an injury, the faster you can remedy it. Some guidelines for when to seek advice are if you have pain accompanied by swelling the area should be evaluated, any swelling, bruising, or lump can warrant medical evaluation. Also, if you have pain after rowing, take a couple of days off to see if it resolves with icing four to five times a day. Try rowing again for a short period, if the pain returns see a doctor or physical therapist.

It is only natural to want to get back to your normal training volume after an injury. How fast you can do that depends on whether you have cross trained during your injury to maintain some cardio-vascular fitness and the severity of your particular injury. A safe general rule is to allow twice the amount of downtime to build back up to your usual routine. So, if you have been off the water for three weeks, allow six weeks to build back up to your regular mileage. You may have to start out with short 20-minute sessions every other day gradually increasing each row by five minutes until you reach 45 minutes. Then begin to alternate one day at 30 minutes with one day at 15 minutes and gradually build from there. This all requires patience but you have to remember why you may have become injured in the first place. Keep the big picture in mind, train safely, and enjoy your rowing.

THE ANATOMY OF A SPORTS MASSAGE

Ancient Greeks and Romans combined exercise with massage in their athletic training for centuries, as did Asians who practiced martial arts. In the 1960s, Russian athletic teams introduced the modern discipline of sports massage when therapists began traveling and working with their teams. Sports massage is an area of massage therapy that is specifically designed to meet the needs of athletes by enhancing recovery, decreasing the likelihood of injury, and acting as a performance aid. Today, regular treatments are included in any serious competitor's schedule. The benefits, however, are available to those of any fitness level. By preventing musculotendinious injuries, reducing the strain of training and the associated chronic stress patterns, sports massage lets you return to maximum training levels quicker, speeds recovery, and can give you a psychological boost by reducing pain and invigorating your muscles. As a part of your preventive approach to athletic training it will keep your soft tissue free of trigger points and adhesions helping your body to reach peak neuromuscular functioning.

There are several important physical effects associated with massage. The stroking movements used draw fluid through blood and lymph vessels by increasing pressure in front of the stroke and creating a vacuum behind. This pumping effect is important to stimulate blood flow to restricted muscles as tight areas drive blood out depriving the tissue of its ability to repair. Deep massage helps pores in tissue membranes to open so fluids can pass through. Increased permeability of membranes assists the removal of metabolic waste products such as lactic acid while encouraging the muscle to absorb oxygen and nutrients for faster recovery. Massage elongates and broadens muscle fiber bundles in ways that cannot be achieved with usual stretching methods. It can also mobilize the fascia surrounding a muscle to release tension or pressure allowing the fibers to become more pliable. Muscles relax with the manual activation of mechanoreceptors, which sense touch, pressure, length, and warmth. Residual scar tissue plus hard training can make tissues stiff and inflexible which can have a negative impact your rowing.

If you have never had a sports massage here is what you can expect. There are three main types of sessions based on time frames. A training massage helps to increase flexibility and range of motion plus recover faster from workouts. The focus is to prevent the development of chronic problems and speed healing from any existing injuries. A session can last from 30 to 90 minutes. A pre-event massage is done before an event to stimulate circulation, calm nervous tension, and prepare the body for performance. It warms muscles and increases flexibility. After 15 to 20 minutes, you will hop off the table ready to race. Post-event treatments are typically given one to two hours after an event to relieve the swelling caused by micro-tears in the muscles, to encourage blood flow so lactic acid can be removed, and alleviate soreness. This is not the time for deep trigger point work but to help the muscles repair themselves; a full body flush can be done in about 30 minutes.

A training massage usually takes place in a clinic or office. When lying down on the massage table you will be draped in a sheet. Only the area being worked on is exposed. A pre-event or post-event massage is often done at a competition site and you will get on the table with your sports clothes on. A variety of strokes can be used depending on the nature of your session. Compression is applied with quick, rhythmic action using the palm, loose fist, or fingertips. It spreads the tissue and softens tight muscles. Jostling and vibration involve picking up tissue and tossing it back and forth, like rocking your quadriceps side to side. It is done briskly to stimulate and warm up tissue before an event or done gently to relax. Tapotement is a type of rhythmic striking that can be done with the fingertips or cupped hands. It is common in pre-event massages for warming up and also used in training massages. Effleurage is a type of long stroke applied in the direction of the heart to increase the drainage of waste products. Friction strokes can be circular, cross-fiber, or linear and move a superficial structure over a deeper structure to mobilize areas that are stuck together and not moving smoothly. Some strokes, such as effleurage, require gliding over the skin so the therapist will use an oil or lotion for others the skin needs to be dry as with friction. It takes about 24 hours for the neurological effects of a massage to be fully integrated into your system.

Your therapist may ask when your last training session was, the type of training, and what areas feel tight, fatigued, or overstressed. Your therapist may also want to know when your next practice or event is and how you felt after your last treatment. Contraindications to massage include, but are not limited to, open wounds, contusions, ruptures, burns, arthritis, gout, bursitis, infections, thrombosis, bleeding disorders, and tumors. If you have any condition that you are not sure of discuss it with your massage therapist to ensure whether it is safe for you to receive massage. Sessions are typically charged according to time and vary depending on the therapist and the setting. Resort rates are usually higher than domestic rates. If you have a specific injury that you need addressed you can book just 30 minutes. Many therapists offer lower rates for packages of five or more appointments.

To find a certified therapist your area, consult these organizations: American Massage Therapy Association (AMTA), www.amtamassage.org/findamassage/locator.htm or call 888-THE-AMTA. Canadian Sport Massage Therapist Association (CSMTA), www.csmta.ca. National Certification Board for Therapeutic Massage and Bodywork (NCBTMB), www.ncbtmb/database/query.asp.

SERIOUS RELAXATION: HOW TO RECOVER FROM THE RACING SEASON

The conclusion of head racing season plays a different role for each rower depending on the type of annual training cycle they are on. For elite and college athletes it is part of the preparation for the next season and will build into more formal training to take place over the winter. For many club and masters rowers the end of the head racing season represents their annual cycle's peak. The need for a definite recovery period is high before entering the next year's cycle of training. It is important to include two to three weeks of regeneration into your training plan. This is when you need to recuperate and to plan for next year's training.

It is easy to neglect taking this break during the year but it is as important to give yourself psychological rest as well as physical rest or attend to injuries that may have cropped up during the season. During your regeneration weeks you should still exercise but it should be relaxed, easy and unstructured. It is a perfect time to cross train if you like or to begin some easy weight lifting to prepare for a more structured program later on. For two to three weeks during a regeneration period your weekly schedule could look like this:

- Two days of passive rest.
- One day of active rest.
- Two days of passive rest.
- Two days of easy training.

Passive Rest

This type of recovery includes activities such as reading, watching television, going to the movies, going to a concert, going out to dinner, or lying in the sun. You are relatively stationary and just taking it easy or getting extra sleep. No more than 30 minutes of walking.

Active Rest

Recovery through light aerobic movement or active rest facilitates faster recovery than total rest due to increased circulation. For a sculler, good choices would be 30 minutes of swimming, one hour of easy cycling or tennis, or a 30-minute brisk walk or jog. Stretching could be included here too.

Easy Training

This is conversational pace, steady aerobic exercise or a light weight workout but no more than 40 minutes in total. As during active rest, this is a good time to mix activities.

Remember that your goals during your regeneration weeks are to reduce stress, have a change of pace from hard training, and take some time out of the boat. Choose things to do that you truly find relaxing, whether it be watching a film, hiking in the mountains for a change of scenery or going to get a good massage. Let your mind wander away from training or work concerns and feel refreshed. Truly enjoy your time off, as there will plenty of solid work to do when you get back into your training routine.

TAKING THE TIME TO UNWIND

The scene was rather surrealistic; body shapes covered head to toe in black mud. Some were basking in the sun. Others were simply strolling along the path between the sulphur pools and the shore. With only their eyes peering out like circles, all were engaged in the process of maximizing the health benefits of the therapeutic sludge. The Ein Gedi Spa is a famous attraction located on the shore of the Dead Sea. People from all over the world visit this unique geographical spot, known as the "emerald of the desert" because of its greenery. Though surrounded by high mountains, the Dead Sea is the lowest point on earth sitting 413 meters below sea level. The air and water quality are exceptional and thought to be ideal for relaxing and re-energizing.

Since I was in the area, I decided to test the waters for myself. The Dead Sea is so dense with salt that you can sit on it which means you can float effortlessly, feet up, and even read a newspaper. You definitely feel ridiculous and realize that rowing would be virtually impossible on it. A 30-minute dip cleanses your skin so your cells breathe better and deeply relaxes your muscles. Slathering yourself in the mineral mud containing calcium, magnesium, potassium, sodium, zinc, iron, and sulphides helps invigorate your peripheral blood supply, boost the strength of your cells and draw toxins out of your body. Then a final rinse with the sulphur water shower concludes the treatments. All are an important part of helping to detoxify and restore balance to your body after a long period of hard training.

Rowers are some of the most motivated athletes. Getting a rower to work hard is never a problem; getting a rower to relax and recover enough is. They often push beyond physical and psychological norms. The need to maintain equilibrium between training, friends, work, school, and recovery always exists. Recovery rates from training vary with different conditions. Here are a few examples. Athletes older than 25 years of age may require longer rest periods after training. Exercising in cold temperatures slows regenerative hormones and increases lactate production at low loads. Decreased range of motion restricts blood supply and compromises muscle activity. The type of exercise affects recovery rates; training endurance has a lower recovery rate than doing sprint training. Psychological factors also affect recovery because negative feelings are able to trigger the release of stress-related hormones and slow the process.

There are many ways to include treatments, such as massage and hydrotherapies, to help you recover. Massage effectively assists the elimination of toxic substances from the tissues, stimulates circulation, and decreases muscle tension. There are over 300 massage modalities and techniques available. Sports massage is a good choice because it precisely applies certain manual maneuvers at different times in the training schedule. For example, a pre-event massage will decrease muscle tension yet keep the body and mind ready for competition. A post-event flush is a total body massage lasting 30 to 40 minutes given soon after a hard training session or race. A flush is defined by the type of superficial strokes used: jostling, compression, effleurage, and spreading which help to increase the elimination of lactic acid and other metabolic waste products. Sessions done on rest days are called maintenance massages and are reserved for deep tissue work and targeted at injury prevention.

Water therapies help the mind and body. Hot showers and baths relax muscles, increase circulation, and improve the quality of sleep. Contrast showers alternating hot to cold water stimulate circulation and saunas allow for vasodilation and perspiration, which eliminates toxins from the muscle cells. Toxins cause fatigue to linger and negatively affect central nervous system stimulation. Saunas taken weekly for a minimum of 15 minutes produce effects which would normally require two hours of rest to achieve. Cross-country skiers routinely build time for saunas into their training plans. A full session can consist of three 15 to 20 minute sessions. After each bout you immediately rinse in a cold-water shower blending it to warm to create a contrast effect. Once wrapped in a robe, relax and cool down for 10 to 15 minutes before the next round. Drinking plenty of fresh water between sessions helps the cleansing process. Stay healthy, fresh, and keep your saw sharpened this winter.

BUSINESS TRAVEL: BATTLE ALONG THE WAY

"What the heck is that?" He opened my box. A seasoned security guard, he looked at the folded skeleton of metal, puzzled, like the guys at gas stations who think your boat is a missile on the roof of your car. But in this Middle Eastern airport the situation was more serious. "It's a rowing machine," I answered, "for exercising." "Well then, put it together and exercise," he said. I put my erg together as a crowd gathered. It took some time. Two sniffing dogs were nearby. Then I started rowing. After a few minutes, I was ordered to stop. The monitor was removed and sent to a scanner for explosive devices. I had to prove I was really a rowing coach so the guard insisted I turn on my laptop and show him some of my e-mails. Four hours had passed. They were still suspicious of me until a young baggage porter stopped and said that his mother has one of those machines. "She even races on it," he added. Only then they decided I could I pack it up and be escorted to the airplane.

I must admit that it was not always so complicated. In Italy and Slovenia, when seeing my machine no questions were asked. When they saw my erg, they just smiled and waved me through. Yes, there are countries where our sport is respected. Having an indoor rower with me was a good way to stay fit when I was away for extended periods of time, but for short trips working out requires creativity, diligence, and organization. For many adults who travel for professional purposes, training on the go is a fact of life. Recently, some masters shared their experiences with me about how they stay on track when away from the boathouse.

The two biggest obstacles for exercising when away are finding the time and the motivation. Work in different continents can mean being in several locations in a short amount of time.

Asian itineraries with appointments in China, Taiwan, Japan, and Korea in the matter of a few days often means a long day in one location and then a short flight or long drive to another. In addition to a tightly packed schedule, business dinners also consume time in the evenings. Staying motivated is tough when you are tired, hungry, and the nearby fitness room is dreary or you feel pressured that you are not getting your workout in and losing shape. A trip is more enjoyable if it isn't preventing you from getting your workout done. All agree that you have to do something each day-no matter what. Be it nothing more than a 20-minute run, a couple weight exercises, or stretching. One missed day easily becomes two or three. Sticking to basic daily maintenance keeps you feeling in sync with your normal routine and goes far in the long haul.

The most effective strategy is planning your training as part of your travel schedule. You'll need to do some work up front. Know what exercise equipment is available at your hotel. Then, for the future, keep your own notes about each location. If you will be in a rowing city, make call a local club ahead of time to inquire if visitors can access an erg or shell. The use of ergs is usually easier than a boat but in some cases you might be able to get a morning row by arrangement. Rowing at a new club, in an interesting setting, is an aspect of business-related travel that is universally met with delight. Commit to setting your alarm clock and getting up early. Define what your workout will be; how long, what routine plus, warm-up, then allow extra time to adjust for any inefficiency. Always pack running shoes, workout gear, and a stretching strap. Sean Maloney of Bair Island Aquatic Club travels overseas 30 percent of the time. He advises, "If you are out running stick on main roads even though in some places the pollution is bad. Taking side roads has led to being attacked by dogs (Thailand and India) and of course getting lost."

Potential illness and changing time zones are major factors to contend with on foreign journeys. Maloney says, "Avoiding illness? No magic remedy. I get sick on trips. Economy class on planes is a big culprit. If you can go business class the air is less crowded with germs. Obviously the basic stuff-never drink tap water in Asia or emerging markets, never eat ice cream, never eat salads unless you are in a good hotel." Eat lightly and stay well hydrated. Taking a multivitamin and extra vitamin C can help keep your resistance up. Carry hand sanitizers with you at all times and wash your hands frequently. On long flights, drink a lot of fluids and eat less than you would when not traveling; bring good snacks with you. Rowers can be more comfortable with upgraded seats that have more room. Otherwise, get up and stretch frequently. To avoid jet lag, try to get into the correct time zone as soon as you can. Resist sleeping a lot on long flights. It is better to get to your hotel when sleep is past due. The first day might be brutal but adjust as soon as you can. For small time changes you can ignore the differences and use the extra time to do something relaxing. Finally, pad your weekly program with two days off so you are sure to get in all the sessions you planned. Do a harder day before you leave and allow for an easier day when you are back home to catch up on needed rest. Pay very close attention to how your body feels as this is when you may likely get sick. Sleep as much as you feel you need to get back in balance. Web site resources for the business traveler include: www.concept2.com, www.rowersalmanac.com, and www.athleticmindedtraveler.com.

EXERCISES TO PREPARE FOR SCULLING CAMP

When sculling camp season is a couple of months away it is the time to begin preparing for your week or weekend at camp. Each day when you are at sculling camp you will spend more time in a shell than you generally do at home. Though you maybe working on technique or doing easy mileage, the increase of time in the boat can lead to some minor aches simply because you are rowing more than you generally do in a day. To prevent blisters rub your hands with rubbing alcohol daily starting two weeks prior to camp. Lack of flexibility in your hamstrings and lower back or inadequate core strength to support your posture are a few factors that can lead to potential discomfort. By starting a regular schedule of flexibility work and core strengthening, you will be well prepared to spend time in the boat working on technique and training. Good flexibility and core strength will greatly improve your ability to learn good sculling technique.

Good rowing technique requires adequate mobility for numerous biomechanical reasons. Restrictions in the hips and ankles necessitate modifications be made through your rigging to achieve the right compression. In extreme cases this can be quite difficult. Making your muscles more elastic will reduce the need for compensation through your equipment, reduce your risk of injury, and help you acquire better stroke length through the water.

Here is a simple exercise prescription for you to start a few months before you go to camp. In addition to your regular sculling, rowing, or erging, four 30-minute sessions per week would be ideal. You can certainly include flexibility daily if you have the time available.

If you have never sculled before you should build up your aerobic endurance with running, walking, biking, or on the indoor rower if you have access to one. When you start sculling you will be focusing on technique and rowing quite lightly so you should maintain your fitness level with cross training.

Basic Preparatory Exercise Program

- Sunday: Aerobic exercise for 60 minutes and flexibility exercises for 30 minutes.
- Monday: Rest day.
- Tuesday: Core strengthening exercises for 15 minutes and flexibility for 15 minutes.
- Wednesday: Core strengthening exercises for 15 minutes, aerobic exercise for 45 minutes, and flexibility exercises for 30 minutes.
- Thursday: Optional day: Aerobic exercise for 45 to 60 minutes.
- Friday:Core strengthening exercises for 30 minutes.
- Saturday: Aerobic exercise for 60 minutes and flexibility exercises for 30 minutes.

Flexibility Exercises

Include a choice from the following exercises. Gently hold each stretch for a count of four then relax and repeat three to four times. Focus on areas that are particularly tight. Do not push any motion that is painful.

- The Rack: Lying on your back, stretch your arms and legs in opposite directions.
- Knee to Chest: Lying on your back, hug one knee to your chest.
- Knee Across: Lying on your back, bring your knee across your body to the floor.

- Leg Up Hamstring: Lying on your back, extend one leg directly up to the ceiling.
- Cobra: Lying on your stomach, raise your upper body off the floor.
- Lying Quadriceps: Lying on your stomach, reach back to hold your heel to your buttocks
- Lying Hip Flexor: Add to the lying quadriceps stretch by raising your knee off the floor.
- Child's Pose: Sit back on your shins and reach your arms above your head.
- Kneeling Hip Flexor: Kneeling on one knee, step your foot out in front of your and lean forward.
- Squatting Achilles: Stand with your feet wider than shoulder-width and squat very low.
- Standing Hamstring: Stand with feet shoulder-width apart and reach for the floor with knees extended.
- Standing Triceps: Reach your hand above your head first, then try to touch the center of your back.
- Triceps and Obliques: Add to the standing triceps stretch by leaning away from your stretching arm.
- Biceps: Interlock your fingers behind your back and raise your arms as high as you can.
- Hug Your Traps: Wrap your arms around you as if giving yourself a hug and tuck your chin to your chest.

More Great Sculling Stretches

This exercise is for your hamstrings and low back. The *hamstring stretch-supine* is done lying down on your back. You will need a boat strap or piece of rope long enough to stirrup around your foot. Hold one rope end in your left hand and the other in your right. Using the contraction of your quadriceps (thigh) muscles will assist the stretching of your hamstrings. Your non-exercising leg should remain flat on the floor. If you have severe low back considerations, then you may flex your non-exercising leg slightly. Keep the exercising leg straight at all times. Lift your leg straight up off the floor by contracting your thigh muscles. Continue as high as you can without bending at the knee. Give brief, gentle overpressure with the rope at the end of the movement as the quadriceps muscles move your leg. Release and return your leg back down to the floor. Repeat two sets of 10 repetitions on your right leg, then on your left leg. If you notice one leg is tighter than the other-common among sweep rowers-do an extra set of 10 repetitions for that leg until you feel balanced. In the event you don't have a rope you can use your hands behind your knee to apply overpressure. Be careful not to allow your knee to bend.

This exercise is for your calf muscle to improve ankle flexibility. The purpose of the *gastrocnemius (calf) stretch* is to lengthen the two-joint gastrocnemius muscle improving your Achilles tendon extensibility. Adequate Achilles tendon length is important for the final one-quarter of the recovery as you approach the shins-vertical position. Sit on the floor with your legs flat. With your exercising leg, keep your knee locked using your thigh muscles. Using the shin muscles, pull your toes towards you. Using a strap or rope, as in our first exercise, apply gentle overpressure at the end of the motion. Make sure the shin muscles continue to be contracted when you apply assistance. Hold briefly then relax your foot letting your toes point away from you. Do two or three sets of 10 repetitions, first the left, then the right. Spend more time on one ankle if you feel an imbalance.

Core Strengthening Exercises

See *On Land: Swiss Ball Stability Exercises* for a complete program of core strengthening exercises. Start out very gradually and progress according to your comfort level.

Measuring Flexibility Gains

Here is a way to measure your flexibility gains once you start your daily program. Put a milk crate against the wall. Sit on the floor. Place your feet flat against the side of the crate. Lean forward and measure the distance between your fingertips and the edge of the crate. The edge is your reference of zero inches; if you cannot reach the edge you have a minus value. The distance you reach beyond the edge has a plus value. Values greater than five inches are good; more than 10 represents excellent low back and hamstring flexibility. Investing in the time to create new habits and prepare your body for sculling this summer will help you scull better at home and during your stay at camp.

MANAGING THE COLLEGE CRUNCH

Every spring, college rowers face juggling intensive practices, traveling to races, writing term papers, and taking exams. Getting good grades and making the varsity boat means you have to do everything a little better than the next guy. So as the heat gets turned up in your seat races, how do you stay glued together until championships and finals?

Sleep, staying organized, and keeping a winning spirit are key to having a great season. Sleep is a luxury in student life but for a college rower it is a must. Complete rest is the way you physiologically restore your capacity to work hard. Aim for nine to 10 hours of sleep per day with most of it at night. If you don't sleep enough at nighttime, make up the balance of hours with naps. Power naps are a very effective way to relax and get focused before stepping in the boat, especially when you row late in the day. Do your best to go to bed before 10:30 pm and get up at the same time every morning. Give yourself good sleeping conditions; make sure your room is dark, quiet, and has fresh air. Don't hesitate to turn off the phone and use earplugs if you need to. Sleep when you are tired. Neurologically speaking, there are times when your brain can take in new information and times when it cannot. If you catch yourself reading the same paragraph in your biomechanics book five times over-and you still don't get it-you'd better put it down and sleep for a few minutes. Trying to force information into your memory banks when you are tired wastes valuable time because your learning is ineffective. By resting a bit, you'll be mentally fresher and, as a result, be able to complete the same work much faster.

Avoid crowding your day. Wake up on time to get to class or practice without rushing. Write down whatever you need to keep track of: competitions, exams, or your work schedule.

Know what you need to do each day. Staying organized is critical to minimizing your stress levels and maximizing your rest time. Do your assignments when they need to be done. With a busy rowing schedule you will only have certain times to designate to each project, whether it be writing a paper or reading a chapter. If you miss your window of opportunity you'll start to fall behind. Trying to play catch up on class work is much more energy consuming than staying on top of it in the first place. Being organized will give you more time to rest and that will ultimately help you learn and compete better.

As a final note, be positive through all your studying and rowing. Clear up any problems you encounter quickly and honestly. Ask for help or advice when you need it. Strive for good relations with your coaches and teammates. It is not always essential to be friends with all of your team's members in order to go fast, but it is important to work towards a common goal inside the boat. Having fun at the boathouse will translate into better practices. Allowing some downtime once a week to forget about school and rowing for a few hours is also a healthy thing to do. Rowing at Boston University in the early eighties, my first year of college rowing was my favorite. It was intense, fun, and successful. We were undefeated in the regular season, won silver at the 1982 E.A.W.R.C Sprints, and took gold at our college nationals. Our novice eight, coached by Holly Hatton, had a wild spirit; we sunk our teeth into each practice, we willingly went after any crew out there. We also savored every stroke of it. So get your rest, stay organized, and go row some outstanding races this season. You will remember them for a long time to come.

GERM WARFARE

Emil Zatopek trained in army boots in the deep snow. The 1952 Olympic champion for the 5k, 10k, and marathon runs never let illness interrupt his training. He just reduced it. Zatopek's case is on my mind this time of year. Winter.

Alice is a masters rower. She wrote me recently saying just when she was gearing up for erg races she is almost always struck by colds. "As luck would have it," another sculler e-mailed, "a houseguest, whom we love and hold dear, for the holidays left a gift that keeps on giving-the flu." At this time of year the list of illnesses that strike motivated rowers is long. Based on an informal count of the athletes I work with, I'd say that 35 to 40 percent of rowers are stricken by colds, the flu, or respiratory infections during the winter. There are many contributing factors. Increased training indoors, children bringing things home, co-workers bringing bugs to the office that their children brought home, outdoor temperatures being highly variable, and holiday fatigue piled on top of doing the interval work that you need to get ready for erg races all work to wear you down. Colds and catching the flu seem to outnumber injuries and if you don't take care of yourself, you'll probably get one or the other. This causes a setback in training that you would rather avoid.

So how do you modify your plan to stay healthy? First you need to assess how you are before you can decide. Monitor your resting heart rate to see if it is elevated compared to normal. As a general rule of thumb, if it is 10 beats higher than normal take a rest day, if it is five beats higher than normal, train but avoid intensive work. If you happen to have a time trial planned, postpone it until you are better and your resting heart rate is normal. Part one of Fritz Hagerman's article, *Training the Energy Systems*, online at www.irow.com, advises, "If you are unusually tired, injured or sick, then taking a day or two off should not be considered a serious training setback. Instead, abstinence of training under any of these conditions is a wise choice. Because most interruptions of training are due to respiratory infections, it is recommended that training be reduced if the respiratory problem is above the neck and cancelled if it is below the neck."

Alice asks: "What's best to get back up to speed?" It really depends on how much time you have had to take off from training. If you have missed two to three days in a week's training, you can start back with a low intensity row and some flexibility work but can continue following your training plan without trying to make up workouts. If you have missed more than three days in a given week, you should revise your training plan to repeat that week. More than a week missed would be reason to return to the phase before your illness and repeat the training that you were not able to do, ensuring the right physiological progression. If you are on the brink of going to an indoor race, monitor your symptoms and use common sense to decide whether or not you should really race. If you are not recovered, the ability to dig deep just may not be there in the second 1,000 meters. Neither will the personal record that you want. Resting and getting back to 100 percent represents better time spent in the long term. Use your downtime productively watching rowing videos or reading training books. Besides that, nothing beats thick blankets, some extra rest and the old-world remedy of a glass of Cognac or warm red wine with cloves. Tough Zatopek might have disagreed with taking it easy but I wonder if that was a reason he lost his hair early? Putting energy into getting well when you are ill and then into getting faster when you are healthy will work better for most of us.

HOLIDAY STRATEGIES

Growing up in Buffalo, New York, often times there was so much snow that you could walk on top of the snowdrifts and touch the tops of the telephone poles. Severe blizzards that made sliding down garage roofs possible were normal to us, and being a pretty social town, parties in Buffalo were plentiful. Thinking back to those truly long winters, I remember that the holiday season seemed to go on forever. When holidays roll around, the nature of their timetables throws schedules out of kilter. Being a person that likes routine, I try to find a way to keep up on my workouts especially around those events when you know that feasting is inevitable. As a high school student, I usually grabbed my cross-country skis and went bushwhacking at the golf course behind my house once the turkey was in the oven. During my college years, I set up a makeshift gym in the basement with weights for doing circuits or bench rows and would disappear down there during winter break the moment the sound of a football game murmured from the television or a deck of cards appeared. When the board games came out, as a rule, it was time for me to go out for a long run in the snowy streets. Whatever your holiday commitments are you should have a general idea of how much training you want to do and come up with a few strategies that can keep you on track or at least keep you guilt-free. You can decide if you are going to train daily and stick as closely to your schedule as possible, go on a maintenance plan, or throw structure to the wind and wait to make your New Year's resolution to get started again.

If you are determined to stay on track, there are ways that you can manage your schedule. When you have houseguests, set a time each day when you go to do your workout. Often mornings are easier before the pace of the day takes over and it becomes hard to get away later on. Going out of the house to the gym or boathouse to train will keep you in your training mindset. When you return home you can shift back into holiday mode. A lot of traveling can also be disruptive to your regular schedule so having some ideas ahead of time about how to manage staying fit when on the road can make it easier to do. If you don't have access to a gym when you travel there are ways that you can still get in good sessions. Running or fast walking can be done in most places. If you need to exercise in your hotel room, carry elastic therapy band with you. With elastic you can do many upper body exercises such as bicep curls, vertical rows, triceps extensions, lateral raises, deltoid raises, or overhead presses in multiple sets or combine with calisthenics. You can jump rope for 30 to 40 minutes or do a workout of squat jumps building up to six sets of 60 repetitions.

Setting up a circuit of 12 stations of different exercises that alternate muscle groups and rotating through them can be an interesting and motivating workout that you can do without a gym. A circuit can be based on a set amount of time such as 75 seconds of exercising with 45 seconds rest for a total of 40 minutes or be based on a set number of repetitions per exercise with a set amount of rest between each circuit. Circuits can be all resistance-based, all calisthenics-based or a combination of both.

Here is a general strength and aerobic endurance circuit using your body weight. Perform the following exercises for 30 minutes continuously: 25 squat thrusts, 30 seconds run in place, 50 sit ups, 30 seconds run in place, 30 push ups, 35 jumping jacks, 25 squat thrusts, 30 seconds run in place, 50 sit ups, 30 seconds run in place, 40 squat jumps, 25 squat thrusts, 30 seconds run in place, 50 sit ups, 30 seconds run in place, 30 push ups, 35 jumping jacks, 25 squat thrusts, 30 seconds run in place, 50 jumping jacks, 30 seconds run in place, 50 sit ups, 30 seconds run in place.

The following circuit is to develop core muscular endurance and explosive use of the legs. Repeat circuit the five times. Rest 10 seconds between each exercise and three minutes between each circuit: 15 standing long jumps, 30 push ups, 15 one-legged squats (may be done standing on a bench) then 15 on the other leg, 50 sculling sit ups, 30 squat jumps, 30 chin ups or dips, 50 standing squats, 10 rotate legs overhead and down to the side, almost touching the floor, 20 box jumps (fingertips touch floor, then jump with two feet onto a bench or 25-inch step, then step down), and 30 abdominal crunches.

If you live in a northern climate, planning a cross-country skiing vacation is one of the best ways to improve your aerobic conditioning and long endurance in addition to adventuring through the woods and fields. You can spend greater lengths of time on skis at your steady state intensity than you typically would run and skiing offers a lower impact activity. A long ski is often from two to three hours at a time. It offers total use of your musculature emphasizing leg, trunk, and respiratory strength. The mechanics of skiing utilize concepts common to rowing: the use of body weight to accelerate past the planted position of the pole, follow through motion of the hands and arms to preserve speed, fine tuned balance, explosive rhythm followed by recovery during every stroke, and a sense of glide. Snowshoeing is another fun winter sport. If you venture to the tropics, go for long hikes, run, swim, play water polo or beach volleyball. Biking, spinning, soccer, basketball or power yoga can also be fresh additions to your training plan.

Going on a maintenance plan might be your best option when you know that your schedule will be too busy to train every day. Aim to do three workouts per week to hold your current state of shape and stretch daily. It could be all aerobic workouts or two aerobic sessions plus one strength session. It will be enough to keep you feeling you good and prevent having to completely rebuild after vacations. When festivities and travel will realistically make it very difficult to stay on a routine. Do the best that you can to resist that third piece of cheesecake, enjoy yourself, and make a date to climb back on the erg even if it is the on the second day of January.

WINTER TRAINING OPPORTUNITIES

How you approach winter training is largely dependent on the climate you live in and the racing season that you are training for. If you are focusing on racing next season, this is a perfect time of year to add variety and cross training to your training regime. The general preparation phase of training that extends through March is the time to work on technical improvements in your stroke under low stress conditions, put in low intensity mileage to develop your aerobic base, and address strengthening issues. Variety is key during these long months of preparation. Here are some ways to vary your program while still working on the proper goals for this time of year.

Cross-country Skiing

Cross-country skiing is one of the best ways to improve your aerobic conditioning and long endurance in addition to adventuring through the woods and fields. You may spend greater lengths of time on skis at your steady state intensity than you typically would run and skiing offers a lower impact activity. A long ski is often several hours at a time. It offers total use of your musculature with emphasis on leg, trunk, and respiratory strength. Many mechanics of skiing utilize concepts common to rowing: the use of body weight to accelerate past the planted position of the pole, follow through motion of the hands and arms to preserve speed, fine tuned balance, explosive rhythm followed by recovery during every stroke, and a sense of glide. Many European cross-country skiers use sculling as a means of training in their off-season to train muscular-endurance. In New England, the names of famous scullers such as Joe Bouscaren, Judy Geer, Dick Dreissigacker, or Ted Van Dusen can be found in the local ski marathon results.

If you are unable to get on snow, roller skis can be a fun and effective dry land variant. There are several types of roller skis on the market ranging from rollers designed for skating on pavement to off-road rollers with six-inch wheels and speed adjusters meant for hard-paced dirt roads and hilly terrain. If you have never skied before it is advisable to take a lesson or two to introduce yourself to the fundamentals of balance, stopping, turning, and going down hills then go out and enjoy some winter training.

Running

Running is an important part of your aerobic foundation. It is an excellent alternative to erging or rowing when you are traveling away from home, unable to get to the gym, or have limited time to train. If you tend to do much of your winter training indoors, running gets you outdoors in the fresh air for a change scenery. During racing season, staying in touch with your running can serve you well when you are unable to get enough warm-up time on the water before your race, need more warm-down after an event, or want to maintain aerobic base.

Circuit Training

If you train with a team or a group of friends, setting up multiple stations of different exercises that alternate muscle groups and rotating through them can be an interesting and motivating workout. There are many variations. Some circuits are based on a set amount of time such as 60 seconds of work with 30 seconds rest for a total of 40 minutes or may be based on a set number of repetitions per exercise (6 x 30 repetitions) with a set amount of rest between each circuit (90 seconds between sets). Circuits can be all resistance-based, all calisthenics-based or a combination of both. You may design your own circuit in your gym or at home depending on the equipment you have to use and the areas you need to address in your conditioning.

Swimming, biking, spinning, hiking, soccer, hockey, basketball or power yoga can also be fresh additions to your training plan. Choose one workout a week to cross train keeping in mind that the intensity of that workout should agree with your overall plan. Be creative and enjoy your winter training.

CHAPTER 3

IN PRACTICE

*ON THE WATER. RUN. RHYTHM. OARHANDLING.
TECHNIQUE.*

TECHNICAL PREPARATION

What is Technical Preparation?

When preparing to perform in rowing there are four major components of training that need to be included in an athlete's regime: physical, technical, tactical, and psychological. It is generally accepted that physical preparation is the main aspect of training required to achieve high performance and certainly is the most time demanding. Technical preparation follows physical preparation as a dominant training factor. Technique can be defined as the specific way an exercise is performed. The ability to execute the cyclical rowing stroke in the most efficient manner increases the likelihood of achieving personal satisfaction and good competitive results. The more mastery an athlete has the less energy required to realize a specific goal. Good technique has a direct relationship to high efficiency.

Technique versus Style

Throughout technical discussions it is important to make a clear distinction between technique and style. Technique training is based on a model of the ideal rowing stroke and this frame of reference forms the rudiments of teaching the skills involved. Coaches and athletes collectively must have an understanding of a model that maximizes both biomechanical and physiological needs. The elements of technique refer to the actual learning of the parts of the stroke. Correct practice and drills are how those elements are learned. The manner in which an individual athlete performs the stroke can be termed style. Style allows for distinctive ways of executing *the fundamentals of an accepted model of the rowing stroke.* It may include traits of the athlete or coach's character and personality or a specific way of performing a movement that is defined by the rower's anatomical or physiological nature. Because of the individual requirements of each athlete to meet the technical challenges posed by the rowing stroke, caution should be used when attempting directly imitate the technique of champion rowers or scullers. A champion's style does not always represent a perfect model of the stroke. Rather, study the technique as an example of how he or she has developed a highly proficient personal style that successfully delivers the compulsory elements of the rowing stroke and use your observations to fit your own individual needs.

Developing Technique

There are many ways to improve technical preparation throughout the year. The following methods are ways to gain a better understanding and learning of technique:

- Personalized instruction with a qualified coach on a regular basis.
- Attend a sculling or rowing camp.
- Defined technical sessions on the water.
- Videotaping with review.
- Practice technical drills to develop stroke components.
- Improve your physical preparation to develop musculature involved in technical skills.
- Correct equipment selection for your body size and weight.
- Properly rig your boat and oars.
- Watch videotapes of international rowing events.

PERIODIZATION OF TECHNIQUE

Watch the final of any world championship singles race and you will see six scullers moving the boat with six different styles. Some have very erect posture with minimal layback, others more of a two-part drive with a definitive legs then back motion; less separated power application versus a more separated power application. You can see variations in hand placement on the oarhandle and the position of the wrist-forearm complex at the release. Though their individual styles contrast one another they are all effectively moving at high boat speeds and stroke rates. The rowing world continually debates and revises the details of stroke style and how to make a boat move better. With good reason, as there is certainly more than one way to skin a cat and accomplish boat run.

Individual style can differ depending on physical strengths, weaknesses, and body shape but there are important technical elements that are satisfied in each approach. To find your own style or coach a crew to uniformity means that you need to have a solid image of how the main elements of correct technique are performed. A good technical model will show you proper entry timing, solid application of power and leg drive, precise blade depth, accurate release timing, and a complete transition to body preparation. Blades are carried off the water and there is minimal check in the run of the boat. The boat will appear to move at a more constant speed versus having dramatic changes in velocity from stroke to stroke. It is easy to understand that we need a technical model to study but not always simple to know which scullers or crews to watch.

During a visit to Florence, Italian sculling coach, Antonio Baldacci and I talked about the importance of good visual examples to help develop skills. Baldacci recommended studying lightweight scullers, particularly women, to get good technical images. He explained that because they are so close in body weight the demands to row well are very high in order to be successful on the international level. Once you have a mental picture, he continued, you then begin to videotape individuals in the boat and work comparing their motions to the ideal.

Periodizing your technique training to compliment your phases of physical work throughout the training year is another important factor to bridge the gap between simply getting fit and applying your fitness to move the boat. The year is divided into four basic phases: general preparation, specific preparation/pre-competitive, specific preparation/ competitive, and a transition period. Based on one peak per year, allot approximately seven months to general preparation, two months to specific preparation/pre-competitive, two months to specific preparation/competitive, and one month to the transitional period. Each phase has it's own physical and technical demands.

The general preparation phase is the time to work on creating a solid foundation of stroke elements. Drill work takes place at the beginning of each practice or can be incorporated into steady rows. The emphasis is on improving weak elements, defining new movements, and solidifying those patterns. Entry timing, connection between the leg drive and oarhandle, posture, head position, hand placement, body preparation, blade depth, release timing, slide control, and carrying the blades off the water need to be evaluated and the priorities set. The specific preparation/pre-competitive phase is time to keep the gains made during the last phase. This is the period of highest physical stress and the goal is for the crew to maintain form with high levels of lactic acid present in the blood and in a fatigued state when high concentration is needed to complete the workout.

When specific preparation enters the competitive time of the year attention should turn back to technique in order to sharpen the skills required for racing. Clean bladework needs to be effective at high tempos and can be trained by doing high stroke rate pieces at one-quarter and half slide. Start sequences and stroke transitions should be included to regularly practice parts of the race plan in practices. The competitive phase is the time to polish the strongest aspects of the stroke and build a crew's confidence but not a good time to make major changes because of the lengthy time it takes to neurologically engrain a new movement pattern. After the season has ended, the transition period is when to address physical limitations that affect your technique. This includes poor posture, limited hamstring extensibility, or weak low back muscles. With land exercises targeted on core strengthening, Swiss ball work, weights, or flexibility you will make gains that will reflect in an improved ability to execute stroke elements and gain stroke length.

ON YOUR OWN: SELF-COACHING

How easy it was. I just had to cross the river. I found the bike in the cellar of a brownstone. With its handlebar streamers, chrome fenders and newspaper boy baskets, the gold 1965 Schwinn took me over the bridge to practice, even in bad weather. A five-minute ride and I was opening the big door of the old Boston University boathouse. The room was noisy and packed with stretching bodies waiting for the line-ups to be set. Each name was neatly printed on a tongue depressor. The sticks were arranged and you knew where you were sitting. The coach posted the workout on the wall then you went out to execute it under his scrutiny. No matter how hard it was, looking back, it was simply a pleasure. Prepared programs and daily feedback are things that slipped way quickly after graduation and real life moves in. College rowing days, though intense, were luxurious from a coaching point of view. Whether you are continuing rowing after university or starting later in life as a master, if you don't belong to a supervised club program you are going to spend a lot of time on the water alone. The good side is you are training, staying fit, and experiencing some quintessential morning rows. The bad side is you may be out there practicing perfect mistakes in that morning mist.

Self-coaching is something every small boat rower does intuitively out of necessity. To be an effective self-coach you first need to get a technical foundation of the stroke. This is where it pays to invest in private lessons or go to a camp. Initial instruction will help you develop an understanding of body position, rhythm, timing, and bladework because you will then be required to render what you have learned from coaching to practice. Steve Maynard-Moody, a professor at University of Kansas and dedicated master sculler, explains that the problem of most who are not on college or national teams is that is that coaching is a rare opportunity, "The difficulty is to learn what good technique feels like." Steve believes that coaches can help by guiding their students to focus on feeling while they are observing them and that as the student you need to find a translation from the words and images of the coach to feel because in the boat you have no shadow. Unlike runners or cross-country skiers, you cannot answer if your posture is good or if you are compressed enough. Periodic coaching helps you continue to refine your technique. We then have to pose the question, how to practice in the between time?

Here are a couple key drills that I assign to my scullers to develop boat sense and serve as good self-coaching tools. They are also effectively used in a pair or double. For rhythm, single stroke pausing at full body preparation when the oars reach the crossover is a foundation drill. The pause position allows you to identify the transition between the acceleration and deceleration phases of the stroke. The position of the crossover is a reference for the completion of one stroke and the beginning of the next. When your wheels start to turn you continue the recovery preparing for the entry. The pause should be definite and blades carried off the water. When the drive, release, and follow through are done correctly you will have momentum and stability resulting in keeping the blades off the water. In the pause position, your body angle is set before your wheels move and then the upper body needs to remain still as you begin to compress the lower body working into the pins to the entry. Once the seat moves, become aware of your pins and blade moving towards the bow. Let the blade dictate when the seat changes direction. Place the blade before you begin to close the handle angle and drive to minimize negative directional forces on the hull. When the pause drill is done correctly you will feel that you have time to work with the run of the hull on the recovery, compress fully, and pay attention to your entry timing. You will develop a sense of the drive and carrying the speed through the release by eliminating any hesitation of the oarhandle as the blade exits. You will begin to find the balance point as a result of the rhythm. You can incorporate sets of 20 strokes into a steady state workout or alternate rowing five minutes with the pause and five minutes without during a steady row.

Rowing square blades is another drill that I ask scullers to learn. It is a difficult drill but improves important aspects of the stroke. When you row square blades you must learn not to over control the oarhandles and to maintain the speed of the handle as they change direction at the entry and the release. If you slow the handle speed at these transitions you will get your blade caught in the water. Work on using pressure into the oarlocks, working toward the blades, and gaining more control with your thumbs as guides on the end of the handles, unweighting slightly allowing an easier change of direction. As you row square blades pay attention to how the water builds against the blade. Gather the pressure at the entry and strive to keep it constant until you release the blade. This will enforce good acceleration of the boat and stroke rhythm. Carry the blades off the water and learn where the height of the shaft is so you can transfer that height to rowing with the blades feathered making sure to clear the water. Listen to how your strokes sound; make them quiet without tearing noises that tell you're losing energy. You can begin to do square blade rowing 10 strokes at a time working up to 10 kilometers on the square. Then begin to practice starts on the square. It is a great confidence builder.

Learning what you and your boat are doing by watching your wake is a critical gauge for steering a straight course, minimizing check, and developing constant boat speed. Rick Butt's, article, *Improve your Rowing by Going on a Tail Watching Trip*, published in the March 2004 edition of *USRowing This Month*, offers solid advice on reading the wake off the stern. Butt writes from the perspective of in the boat and from a coaching launch. In the boat, he advises to monitor any side-to-side motion of the stern that can indicate poor entry timing causing the boat to twist throughout the stroke cycle. By watching the "V" shaped wake expand and contract with each stroke boat check can be detected; keep the wake constant. From the coaching launch, one can see clearly if there are side-to-side stern movements but most importantly a coach can judge the rhythm of the stroke. Butt says, "The closer the tail comes to moving steadily without slowing, the better the rhythm. Frankly, I think the rhythm is by far the most important factor. It is often the difficult for the rowers to determine, and even more difficult for them to fix without outside observers." There is no shortage of details to work when you are practicing alone and you can make significant gains. It is an investment in time and money to get coaching, but if you are outside a structured program, to keep advancing your technique the feedback is a must.

HEAD IN THE RIGHT DIRECTION

Each season getting back on the water to start coaching brings with it fresh eyes. Working with a variety of scullers with different levels of experience from all around the continent, I am always interested to see the trends of what scullers seem to be learning, or not learning, as they enter the sport as novices or move from sweep to singles. Some of the technical flaws that are very common and that I am seeing a lot of are overreaching into the entry, skying the blade at the entry, and rushing the slide. These are all elements that can, to a large degree, be corrected by improving the sculler's awareness of moving in the direction of the boat.

We are part of a larger system when we row. Our bodies need to work in conjunction with the boat, the oars, the oarlocks, and the water to scull and row effectively. All your motions should be aimed at helping the boat move forward without checking, pitching, or rolling. Your intentional thinking needs to be in the same direction as the boat travels. To be a body in isolation attempting to take control over the equipment, sets us up for those technique mistakes, which learned as a novice, can be difficult to remedy further down the line especially if you race a lot and don't have the water time to spend re-learning your stroke.

Some aspects of sculling are counter-intuitive and interfere with learning good technique. The first is that we are not facing the direction that we are traveling. With eyes looking towards the stern the sculler tends to want to move the body and hands to the stern, which is in opposition to the direction of the travel of the boat. I often tell scullers that one needs to scull with eyes in the back of your head to stay oriented to where the boat is going and where the blades are at all times when you cannot see them. As soon as a sculler begins to tune into the direction that the boat is going they start sorting out reference points that support the new way of thinking and sculling. Rushing the slide is a symptom of not staying connected to the pins and not working with the run of the shell. Slide rushers tend to want to do what they want with disregard for the boat so every attempt they make at going faster seems only to disturb the boat more. Recovery rhythm is negatively affected by rushing the slide and you will commonly see the reverse rhythm of the hands slow from the release to the crossover then fast speed when the wheels of the seat start turning. Sparks fly. Once the scullers begins to take their focus off the stern, shifts it to where the boat is going, and lets the boat move under them, they begin to get some control over their motions. Starting to pay attention to the speed of the boat traveling through the water will lengthen their effective distance per stroke.

Secondly, it is natural to want to control movements from the hands; however over-gripping makes the oarhandles slower at the transition points of entry and release. It causes digging the blades in deep when the blades will set themselves in the water. Controlling from the hands also causes problems learning the entry timing because it is easy to be too oriented sternwards and fall through the oarhandles- losing the pin support- as one desires to go for more absolute length. When you observe a sculler that is overreaching their upper body into the stern you will see their back extended in an unstable position and shoulder blades are no longer stable against the rib cage. This position affects the beginning of the drive and missed entry timing because the sculler has no sense of where the blade is, relative to the water or where the pin is. The pin is your only reference to the boat's stability and travel speed. Learning where the blades are, particularly the lower edges, as they move to the bow for the entry gives the sculler another reference point to guide the timing of the catch that is more precise than just from the handles. We also need to be aware that the oars are moving in an arc around a pin, versus being linear such as the handle of an erg, so keeping lateral contact into the oarlocks throughout the stroke cycle creates a three-dimensional stable structure supporting your body weight. One should take advantage of this source of stability throughout the stroke cycle.

Single stroke pausing at full body preparation when the oars reach the crossover is a drill that can assist to breakdown the stroke and isolate movements. I use this as a foundation drill. The pause position allows you to identify the transition between the acceleration and deceleration phases of the stroke. The position of the crossover is a reference for the completion of one stroke and the beginning of the next. When your wheels start to turn you can focus on relaxing the legs allowing the boat to move under you as you continue the recovery, preparing for the entry. The pause should be definite and blades carried off the water. When the drive, release, and follow through are done correctly in combination with pressure into the oarlocks you will have momentum and balance resulting in keeping the blades off the water. In the pause position, your body angle is set before your wheels move and then the upper body needs to remain still as you begin to compress the lower body allowing the boat to run under you into the entry. Once the seat moves, become aware of your blade moving towards the bow even though it is behind you. Let the blade entry dictate when the seat changes direction. Place the blade before you begin to drive and as the oarhandles complete opening to minimize negative directional forces on the hull. Take the entry at the speed of the boat with little splash.

When the pause drill is done correctly you will feel that you have time to work with the run of the hull on the recovery, compress fully, and pay attention to your timing. You will develop a sense of the drive and carrying the speed through the release by eliminating any hesitation of the oarhandle as the blade exits. You will begin to find the balance point as a result of the rhythm. You can incorporate sets of 20 strokes into a steady state workout or alternate rowing five minutes with the pause and five minutes without during a steady row. A drill that increases awareness of using the support of the oarlocks is to row for sets of 20 strokes and at each point of the entry, mid-drive, release, and mid-recovery you press into the oarlocks as a reminder to maintain contact throughout the stroke cycle. Another drill is to row steady and alternate shifting your awareness to various points of contact with the boat so you row 20 strokes focusing on contact with the footstretchers, then the seat, then the oarlocks, then the handles in the fingers. Gradually you will learn how you work with your boat. Lastly, as you are sculling steady, practice trying to visualize where the blades are from mid-recovery to the entry. If you are focused on the direction of the blades and where the boat is moving it will be a good step towards improving your recovery rhythm and entry timing.

CONNECT TO YOUR BOAT

Quality practice is an important part of improving your skills in the boat. It is especially critical when your water time is limited because of work or school schedules. Paying attention to your contact points with the equipment and the sounds of your stroke will help you learn to be more aware of the boat and how well you are moving the boat.

Feeling connected, stable, and powerful comes from sensing the pressures of the water acting on the blade, the collar pressing against the pin in the direction of the blade, the feet in contact with the footplate, and staying even on the seat. One exercise that I suggest to scullers is to shift their attention to various pressure points while rowing. Practice first during steady state and then when doing race pace work. For example, spend one minute focused on feeling constant pressure of the water against the blade so it is anchored, steady, and not bouncing or slipping during the drive. Then move inboard and row one minute with concentration on contact between the collar and the pin throughout the entire stroke. Feel your thumbs and index fingers positioned on the end of the handles while using core strength to maintain pressure into the oarlock, following the handle's path around the pin. Next, shift your attention to the feel of the seat under you for one minute. Make sure you are centered, sensing the hull running out, creating a platform. Move your attention for another minute to the connection between the soles of your feet and the footplate. Do not loose contact with the soles of your feet on the recovery. If you let the boat come under you on the recovery you can subtly sense this. On the drive keep solid contact with the stretcher through the release so your weight transitions smoothly out of the bow. During your longer rows include some attention to these details and then as you increase your pace.

Sound tells you about your stroke quality. Listening to the boat and the water while rowing is a natural source of feedback. Strive for quiet bladework. Hold the water and be precise; avoid ripping, splashing, or getting stuck. Learn how your boat sounds when you are rowing well and getting good run. Then, combine attending to the sound of the boat with kinesthetic feedback and row with your eyes closed. Do this in a safe environment or with a coach boat watching out for you. Not relying on sight teaches you to pay attention to other senses. For advanced work, you can practice starts and accelerations with your eyes closed. The more aware you are of what your body is doing and what your hull feels like, the more you will become sensitive to small details and learn to make subtle changes in your stroke. When you make a positive correction a boat will respond to it.

FEELING RUN

How far can you make the shell travel in one stroke? Sense of glide is an important quality we learn by developing both skill and intuition in the boat. Careful movement training can help you learn to feel run. The better the run of the boat for each stroke cycle the more speed you have. Incremental gains matter; imagine this season that you add five centimeters of distance per stroke. A head race can take a single sculler about 600 strokes, so that would be a gain of 30 meters in distance. In a single, this represents about three and a half boat lengths. With those extra lengths where would that have placed you in the Head of the Charles last year? Improving your boat glide per stroke should be a key aim of your training on the water.

Drills play an important role in feeling run because well-chosen exercises refine your skill level and make you more sensitive. Rowing is a cyclical sport. We learn one stroke sequence and then repeat it thousands of times. The drive emphasizes the propulsion, the follow through the recovery. Movement training for run uses single stroke work or slow rating work so you can solidify small changes in the basic cycle and then gradually build the new movement pattern up to race pace. Here is one drill that you can include in your repertoire.

Rowing with a pause at one-quarter slide and holding the pause until the shell almost comes to rest is an excellent way to develop your sense of run. Both drive and recovery phases should be paid attention to. During the drive you want to sense that your body motions are coordinated and pick up the speed of the hull. Avoid any abrupt actions that work against the boat. Gather, and then hold pressure on the face of the blade as you begin to accelerate the boat. Aim to feel the blade set and body collected. Release the blade cleanly and quickly from the water pocket without a lot of stress. The boat is gaining velocity at this point so maintaining hull speed as the blade exits the water is our key mechanical objective. A terrific leg drive is negated if your blade gets stuck putting on the brakes. Come out of the bow as fluidly as possible to preserve speed. This does not imply to rush out of bow. Feel the momentum that you have built up during the drive. Time the direction change of the handle and upper body to carry your speed into the first half of the recovery. Be conscious of carrying your motion all the way through the perpendicular point of the recovery until the knees rise slightly. Pause here and keep your attention on the hull as the boat glides. Once the boat has almost stopped, carefully complete the recovery by allowing the boat to travel under you, composing yourself for the entry so the timing is precise and does not interrupt the flow of the boat. In the second half of the recovery, be patient and do not roll faster than the speed of the hull; match the hull speed by staying in contact with your oarlocks as a guide you. Build up to rowing on the pause for 30 minutes preferably on a day with quiet water conditions. This drill requires patience and intense attention but the devil is in the details and every extra centimeter gained counts on the race course.

FINDING BALANCE

At first you will feel like a drunken dragonfly trying to find
the right pose to keep your blades from touching the water. Sit
in your single, press both handles down to your lap so they come
high off the water and learn to balance the hull. Classic coach,
Steve Fairbairn, wrote in *Chat XIII: The foundation of rowing for
beginners, but good practice for all*, that this is the best exercise
to learn how to balance in the boat. In the publication *Rowing
Faster*, Volker Nolte writes "Balance allows rowers to keep their
blades off the water, keep the boat from rolling, and cost the
least amount of work. When athletes start rowing on the water
after a long period of training on the ergometer, they find they
have to exert more energy in the boat to maintain balance. Any
rolling of the boat requires rowers to contract muscles not only
to even out the boat but to stabilize their bodies." The recovery
phase of the stroke demands good balance to achieve a sense
of lightness and preserve boat speed. In the book, *Mechanics
of Sport*, Gerry Carr states, "Equilibrium (or balance) implies
coordination and control. An athlete with great balance can
maintain a state of equilibrium and neutralize those forces that
would disrupt performance." Carr adds, "Athletes must maintain
their balance in skills in which there is little movement, and in
skills that are highly dynamic. The enemy that athletes fight
while trying to maintain balance can be any external force.
Gravity, friction, air resistance, or force applied against them by
opponents can destroy their performance."

In rowing and sculling the lack of balance can dramatically
slow your boat speed because you cannot get your blades off
the water and devastate your race if you are unable to cope with
rough conditions and are floundering down the course catching
crab after crab. If you are not able to keep your blades off the

water on the recovery or cannot row with fully square blades for at least 1,000 meters you need to improve your balance.

Balance training should be a routine part of your workout schedule until you can clear your blades from the water and make the boat a solid platform. You can easily include land exercises in your warm-up; do specific types of cross training, and on-water drills to improve your hull stability, which will directly translate into more speed.

Dry land exercises are done with and without props. The following exercises use your body weight only. A *V-sit* is a core strength exercise that also emphasizes balance. From a lying position on the floor with arms overhead, lift your legs 45 degrees from the floor, then your torso 45 degrees. Hold the "V" position for a count of five and then lower gently. Repeat up to 10 times. This is akin to the ashtanga yoga pose called navasana, which is held for five breaths. A *sculling sit up* is a similar motion in that you are balancing on your ischial tuberosities (sit-bones) except you bring your knees to your chest in a crunch motion and your arms are parallel to the floor. You should aim to build up to a set of 50 repetitions. *One-legged squats* may be done standing on a step or bench. Extend one leg in front of you for balance, squat on one leg until your thigh is parallel to the floor. If you need extra stability, put a light hand on a railing or the wall. Practice 15 repetitions on each leg. Hopping on one leg uphill or in the sand dunes is also an excellent exercise and should be done in sets of 15 to 20 hops on each leg alternating for three to four sets.

With props you can continue working on balance and equilibrium with increasing challenge. Walking a tight rope was a common training exercise for Norwegian biathlete, Ole Einar Bjoerndalen, four-time Olympic Champion and currently the most decorated in the sport. Early in his career, this practice helped him develop rock-solid stability on his cross-country racing skis. If you don't happen to have a tight rope hanging around, take a roll of athletic tape and stick it to the floor for about four meters; practice walking on it in with bare feet. You can use a balance beam or the steel rail of the train track. Performing squats on a balance board is an excellent exercise too. You can purchase commercial balance boards from medical companies or use a small stick with a plank across it, seesaw style, that you can stand on and squat stabilizing the board level until your thighs are parallel. This can then be done with a weight bar across your shoulders. The *Swiss therapy ball* gives you many options for developing steadiness. An important exercise is called *sculling balance*. You sit on top of the ball; slowly raise both arms and feet. When you can comfortably hold this position begin to simulate the sculling motion with your arms and legs. Make sure that you are secure sitting with just your arms and feet raised first before you attempt this. In the four-point dog pose, you balance with both hands and knees on the ball for the maximum amount of time. When you have mastered that go to three-point dog. Start in four-point dog position, then go around in a circle and remove one limb at a time holding each three-point position for ten seconds. The next in the progression is two-point dog; extend your right leg and left arm, hold for 10 seconds, then switch to your left leg and right arm extended for five to 10 seconds. Grand mastery of the Swiss ball is when you can stand on it-this can take months. Start in four-point dog; gradually move to kneeling, then kneeling one leg, then standing. Be attentive when working with the Swiss ball; practice in an open space on a carpeted surface or mat away from any potential obstacles.

Cross training with inline skating, ice-skating, gymnastics, tango lessons, ballet or yoga classes are all fun ways to improve your equilibrium. Both cross-country skiing techniques, skating and diagonal stride, are extremely good for developing balance especially when drilling without poles, in addition to the aerobic benefits.

The drills on the water that will teach you hull stability include static drills such as sitting at the entry with the blades buried, stable against the oarlocks, gently bobbing the blade in and out of the water until you get comfortable enough that you can let the blades sit in the water and lightly lift your hands off the handles. Bob your oarhandles in the release position too. This is important for learning a clean extraction from the water. All varieties of pause drills done on the recovery demand that you keep the blades off the water. Rowing with square blades on the recovery or the drill where you feather-square-feather during one recovery will focus your attention on the movement of the hull and staying set. One of my favorite drills is rowing with eyes closed. You develop a special sensitivity to the quality of the boat run and can feel where your center of gravity is. It is best to have a coach boat guiding you for this drill. As you continue to master balance the time you spend on the river messing about in boats will become more enjoyable and speedy.

HOW TO IMPROVE RHYTHM

When we practice moving the boat, whether it is a single or a team boat, the rhythm of the stroke is part of how well the boat travels through the water. Good quality boat run relies on a powerful drive followed by the transfer of weight out of the bow and a recovery speed that does not interrupt the run of the boat while compressing into the entry position. A common fault is for a rower to lack contrast between the acceleration and deceleration phases of the stroke or to fail to follow through with the hands and body once the leg drive is complete before the boat comes up under the seat into the entry. This creates a rushed sense to the stroke and the rower does not get the benefit of the relaxation afforded while on the slide which leads to a greater stroke efficiency.

Walter is a middle-aged lightweight masters sculler that I worked with recently. When watching him scull he looked like he was moving very fast inside the boat relative to the speed the boat was moving. He looked like he was trying hard to go faster but seemed to be tiring himself out too much. What was most noticeable was at the end of the leg drive as the blade came out of the water, he paused and then his legs, body, and arms started to move on the slide together. The stroke had an end-to-end appearance versus a cyclical flow. We needed to adjust his rhythm. We started first by having Walter stop and sit at the release position, then to go to arms-body away. It is at this point that we talked about the crossover of the oars as being a reference point in the stroke for the transition of the boat's speed. It was important that Walter create a new image of the stroke that included a better follow through motion of the arms and body out of bow so he didn't lose his boat speed at the release when pausing. I asked him to continue the acceleration of the stroke through to this point to keep the boat speed as the oars come out of the water and change direction.

The first drill that we worked on to improve setting of the body angle was pausing arms-body away each stroke. The pause was a definite, "one-1,000-two-1,000-row," tempo so there was adequate time for him to check that his posture was comfortable and head was up. After breaking the pause we worked on keeping the weight of the upper body even and letting the boat run under the seat to compress into the entry matching the speed of the boat. We did about 10 minutes of single-stroke pause drills then we began to alternate one stroke on the pause/one continuous stroke for 10 minutes. The goal of the continuous stroke was to maintain the rhythm of the stroke felt during the pause drill but to eliminate any break in phases so the recovery speed shifted smoothly. We then began to row pausing every fifth stroke to reinforce the contrast of the rhythm of the drive/follow through letting the hull run on the recovery. These exercises made the boat feel very different to Walter but he said that he felt he could apply his power better through the legs, carry the acceleration of the boat, and then relax more on the slide because he was stable. I then asked Walter to begin working at lower strokes rates such as 18 or 20 strokes per minute to concentrate on maintaining his new sense of rhythm. One workout I suggested was to row 2 x 30 minutes with five minutes rest between. Within each 30 minutes alternate three minutes pausing arms/body away at 14 strokes per minute and two minutes at 18 strokes per minute. Walter could feel that he was getting more boat run per stroke and planned to devote his upcoming steady state training to making this new rhythm feel very natural.

REFINING YOUR OARHANDLING

Training on the ergometer prepares our bodies and minds for eventual work in the boat. However there is an aspect of technique that we are not able to practice well on the ergometer-the action of the hands during the stroke in the boat. On land, we lack the motion of the arc of the handles, the feeling of weight of the oars in the hands, pressure into the pins, and the support of the oarlocks on the recovery. Upon returning to the shell dedicate time to improving your dexterity and proper positioning of the hands. A review of the hand pattern in sculling with a discussion of common flaws and drills will help focus your attention to detail in your shell.

Three basic functions of the hands during the sculling stroke are providing connection for power transmission onto the blade, contributing to stability in the boat, and controlling the blade's entry and exit from the water. Commentary from the DVD, *Effective Sculling Technique*, sets a good stage for us, "An effective part of sculling is the position of the hand on the handle of the sculls. When gripping the oar the hand must be placed so the wrist remains flat and the forearm linear with the wrist when applying pressure onto the handle at the beginning of the drive phase of the stroke. The fingers act as a hook at this point, and along with a relaxed arm and shoulder system are simply acting as a transmitter of energy onto the handle from a powerful leg drive. Similar to many other sports that utilize a handle such as golf, baseball, and hockey, the grip and the positioning of the hand has a significant impact on the ability to transmit energy. The grip on the handle must be relaxed and the sculler must be able to feel the weight of the oar in the hands to control balance in the boat."

To scull efficiently, refine your hand motions during the stroke and develop a consistent pattern. At the entry of the blade, the forearm, wrist, and back of the hand are in line. The hand applies pressure against the pin in the direction of the blade as the arms open in an arc. The index finger is close to the thumb at the end of the handle so the hand is as far away from the pin as possible providing better leverage. Both hands should be at the same height. The blade is placed with a minimal rising of the handles. At mid-drive when the oars are at 90 degrees to the boat and crossing over, the left hand is slightly in front of the right hand without separation. Wrists are flat, the handle is held in the hook of the fingers. The palm does not touch the handle. The ridge of your closest knuckles is positioned slightly towards you versus too far over the top of the handle and you feel the handle press against the inside of your fingers. The level of the hands should be in line with your center of gravity. To find that point, squat down as low as you can and hold your hands in front of you for balance. The height of your hands is close to your center of gravity. Set the starboard oarlock one to two centimeters higher to allow the boat to stay level when making the crossover.

Approaching the end of the drive, elbows draw through keeping the forearms level to the water and wrists flat. Keep the handles in front of the torso. Hands should finish uniformly with spacing of a fist-width or a little more. To accomplish this, the left hand will have to come in a bit faster than the right hand. Maintain pressure so the collar is against the oarlock providing stability. Thompson writes in *Sculling Training, Technique, and Performance*, "As the drive comes to completion with the draw of your arms, you must release the power before the handles reach your body. Once the power is released, your hands, pivoting from the elbow, should apply a downward pressure. This sequence of movements will extract the blade from the water." To feather keeping the wrist flat, raise the middle knuckles and depress the knuckles closest to you allowing the handle to roll out slightly in the fingers until the sleeve falls flat in the oarlock. The pivot point is at the knuckles closest to you. Hand levels travel the body, parallel to the thighs, and then the water. At the recovery's crossover the left hand is slightly above and to the stern. The right hand follows it. To square the blade, lower the middle knuckle so the fingers roll down.

Common hand-related flaws include: excessive squeezing of the handle, sculling with palms on the handle, the left hand pulling up over the right hand on the drive, and uneven hands at the entry or release. The drill of rowing with the fingers open on the handle during the recovery produces relaxation and a feeling for keeping the weight of the handle under the roots of the fingers. Pausing arms-body away on the recovery allows a moment to check the position of the hands at the crossover giving a reference for the same point on the drive's crossover. The delayed feather drill, tapping down of the handle so the blades come out fully squared and clean, will require even, loose hands at the release. A simple stationary drill for level hands at the entry is to sit at full compression with the arms open and blades buried, evenly bobbing the blades in an out of the water while maintaining pressure against the collar toward the bow. Hands are sensitive instruments capable of great precision; refinement of your oarhandling will cultivate a better stroke.

CASE STUDY: BLADES

During the season I work on the water with many scullers of different abilities and competitive goals. It is common to see recurring faults in both novice and experience rowers. Rowing with the blades too deep in the water is one widespread mistake.

When Mary came to sculling camp this season she was fit, interested in going faster in her single, and wanted to win a few races. There was no doubt that she was willing to do the training that she needed to do. As soon as I asked Mary to take some strokes at a rating higher than 28 strokes per minutes, she started to tense her hands and the shafts of the blades were covered about a meter in the water as she tried to increase her pressure. At the sight of those blades so deep in the water we had to stop, re-group, and go back to some basics.

In order to re-educate Mary's sense of blade depth we went through a few exercises. I instructed Mary, "Sit balanced in the boat with your hands and body away, blades flat on the water, now square your blades and let them float. Almost take your hands off the handles; See where the handles are when you let the water support the blades? This is where your handle levels need to be when the blades are at the correct depth. Now let your hands follow where the oarhandles want to be as you guide the handles toward you." The next step was to reposition Mary's hands so her thumbs were on the end of the handles and she was applying subtle pressure laterally into the oarlocks from her trunk, "When you keep pressure into the oarlocks, you are able to relax your fingers more because the thumb guides the handle." Mary grasped this and believed that the blades would truly set themselves in the water as they were designed to do but as soon as I asked her to start paddling again the temptation to pull hard over-powered the delicacies she had just experienced while letting the blades float so we had to try something else. "OK," I said, "come up to the entry to take a stroke, but once the blades are set in the water lift your middle, ring, and little finger off the handles so you cannot pull and you must float the oar through the water feeling where the correct blade depth is. The top edge of the blade is just under the surface of the water-minimal shaft is in the water." Mary was able to do this and seemed to finally buy into the fact that there was no need to control the handle too much. We then took the same feelings of relaxed hands and applied it to regular strokes.

As Mary was able to sense better where she wanted to feel the blade in the water, she was able to focus more on staying relaxed through her shoulders and letting her hands be guided by the level of the handles. We concluded the day's session with an exercise in rowing circles with one hand. I asked Mary to keep one blade on the water and row around in a circle with the other hand. The purpose being to watch her blade while it is in the water and to solidify using the blade level in the water as an indicator for where she wants her hands to be inboard through the release.

GOOD BLADE DEPTH AT YOUR FINGERTIPS

Blade depth is one of the aspects of technique that needs careful attention. Rowing too deep causes a myriad of problems such as getting caught at the release or increasing the amount of vertical motion going on in the stroke. I recently did a group lesson with some intermediate scullers; here is how we worked on blade depth to help move the boat better.

First, to get a sense of where the blade will sit naturally, I had the scullers sit at the release and hold the oar using their thumb only on the end of the handle. By keeping pressure against the oarlock, they had control of the handle but allowed the blade to sit where it wanted to in the water. Then, they lightly placed their fingers on the blade without disturbing the height in the water. Next, we did a drill called *rowing in circles*. With one blade feathered flat on the water and the boat balanced, row with one oar. The boat will move in a circle, but the advantage of this drill is that they were able to watch what the blade was doing during the stroke. I explained that by accomplishing the right action in the water your inboard handle levels would be correct as a result. I asked the scullers to keep the top edge of the blade level with the surface of the water; this way they had a concrete reference point for where the blade level should be while in the water.

Allowing the blades to sit in the water requires light hands taking care not to overpower the stroke and lift with the upper body during the drive. I like to use *two-finger rowing* as a way to demonstrate how little effort you need to control the oar. I instructed the group to use regular hand placement while on the recovery, place the blade at the entry and once the blades are in the water lift the middle, ring, and small fingers off the handle so they are drawing the handles with the thumb and index finger only. In this drill one cannot pull so you automatically can feel where the blade wants to sit. Another variation we did was *rowing middle finger only* where after the entry, they used only the middle finger to draw the handles through the stroke.

The final drill we did during the session was *half-blade rowing*. The goal of this drill was to feel how to control the blade keeping only the lower half of the blade in the water and the shaft completely out of the water. This requires focusing on the point of contact between the lower edge of the blade and the water's surface. Learning when this happens helps learn the sense of the blade's size and action. It will also help you learn an important frame of reference for developing good entry timing and for improving starts this season.

IMPROVING BLADE DEPTH

During the on-water season I work with scullers of different abilities and competitive goals. Certain faults tend to repeat. A pervasive flaw is rowing with the blades too deep in the water. Having the shaft buried too far can make raising your ratings difficult and interfere with releases at the end of the drive.

To develop your sense of blade depth, go through a few exercises: Sit balanced in the boat with your hands and body away, blades flat on the water, square your blades and let them float but keep slight pressure into the oarlocks laterally. Unweight your hands on the handles and see where the handles are when you let the water support the blades. This is where your handle levels are when the blades are at the correct depth. Next, let your hands follow where the oarhandles want to be as you guide the handles toward you. The next step is to reposition your hands so your thumbs are on the end of the handles aware of subtle contact into the oarlocks and your index finger is close to your thumb. When you apply pressure through your trunk into the oarlocks, you are better able to relax your fingers because the thumb can help guide the handle.

Another useful exercise is to come up to the entry to take a stroke, once the blades are set in the water lift all your fingers off the handle except for your middle finger and float the oar through the water feeling where the correct blade depth is. The top edge of the blade is just under the surface of the water and minimal shaft is in the water. Take the same feelings of relaxed hands and apply it to regular strokes. Sense the blade in the water, focus more on staying relaxed through your shoulders, and let your hands be guided by the level of the handles. Conclude a day's session with an exercise in rowing circles with one hand. Keep one blade feathered on the water and row in a circle with the other hand. Look at your blade while it is in the water and solidify using the blade level in the water as an indicator for where you want your hands to be through the release.

BASIC MANEUVERING

When you start learning how to scull in a single, you will need to learn the basics of maneuvering your shell. Here are some exercises to begin getting comfortable in your single.

Rowing Circles with One Blade

Start from the release position, blades flat on the water, boat balanced. Row with one oar only, leaving the other oar feathered on the water for stability. The stabilizing oarhandle should be held against the body. Follow the blade with your eyes to see the effect of your actions through the water. Try placing the blade in the water, letting the handle go free to see the natural depth of the blade, and then placing your hand back on the handle to follow the movement of the oar. Row yourself in a full circle with one oar and then switch and row around in the other direction with the other oar. Use the least possible power and a loose grasp.

Stopping

Learn how to stop rapidly. From a moving position, at the release, square the blades and press them into the water for a braking effect. Lean your body against the handles if needed.

Backing

Backing is when you move the boat towards the stern. First begin by practicing gliding up and down the slide keeping the blades slightly tilted on the surface of the water. Then practice backing with one hand only, the other rests near your body. Start from the finish position, square one blade in the water, letting the blade float; push your hands away from your body. At the end of the stroke, turn the blade feathered with the concave surface facing the water so the tip of the blade skims the water as you bring your hand back to your body. Try 10 strokes and then switch to the other hand. Then use both together. When you are comfortable with the backing motion you may add in slide length as you push away to make the stroke longer. Work up to backing for 50 strokes.

River Turns

Once you are able to back the boat down, you are ready to learn a river turn. You move your hands together but alternate the position of the blades. Using arms-body only, push your hands away from you with the port blade squared and the starboard blade feathered on the water; port backs, starboard is feathered on the water. Then take a stroke with the starboard blade as the port blade is feathered and skims the water; starboard rows, port is feathered. When you have mastered this you can lengthen your slide to take longer strokes. This is a quicker, more efficient way to turn the boat than simply rowing yourself around with one oar, especially if the water is fast or there is strong wind.

ROWER'S GUIDE TO ROUGHING IT

The August 2003 *Rowing News* cover read "Hurricane Schinias!" featuring the U.S. junior men's eight buried in waves moments before they swam to the finish line at the Junior World Rowing Championships in Greece. The picture reminded of my own Greek experience. Years ago, when I was racing at Poros Island in the Aegean Sea, I had the pleasure of being waked by a navy destroyer. Not only did my oars pierce into the walls of the wakes up to the riggers but any site of land quickly disappeared when I was in down in the bottom of the dip. There was a moment when I thought I'd be swallowed at the 500-meter mark. You will race on rough courses in unpredictable circumstances; I'd go as far as to say 50 percent of the time. So, as much as we like to be romantic savoring those morning rows on placid water chasing the perfect stroke, we have to face reality and learn how to handle wind-driven waves or breaking rollers. Athletes aiming for Athens are getting ready for some potentially serious rock and roll in the Olympic lanes but any racecourse can dish out less than ideal circumstances; learning to handle environmental situations is going to help you race your single better or keep your crew together.

U.S. national team sculler, Rachel Anderson, says, "the main thing is to stay calm and keep power application low and stable, i.e. in the legs rather than tensing up and using more upper body and back. Lisa [Schlenker] is great about reminding me to relax my neck, which has the effect of loosening everything from my shoulders to lats to the grip on the oars. I think square blade rowing is good practice for rowing in rough water and also thinking about carrying the blades higher off the water so you don't slap so much, thereby, keeping the boat running out as well as possible. In short, stable upper bodies; just push the knees down on the drive, loose shoulders, and blades high off the water on the recovery. As unpleasant as it is, I always feel like I am rowing better after I come out of rough water and back into calm."

Ted Swinford, 1986 world champion in the men's straight four, is a master coach when comes to teaching how to row well in wind, swells, and wakes. In the winter of 2000, Ted coached me in the single and the double while training in Sarasota, Florida. Since late afternoons could be quite rough on the Intracoastal Waterway we spent a lot of practice time in tricky conditions. We used the pause drill with arms-body away in several ways. First was to keep the momentum of the hull after the release so the boat kept its run and remained stable. Second was to completely prepare the body before any slide motion with the blades clear of the water and then to move on the slide without changing the trunk position coming into the entry. In effect we used the pause drill to be precise about making sure to do Part A-setting the body angle, before Part B-complete the slide keeping the lower body relaxed and staying connected to the speed of the boat. Most importantly it helped to develop a very stable upper body, using the support of the oarlocks that was able to absorb any changing handle motions resulting from blades get bounced by the waves. Collars need to maintain subtle contact with the oarlocks with the application of pressure coming through the hands from the trunk muscles. With outboard control, lighter hands can adjust for uneven strokes without affecting the trunk position and will not disturb the run. We also practiced square blades in very difficult conditions so a different balance point can be learned and to get comfortable carrying the oar shaft higher off the water. Starts on the square were a Swinford specialty to develop poise and clean bladework. Resisting crabs came from loosening up the hands and letting the water correct the blade versus trying to control it.

When you are coaching crews, expose them to wind, waves, the boat out of balance, and to catching crabs so they build self-assurance in practice. *The GDR Text of Oarsmanship:*

Rowing Rudern recommends, "train first on calm water, then in moderately turbulent, and finally in very difficult conditions." Staging time trials in bad water as well as flat will teach the crew to pull through mistakes and help them develop recovery strategies as a team. Race simulations should include planned crabs, jumped slides, and staged breakage. This is especially true for starts where a race can be compromised if the crew doesn't get away clean. Anderson says that rowing with ease in rough water comes with time, as it is a function of comfort level and confidence in the boat. Just as cross-country skiers let their feet find out how to read the track, we can learn how to let our hulls hold steady in the turbulence and put our skills to the racing.

CHRONIC OVERREACHERS

Early June marks the transition from the intense racing of the college year to the start of club and masters sprint events. Putting your boat in the water for a morning row when the temperature is still cool, but you know the day is going to be a hot one, generates an image of a classical summer practice to me. It is a quieter time of the rowing year but one filled with the anticipation of working towards racing at big regattas in August. We start thinking about how to improve our starts, stroke rates, entries, and power through the water. To get a clean blade entry into the water for effective stroke length and a strong drive, you have to set yourself up for it. So at this time technique work is focused on precision at the top of the slide because as the racing stroke rates rise, timing issues become more pronounced.

A flaw that interferes with the timing of the entry and leg application is to overreach through the upper body into the entry position in an attempt to get a longer stroke. It is apparent that the rower's seat stops moving but the hands keep extending to the stern. This compromises the upper body posture at the entry causing a loss of stability due to losing contact with the oarlock pin and weakens the connection to the leg drive because the lower back is not in a strong position. Instability occurs at a point in the stroke where accuracy is needed so one can put the blades directly into the water as the angle of the hands is opening up. Without a stable platform it is difficult to place the blade into the water confidently. Correcting overreaching takes a lot of concentrated work on the part of the oarsman and the coach. The athlete needs to learn a different approach to the second half of the recovery, adjust to a new rhythm, and change the timing of the blade entry. The coach has to facilitate creating a new image in the athlete's mind of how to produce the motion and then has to groove in that movement pattern.

Here is a case study of one approach to correct overreaching. Josh rows for a high school sweep team and wants to train in a single. He presented as trying to get a very long stroke into the front end that was making him unsteady before placing the blade and he was complaining of his lower back pain. I began by having Josh sit at the release position, correcting his posture so his head and chest were up, abdominal and lower back muscles were firm. Josh looked balanced over the seat. Then I asked him to come to the arms-body away position on the recovery. He transitioned his weight out of the bow of the boat but still maintained his good posture and head position. Next, I asked him to start compressing slowly. When he started to move his seat on the recovery he also continued to stretch through his shoulders until he reached the end of the slide. By this point he had lost his posture, his head was down, and the stability of the hull was gone.

We had to revise how Josh understood the recovery. In his attempt to row longer, I explained, he was moving his weight too far towards the stern of the boat in an opposite direction than the boat is traveling and that motions need to keep the hull stable as the hands are opening. I continued, "This stroke, set your body angle out of bow, now keep your body in this position and feel the boat run under you as you compress; keep contact with the collars against the oarlocks as a guide to the speed. Let the stern come towards you. Allow your legs to relax. Think of the boat moving in the direction of the finish line." Josh was able to make a small change but really wanted to continue stretching too far into the stern. "Posture is as important here as it is in the weight room. A power clean requires your lower back to be firm and your head up. Working on the entry is the same." I clarified, "Maintain your posture as the boat travels under you so when the blades engage the water your legs are linked to the handle through the direct connection of your trunk. If you loose your posture the impact of your legs will be absorbed through the spine instead of transmitting that power to your oarhandle. As soon as the blade is set the oarhandles will start to come to you."

We spent most of our session using the pause drill at arms-body away position. We worked on preparing the upper body, setting Josh's posture, pausing briefly, then putting the focus of recovery into the lower body to let the boat travel under him. So once the seat started to move the upper body remained stable except for the arms opening up with the oarhandles. The stability resulted from working around the pin and in the direction of the blade.

Josh had to resist the temptation to go too long and perceived his stroke was shorter than he was used to. In keeping his body position, though, he was able to get better leg compression, entry angle, and the timing of the entry began to improve. After doing the pause drills, Josh worked on three-quarter slide rowing to work on isolating his lower body moving while keeping his body stable. He said visualizing where the blades are when nearing the water helped him feel balanced and that he didn't feel like he was collapsing through the handles. Josh started working with the support of the oarlocks to keep his trunk steady. He also focused on keeping his shoulder blades firm against his rib cage. Off the water I recommended that he do ball stabilization exercises, sit ups, push ups, and strengthening focused on core strength of the trunk and the scapulae.

It takes many miles and patience to solidify the different feeling of more stable posture but the stronger body position will help Josh use his body weight better in his sweep rowing, as well as, protect him from the risk of lower back injuries. Developing a mental image of the blades moving to the bow as you compress and moving your hips through the pin assists in becoming aware of where the blades are as they approach the water for an exact entry. Correcting overreaching is a good investment in your future boat speed.

EARLY QUALITY

Used properly Jack Daniels is a beneficial part of your training. Now is the time to move from the foundation work you've done during the off-season to a pre-competitive focus. In *Jack Daniels Running Formula*, the well-known physiologist and running coach describes this time of the year as the phase of early quality training. By rowing definition this is our spring season and the goal is to prepare for the type of rowing that will be most important in the competitive phase. This is when you improve stroke mechanics, continue strengthening, introduce easy speed work, and start doing intervals with plenty of recovery time because the next stage of the year will be the most stressful in terms of preparation for competition.

Transitioning from the erg to the shell might take weeks. As the smaller spinal and trunk muscles adapt, they can exhaust rapidly long before your postural core muscles especially when sculling in a reactive single or rowing with an unstable novice crew. Initially, keep your boatmanship centered on form and balance. Medium to low intensity steady state rows are the best way to maintain your aerobic base and give you the time to pattern correct movements. The drills you choose should address your weaknesses and be done when you are fresh. Once warming up is finished, the first part of your practice on the water should include drills. Afterward move on to the body of the practice. Technical sessions alone ought to be less than 60 minutes. Due to the high level of concentration required they are mentally demanding, when fatigue builds up the exercises should end for that session. While getting accustomed to being back in the boat it may be difficult to maintain the high aerobic output you have been doing on the erg so I suggest doing combination erg and water workouts. If the main point of the practice is technical but will include some power pieces towards the end, do your warm-up and drills in the boat, then come off the water and do the power pieces on the erg. Or if you plan long intervals for improving your maximum oxygen uptake followed by a steady state recovery row, do the long intervals on the erg to insure the right intensity then go out in the boat for your recovery row. This is a very effective way to get the conditioning needed while you increase your comfort and power level in the boat.

Training during the pre-competitive phase has a balance of technique, aerobic endurance, and controlled intervals. Drills to improve rowing technique should emphasize timing and correct body positions, steady state rows with 10-stroke accelerations every five to seven minutes will develop an easy sense of speed or help introduce moving starts, short intervals such as repeats of 250 meters or 500 meters with up to three times the rest, to keep lactic acid levels low will provide some initial high quality strokes, and long intervals from two minutes up to 15 minutes with rest lengths that allow for the intensity to be maintained during each interval are varied within the weekly plan. During a cycle of four to eight weeks, following the wave principle of alternating phases of increasing and decreasing workload is more efficient than a continuous method of loading. The *FISA Coaching Development Handbook Level One* explains, "The wave principle requires that a training load increase must be followed by a decrease in training load during which the athlete's body is able to recover and adapt to the training load. This enables the athlete to be subjected to progressively increasing training loads." Good improvement results if the load is increased over three sessions in a row up to maximum capability. For five or more sessions per week an example pattern is 50 percent, 75 percent, 100 percent, followed by an easy workout or a rest. For fewer sessions per week it is better to alternate one day off after each session and design the work to be at it's highest on the weekend.

Begin your daily practices with a warm-up and drills followed by the main workout. Include your flexibility exercises at the end of each training session to improve the resting length of the muscles and joint mobility. Maximum strength weights twice per week will increase the ability of the muscles to recruit more fibers per contraction and then gradually start to transition to power; decreasing the weight, increasing the repetitions adding an element of speed to lifts. A strong advocate of efficient training methods and preventing overtraining, Jack Daniels advises his athletes not to overdo their efforts for the requirements of the session, holding paces in control so that low intensity is low and high intensity is high sets you up for good results later in the season.

HURRY SLOWLY BACK TO THE WATER

At last the river thawed. All winter you have practiced indoors religiously. Now your instincts tell you to seize your oars and row, rejoicing that erging is over once again. No doubt it feels good to go pump out a 20k row with wild abandon, toss in some starts, and sweat. You'll be euphoric; you'll probably also have blisters, sore muscles, balance and bladework problems. So, if your goal this season is to move your boat more meters per second, should you really just go tear up the waterways? Paying attention to details, while easing back into your shell will pay out better dividends later in the season. Avoiding a madcap approach might also mean a little more erging.

Allow yourself a tuning period of a few weeks when getting back on the water. Give your hands time to adjust to a different handle size or texture. Check that your grips are in good shape and replace them if you need to. Remember that you haven't feathered an oar all winter so you will have to be aware of correct hand placement and oarhandle manipulation from the start. Sweep rowers again need to isolate the functions of their hands so the inside hand feathers and the outside hand controls the height. Scullers should keep the thumbs at the handle's end and resist palming the narrow handles. Attending to flat wrists and keeping the weight of the forearms uniform is important to minimize extra motion.

The boat is a reactive environment, so many smaller trunk muscles that have not been used during the winter will fatigue before your larger power muscles will. Your initial sessions are, in effect, limited by the endurance capacity of your stabilizing core muscles. When you start to fatigue and catch yourself balancing the boat by swaying your knees you need to go back to the dock. During the early season, care needs to be taken to row well and prevent any type of overuse syndrome that will linger into the season. Keeping in mind that a muscle strain can typically take six to eight weeks to heal.

Scandinavian cross-country skiers have a training motto that says, "Hurry slowly." When you get back in your boat this season, put technical emphasis on balance and bladework. This will take patient kilometers of low rate work between 16 to 20 strokes per minute and exercises for the entry and release such as pausing at half-slide, one-quarter-slide-rowing, or legs-only. Groove in good movement patterns, but be aware that you also can't afford to lose fitness. This is where the erg comes in. The initial transition to the water requires lower power applications until you are comfortable, so putting in some work on the erg can be key to keeping your fitness level up during the transition time. Do your workouts that are above steady state intensity on the erg so you can work at a high enough aerobic level. Gradually, build the pressure up on the water until you can maintain technique under more stress. Being diligent and taking the time to practice good bladework will give you more boat speed once you start ramping up to race cadences later in the season. Next time you get ready to push off the dock for your distance row, remember another rowing proverb, "If you can't do it slow, you can't do it fast."

WHY ROW SLOW?

The coach's fangs sharpen. The rowers start feeling the lactic acid levels rising in their blood as they watch their coach jot down a race pace practice on the chalk board; two sets of 6 x 500-meter pieces with one minute rest between pieces; 10 minutes between sets. That should satisfy your desire to row over the edge and see how hard you can push yourself; but is that really tougher than 4 x 30 minutes at stroke rate 16 in silence?

When I start working with an athlete, I ask what their favorite and least favorite types of workouts are. You'd be surprised how often I hear, "I like challenging ones! I prefer shorter pieces. Super long boring pieces are hard." This week an athlete was asking me, "Why do I have to learn to row at low stroke rates?" I always find this interesting because long rows were always a favorite part of my training on the water or the erg. There were many 25-kilometer rows in my single down on the west coast of Florida when I would feel like I set out on a technical adventure of sorts. There were events in every row; drawbridges going up, better catch timing, manta rays launching themselves over my blades, revelations while rowing with squared blades. Once, in Sarasota Bay, I even met a guy with a cat sleeping in an open water boat complete with a tent over it. Turned out he was from Maine and had rowed down the Mississippi and was now following the Intracoastal Waterway back up the east coast. The most important feature of my long rows was that I found I could create space in the stroke to find new details and the lengthy sessions gave me the luxury of time to refine them.

Stroke rhythm needs to be developed at slower stroke rates of 16 to 20 strokes per minute before you can apply it to higher speeds. Good strokes rely on maintaining a relationship between the acceleration and deceleration phases of the stroke to keep the boat moving as close to average speed as possible. Ratio between the time on the drive and time spent on the recovery is usually one to one or one to three; only at very high race cadences will the ratio be closer to one to one. Alternating an explosive drive with muscular relaxation on the recovery is an important skill to develop for efficiency. Active relaxation and posture needs to be comfortably maintained as the boat runs under you. The hull approaches its slowest speed as you near the entry and its fastest speed after the moment of release. So, these transition areas have to be mastered to keep the hull steady as your speeds climb.

Good breathing habits help rhythm and is better patterned at slower rates. To breathe fully the posture of the upper body needs to be straight so the diaphragm can act freely. As in weightlifting, work is performed with the breath held under pressure. Exhale at the release then breathe in during the recovery just before and during the entry. When racing your breathing rate is elevated and a second exhalation is needed on the recovery to expel additional carbon dioxide. As you build your paces you will accustom yourself to comfortable breathing patterns.

Controlled movements and good bladework positively affect the set of the boat. Rowing at low rates extends the recovery phase, demands attention to detail, and teaches you to stabilize the boat. Balance is the result of all the elements of the stroke working together. It allows you to keep your blades above the water during the recovery and then use the boat as a platform for levering your weight. Fluidity will maintain balance just as abrupt, rough motions will disturb it. The set of the boat becomes very important in competitive rowing especially in bad water conditions. Equilibrium is trained at lower ratings.

Making every individual stroke a drill will teach you to feel boat run. Body movement training to improve run through slow rating work will solidify small changes in your stroke cycle. Both drive and recovery phases should be paid attention to. During the drive you want to sense that your body motions to be coordinated and legs to pick up the speed of the hull after the entry. Avoid any abrupt actions that work against the boat. Gather, and then hold pressure on the blade as the boat accelerates. Aim to feel the blade anchored and body collected. Release the blade cleanly and quickly from the water pocket without a lot of stress. Maintaining hull velocity as the blade exits the water is one of our key mechanical objectives at low rates. A terrific leg drive is negated if your blade gets stuck and puts on the brakes. Come out of the bow as smoothly as you can to preserve speed. This does not mean to rush out of bow. Feel the momentum that you have built up during the drive. Time the direction change of the handle and upper body to carry your speed into the first half of the recovery. Be conscious of carrying your acceleration all the way through to the perpendicular point of the recovery until the knees rise slightly. Keep your attention in the hull as the boat glides. Carefully complete the recovery by drawing the boat under you; compose yourself for the entry so the timing is precise and does not interrupt the flow of the boat. In the second half of the recovery, be patient and do not roll faster than the speed of the hull itself; attempt to match the hull speed. This requires good attention span and connection to your boat through the oarlocks.

Long, low rows develop important psychological aspects of training in addition to the physiological benefits. Concentration and keeping your mind in your boat is a key skill of racing. These rows are part of your mental training for race day. Focus and being present every stroke requires practice. In teamboats there should be no talking during a session as it serves to distract from the task at hand. In Jim Joy's article, *Effortless Power or Powerless Effort*, some of the key points Joy mentions can be strived for through low stroke rate practices. Joy writes, "The foundation is the subtle movement of the swing-trunk, legs, arms," he continues, "Stay focused in the present on the *what is* not the *what should be* and he emphasizes mindfulness, being fully aware, and attentive. Place importance on relaxation in movement with no unnecessary movements; timing, accuracy, and balance in the delivery of power. Joy's principles of effortless power include: being calm, relaxing, centering, being whole, and being present. Taking the time to row slowly will help you to become more proficient and aware of your stroke. Going fast will follow shortly.

CHANNELING THE RATE MONGER

You are willing to put yourself in the position to see how fast you can make your boat go. You've decided to race. Not an easy task so there are a lot of things you need to have in your bag of tricks before you back your stern into the stake boats; fitness, determination, sharp bladework, a good start, and a killer sprint. With the summer's championships not far away, now is the time to practice transitioning your stroke rates up. In order to make a move on another boat or know that your final 30 strokes will be there on demand, higher strokes are a must.

Rating transitions are when you shift from one rating to another. A single stroke will determine either a drop or a raise in your strokes per minute. It is something you and your crew have to commit to so the rhythm change will follow smoothly without breaking the flow of the piece or race. Leg drive, handle speed, and relaxation are important in jacking the rates up. When you want to increase your rate of striking make sure to keep the leg drive sharp. Once you begin to drive, fully complete it, especially the last one-quarter of the slide. This is an area where many rowers under-utilize their momentum and let the legs slack off. Strong legs through the entire drive will help you to increase the velocity of the handle.

To move the rating up you need to generate more handle speed through the release and in the first half of the recovery. Timing of the release is important to keep the handles moving. Strive to find the timing between the completion of the leg drive and the release to give your boat optimum glide. Avoid muscling the motion thus slowing down your oar. A good shift to a higher rating feels light, quick, and collected. The increased boat speed seems immediate. Approaching that stroke be mentally prepared to give a 110 percent leg drive and let the handle rebound away from your body as the blade comes out of the water. Good posture, pressure into the oarlocks, and releasing the tension of your hands will create an elastic sense of movement in the oarhandles. A clean exit from the water is a must.

To practice rowing higher, start at lower ratings and gradually increase. Initially, you can embed acceleration 15-stroke pieces into your steady state rowing by going from a base rate of 18 to 20 up to 35+ strokes per minute. Then do a workout with a set number of pieces at determined rate changes such as 10 x 20-stroke pieces where you start at a base rate for 10 strokes and increase by two strokes per minute for the second 10. During 30- or 40-stroke pieces you can build from to a base race pace for the first 10 strokes and then increase the stroke rate by two every five strokes. Aim for hitting some maximums where you can still hold technique together. During the racing season have dedicated practice sessions to learn how to swing from one rating to another. On a daily basis include some short accelerations before going into the dock. Finding how to activate your extra gear ahead of time will help you to confidently execute your race plan and get the results you are looking for.

SPECIFIC STRENGTH: THE BUNGEE ROW

Making a smooth transition from the winter weight room sessions to strength training on the water can be a fun, valuable part of your race preparation and something you can include as part of your weekly diet of workouts throughout the season. The *bungee row* is used as a means to perform strengthening exercises while rowing in the boat. Wrapping an elastic bungee cord around the hull of the boat to the stern of the coxswain or sculler's feet will provide a substantial amount of drag to slow the hull speed during the recovery making the boat feel heavy. This series can replace one of your weight room sessions. It is cautioned that this is an exercise to be done specifically for strength and muscle fiber recruitment. It is not advised to row long miles this way with the thought that more is better because muscle firing will be trained to react too slowly than what is needed for racing.

- Repeat four sets of 10 strokes, stroke rate 10. Maximum effort.
- Rest one minute between each set.
- Repeat the series four times; rest three minutes between each series.
- Warm up thoroughly before you start. The entire workout will take 41 minutes.

For sculling, rowing 10 strokes per minute is a challenge for balance and concentration. You may need to insert a brief pause with arms-body away to maintain the correct rating. For sweep rowing, this drill can be performed all eight or for added resistance alternating stern-four and bow-four every 10 strokes. Rowing 10 strokes per minute can be a significant technical challenge in a pair, as well.

SMALL BOATS NOW FOR THE BIG BOAT LATER

Sitting on the starting line in the two-seat of the second varsity boat, you remember your seat racing results in the spring. You wanted to make the first boat but didn't. As scholastic rowing comes to a conclusion, you now can already start working towards next year's varsity eight. Whether you are a high school or college rower, the solution for improving over the summer can be summed up in three words: Row small boats.

Water time in singles and pairs will teach you balance, bladework, and most importantly, how to move a shell with good run. These two boat classes are very sensitive and you'll find it doesn't take too many miles to learn a lot about blade depth or the value of clean releases. If you have the option, learn to scull over the summer. It will surely help your sweep rowing in the fall. The rationale for this is straightforward. Sculling is a symmetrical motion that incorporates equal learning on both sides of the body. The movements of the hands are finer and the balance of the single more delicate than any other hull size. By sculling you acquire watermanship, finesse, and a repertoire of skills that can later be applied to sweep rowing in a bigger boats. Pair rowing technique is as subtle as in a single so it too will give you a big technical boost, especially if you can row both sides.

Long, slow distance rowing will develop your base aerobic endurance and skill over the summer. It is better to come back to your team strong in September strong than having to get back into shape only when the school year starts. Check out rowing clubs in your area to see what your sculling options might be and what type of coaching is available. You can also consider a camp for a week or two to get coaching and then know what to work on when you get home. If your local club has a summer sweep program, see if it is possible to do some sculling in your free time in addition to the team practices. These rows can be targeted primarily on learning technique and do not have to be intensive. You can do a lot of drills such as square blades, pause drills, square blades/feet-out rowing, or learn to do things like the *Swinford Switch* where you scull with the port blade squared and the starboard blade feathered for 10 strokes and then in one stroke, switch to the port blade feathered and the starboard blade squared for 10. This is an excellent drill for right-left coordination. Or learn to change the oars from one side of the single to the other without falling in. Perhaps you shouldn't do this one in your dad's new Filippi but the creative opportunities are endless. Small boat rowing over the summer can be the key to jumping up to the next level and sitting in exactly the seat you want next season.

TECHNICAL IMPROVEMENT FOR MASTERS
2001 USROWING CONFERENCE PRESENTATION

Part One
What is Technical Preparation?

When preparing to perform in rowing there are four major components of training that need to be included in a masters athlete's regime: physical, technical, tactical, and psychological. It is generally accepted that physical preparation is the main aspect of training required for fitness or performance and certainly is the most time demanding. Technical preparation follows physical preparation as a dominant training factor. Technique is dependent on physical preparation and relies on adequate strength levels to meet the demands of the stroke.

Technique can be defined as *the method of performing the stroke*. It is how you move the boat. Developing your ability to execute the cyclical rowing stroke in the most efficient manner increases your likelihood of achieving personal satisfaction and good competitive results while reducing the risk of back or rib injuries. The more mastery you have the less energy required to realize a specific goal. Good technique is directly related to high economy.

Technique versus Style

Throughout technical discussions it is important to make a clear distinction between technique and style. Technique training is based on a model of the ideal rowing stroke and this frame of reference forms the rudiments of teaching the skills involved. Coaches and athletes collectively must have an understanding of a model that maximizes both biomechanical and physiological needs. A technical model must also be flexible as developments in equipment or new scientific findings may influence current thought and practice. A model is malleable.

The elements of technique refer to learning the parts of the stroke. Correct practice of the stroke as a whole in combination with drills is how those elements are learned. The manner in which an individual performs the stroke can be termed one's style. Style incorporates distinct ways of executing *the fundamentals of an accepted model of the rowing stroke.* It may include traits of the athlete or coach's character and personality or be a specific way of performing a movement that is defined by the rower's anatomical or physiological nature.

Because you have individual requirements to meet the technical challenges posed by the rowing stroke, use caution when attempting to directly imitate the technique of champion rowers or scullers. A champion's style does not always represent a perfect model of the stroke. Their style is the result of how they have solved their own technical issues. Study their technique as an example of how he or she has developed their own highly proficient, personal style that successfully executes the elements of the rowing stroke. Use your observations to influence your own individual needs.

Methods to Improve Technical Training

Improving technical preparation may take place throughout the year: both on and off the water. The following suggestions are ways that you can better understand and learn technique:

- Improve physical preparation to develop the musculature involved in technical skills.
- Develop an ideal visual model of the stroke.

- Schedule personalized instruction with a qualified coach on a regular basis.
- Attend a sculling or rowing camp.
- Include dedicated technical sessions on the water during each week's training.
- Perform technical drills to develop stroke components.
- Get videotaped and reviewed.
- Correct equipment selection for your body size and weight.
- Proper rigging of your boat and oars.
- Watch videotapes of international rowing events.
- Read texts about rowing and sculling.
- Practice.

Factors Affecting Technique

Physical preparation, how fit or strong you are, has a major influence on your technique. In order to execute the stroke correctly one needs to have adequate leg strength, core body strength and cardio-vascular conditioning. Poor physical conditioning will limit your ability to acquire new skills and decreases your chances to maintain proper technique under the stress of fatigue. Technical deterioration is often the result of a decline in physical fitness. For example, without core trunk stability and lower back strength it becomes very difficult for one to maintain posture through the drive often causing the body weight to collapse at the release. In another case, without leg power a sculler cannot properly initiate the acceleration of the body weight that is an essential component of the stroke.

Lack of flexibility can also be a limiting factor in achieving good technique. The compressed lower body pose at the entry requires both hamstring and low back flexibility to meet the demands of the position. Either leg compression or upper body posture is compromised when flexibility is lacking. Poor hamstring elasticity will affect your ability to set your body preparation after the release while keeping your legs extended. Flexibility can be improved with practice and it is to every sculler's benefit to incorporate some stretching into daily training sessions. Finally, check that the boat you are rowing is in correct adjustment. Improper rigging is another factor than could affect your technique adversely.

◆

Part Two
Learning and Perfecting Skill

Developing your sculling technique and acquiring the skills to scull effectively requires thousands of repetitions of the stroke cycle. Thorndike's law of exercise states that, "without an immense number of repetitions, a skill cannot become automatized or reach a high level of technical stability." Whether you are new to sculling or have several years of experience, the pursuit of technical proficiency will play a role in your athletic career. The mastery of technique is limitless. Often a main objective of training for the duration of one's sculling life, good technique contributes to reaching competitive results, as well as, enjoying of the aesthetics of the movement itself. But how do we actually learn new motor skills and patterns? How is skilled movement achieved and how do we create new habits? The following section addresses the concepts of how movement is generated and learned. Also considered are the learning styles of the athlete, the art of practice and using feedback.

The Stages of Motor Learning

How do we learn to become better scullers or rowers and accomplish new tasks? Some of the factors to consider are what stage of motor learning you are currently in, how do you learn best, what is the learning environment, and what other barriers may exist?

Skill acquisition takes place in stages. The initial stage of motor learning can often answer the question, "was the movement pattern effective or not?" Trial and error strategies are usually used during this phase the help the learner develop a general idea of the desired movement. Consider learning the sculling stroke. You cognitively focus on the stroke by taking a sculling lesson, reading books, or watching other scullers train on a nearby river. Regardless of the time spent mentally rehearsing the stroke, the actual performance of the stroke means that now your body must do what you have been taught, read about, or watched. At this point in learning, success may be considered staying upright in the boat or keeping the oars in the water without going too deep. At this stage it is easy to become overwhelmed with details such as correct hand placement on the oars, proper posture, eye focus, correct acceleration on the drive, or relaxation on the recovery. This phase of learning is cognitively demanding for the novice sculler and the complexity of the task will directly influence the length of time it takes to become comfortable with the new skill on a basic level.

The trial and error nature of this initial phase is largely due to poor neuromuscular coordination and extra movements occurring. It is normal to experience a heightened distribution of nervous impulses, stimulating extra muscles, when old habits are being interrupted and new habits are being formed. Once the motor skill is established and adequate coordination is present the basic stereotype of the skill is formed.

Late stages of learning correspond with an automatic phase leading to mastery. During this stage the athlete learns fine movements, subtleties, efficiency, as well as the ability to perform the skill in various environmental conditions. Through experience, an athlete develops resources and a repertoire of responses relating to both self and environment. For example, a sculler may release the blades from the water symmetrically seven of 10 times. Error detection for an unbalanced release would include visual feedback, seeing one blade come out ahead of the other, and tactile feedback, feeling one oar in the air and the other still underwater. This sensory feedback combined with the actual outcome of the motion and memory of previous successful experiences can all help the sculler further execute clean releases from the water so a higher ratio of success is achieved.

Eventually, when a skill requires less cognitive demand or awareness of how to move than previously required, an automatic stage of movement is reached. During this period, the sculler may not have to think about each element of the stroke but will be able to execute the stroke as a whole. The degree of skill achieved by an athlete depends on the athlete's ability to analyze and solve movement problems, use resources and remain motivated in a variety of situations. Practice in diverse conditions develops skills in diverse conditions.

Perfecting skill is an ongoing athletic focus and is aimed at fine-tuning technique and then adapting the technique for competitions or maximal performance. This final phase of refinement is dependent on earlier learning, which emphasized perfecting the separate elements, integrating the elements into a whole, and developing the physical musculoskeletal requirements to support the technique being learned.

The Steps of Learning to Scull

- Proper handling of the sculls with minimal power application. Developing basic maneuvering of the boat.
- Mastery of the sculling motion in a wide beam boat or team boat. Emphasis on learning the drive and use of body weight.
- Transitioning to balancing a racing single with medium power application.
- Command over a racing single with technique maintained under various weather and water conditions.

Learning Style and Environmental Influences

Individual learning style has an effect on learning new skills. Using your natural preferred style or being aware of your own learning style can optimize how you integrate new information into your rowing skills. Motor skills most often benefit from progressive pictures, step-by-step modeling, and repetition. If you respond well to visual input then demonstration, modeling an instructor, watching videotapes, or rowing in a team boat with other scullers, will help you create the visual image you need to improve your stroke. Kinesthetic input would include learning from how the motion feels by practice or by having a coach guide you through the movements. When you envision yourself rowing you can note whether you *see yourself* (visual imaging) rowing or rather you *sense* (kinesthetic imaging) what the stroke feels like without having an actual picture in your mind. One way will usually be dominant but you may discover that you have a combination of images too.

It is important for you and your coach to be aware of what stage you are at in rowing in order to progress your skills at a reasonable pace; one that agrees with your current level of understanding and ability to concentrate on the task at hand. A coach needs to know what you want to do or *can do* and needs to grade the demands of the training session accordingly. If the level of difficulty of a given task is too complex or challenging, frustrations, anxiety, worry, and often failure results with a decline in performance and motivation. When skill level is higher that the task requirements then boredom can result. The correct balance between demands of the exercise and existing skill level creates the conditions for a flow experience, which ultimately results in creativity, mastery, and competence. In sport, experiencing success is critical. Your training regime must be designed to offer success, plus a challenge to spur you on to the next level of competence.

A favorable learning environment can support better acquisition of motor skills. In sculling or rowing this could include: the type of water to be rowed on, air temperature, wind speed, amount of boat traffic on the water, quality of equipment, stability of the boat, weight of the boat, access to indoor training facilities, a boathouse or tanks, docking facilities, access to videotaping, or supervision of a coach. As a novice sculler, you will benefit from learning in a more stable environment of flat water, no wind, and a wide beam boat. The initial learning of the exercise accounts for some rigidity of movement, improper use of the body, and inappropriate pauses in the continuity of the motion making the stroke rough. The strategy of using a more stable boat allows you to break the stroke into steps and go slow in order to facilitate the correct information processing and make modifications in the movement by simplifying and stabilizing the environment. Such learning can also take place in indoor rowing tanks or on indoor rowing machines but then must transfer to the natural setting where the rower learns how to row on the water. Competitive and highly skilled scullers can also benefit from periodic outings in a stable boat when a precise detail of the stroke is being refined and can transfer the learning to their performance boat. The perfection of skill continually challenges the sculler to apply their skills in multiple situations, to both different environmental and competitive conditions.

What is Practice?

Practice is necessary for motor learning to occur. *Learning by doing* stresses the active participation of the athlete in performing new skills. Practice is more than just the repetition of a movement and should engage the athlete in solving specific problems or requirements based on the situation at hand. *Discovery learning* is when the athlete learns actively through trial and error and through experience. Learners have been found to acquire skills better when they discover their own solutions versus being shielded from error through guidance. Physical and verbal guidance is an important part of coaching an athlete to improve their skills and certainly plays an appropriate role when learning new elements helping to understand the motion, reduce fear, or promote safety. There is, however, great value in a sculler putting in miles on their own to work out certain technical elements. A goal of training may be to reduce the level of guidance a sculler or crew needs to perform a particular task.

Although practice is commonly considered to be a physical act, it includes mental practice as well. Both are an effective part of a training regime. It is well documented that imagining oneself *doing* something (mental imagery) activates some of the same nervous activity as does performing the actual movement; tendon reflexes increase and motor control areas of the basal ganglia are heightened. Three to five minutes of mental training sessions can be very beneficial if an athlete is unable to attend practice, is injured and cannot row, needs to conserve energy such as prior to racing, or needs to rehearse the race plan.

Blocked versus Random Practice

Practicing a movement repetitively or working on one skill at a time is termed *blocked practice.* In early stages of learning *blocked practice* is slightly more effective than *random practice* because the athlete can concentrate on one thing at a time. However, once a movement or skill has been performed successfully *random practice*, which introduces variety and mixed skills to the training situation, has been proven to improve motor learning retention more so than *blocked practice* over time. One can practice racing starts by repeating the first stroke several times then progressing to the first two strokes up to the first five strokes. This would be *blocked practice. Random practice* would include practicing the racing starts in different wind and water conditions, combined with transitions to base race pace, or from a moving position (flying starts) during a steady state row intermittently on the coach's command. The nature of *random practice* requires more integration of movement patterns because a second pattern is superimposed on the first one. The athlete must in essence forget the first pattern when the second pattern is introduced and then regenerate the primary pattern again when returning to the first pattern. The process of returning to and recreating the movement pattern speeds up the learning process.

To clarify, the sculling stroke is a continuous skill, which has no distinct beginning or end. An example of *blocked practice* of a sculling skill would be performing placement drills; starting from the release, moving on the recovery, and placing the blade in the water as the conclusion of the recovery. Introducing *random practice* could include full-stroke steady state rowing and combining attention to both a clean release and then proper entry timing. By rowing full strokes and shifting attention to different movements within the stroke, you are allowed to forget within the context of the entire stroke and the bring attention back to the entry during the recovery. The technical goal would be to execute the blade placement dynamically with the precision it was learned in an isolated manner during the drill.

Part-task versus Whole-task Practice

In sculling, the translation is part-stroke versus whole-stroke practice. The stroke can be broken down into steps (entry, drive, release, recovery) or phases (acceleration, deceleration) and be taught as separate tasks when we do drills such as pausing arms-body away or time-on-the-slide. The stroke can also be practiced as a whole; rowing steady and focusing on an element within the context of the stroke cycle, i.e. feathering the blade. The goal of *part-task practice* is to transfer the skills learned to the performance of the whole skill and is very effective if the steps are progressive and integrate with the practice of the whole-task. In a continuous skill as rowing it is reasonable and beneficial to practice component parts (drills) and the whole cycle (full strokes) during the same session. More attention will be devoted to technical drills and error corrections later in this chapter.

Intrinsic versus Extrinsic Feedback

To perfect your sculling stroke, feedback is needed during all stages of learning and mastery. Feedback is categorized as either *intrinsic* or *extrinsic*. *Intrinsic feedback* is the information we receive from our sensory systems such as vision (you can see your blade is washing out at the end of the drive), proprioception (you can sense that you are dropping your wrists at the release), and cognition (you can judge how you need to adjust your handle height at the entry). Kinesthetic feedback is internal information that your body gives about its position in space and motion. This type of feedback and feedback about balance is generated by the vestibular system, visual system, as well as, special stretch sensors called muscle spindles located within the muscle fibers and golgi tendon organs which are found near the junctions of tendons with muscles. *Intrinsic feedback* is highly significant for learning the sculling stroke due to the need for stability combined with the accurate timing of good bladework that is mandatory for good performance.

Extrinsic feedback is information that comes to you from external sources. This could be from a human (coach) or non-human environment (water or boat). Generally, frequent extrinsic feedback is needed for learning new skills but should gradually become intermittent in order to enhance performance. The feedback you receive can focus on information regarding the result or outcome of the movement, "You came off the starting line at 45 strokes per minute." This type of information is termed *knowledge of result*. Verbal or non-verbal feedback that focuses on the position or movement pattern used is termed *knowledge of performance*, "Your hands were too high at the entry; keep your wrists level at the release." *Knowledge of performance* is a more beneficial form of feedback for motor learning and motor teaching, but the combination of *knowledge of result* and *knowledge of performance* is better than one or the other in isolation. Proper and frequent feedback can have a highly motivating effect on an athlete, supplying the information required to detect and correct errors, as well as, providing positive reinforcement for good execution of the stroke.

When to Practice Technique

Following physical preparation as the primary training factor, technical training is next on the list of priorities. Devoting attention to technical training can reap greater benefits if done at the correct time of the year and at the proper time in a training session. Technical work should be done in a rested, unstressed state because of the concentration needed to develop confidence in the technique. Technique is best changed when you are not fatigued. Once changed you must learn to perform correctly at race speed. This is also learned best when not fatigued. Finally, you must be able to make the transition to maintain correct technique when under race stress. This preparation requires a great deal of time and is an ongoing part of training in the sport.

Within the annual cycle of training, much of the improvement in technical training is done during the preparation phase, which emphasizes general and specific endurance. Next, during the following pre-competitive phase, technical changes need to be maintained. This period of training produces high levels of fatigue and technical training is not optimum at this time. The later competitive phase, which includes sharpening and peaking, again calls for a return to technical training to perfect skill and apply it to racing situations.

On a daily level, technical work should be done at the beginning of the training session and may be included as part of the warm-up. Again, technical changes are best produced in a rested, concentrated state. Perform the elements or drills that you acquired in the previous training session, continue to perfect the skills that you are working on, and gradually apply those skills in conditions identical to competition. Designating an entire session to technique is a necessary part of the weekly training cycle and should be limited to a maximum of one hour. Because of the high degree of concentration required it is easy to become quite fatigued by the end of such a session. Rest days should be scheduled separately.

Causes of Technical Error

Technical improvement can often be delayed because of incorrect learning. The quicker an error can be corrected the faster the rate of progress. Mistakes have causes and identifying the grounds for the fault help direct the corrective route to take. An athlete may be responsible for faulty technique due to psychological limitation (satisfaction with a low level of skill), poor physical preparation (strength, coordination), misunderstanding of the correct movement pattern, fatigue, incorrect grasp of the handles, or morale (lack of confidence or fear). The approach of a coach can also cause technical problems due to an inadequate or incorrect teaching style, an inability to individualize teaching based on an athlete's needs, or a coaching style that is characterized by lack of patience. On the non-human level, the use of poor quality equipment, adverse weather conditions (cold, wind, waves), and an unorganized training program can contribute heavily to your technical troubles and insufficiencies.

Videotaping: A Tool for Analysis

Over the course of the season it is important to have feedback about your technique and to have some way of monitoring your technical progress. The analysis of videotape is a good way to identify faults and to recognize improvements in your technique. It also gives you and your coach an opportunity to work together in assessing your level of skill.

Videotaping is best done from a motorboat with one person driving and another filming. From the launch you can film the boat from the either side, each individual at the level of the rigger, as well as, from the stern or a 45-degree angle. Keep the motorboat at a speed equal to the speed of the shell when filming. It is also possible to film from land by having a boat row by or away from the camera. If it is possible, shooting from a bridge to get on overhead view is another very useful and revealing vantage point.

To videotape yourself rowing on the erg, setting up the camera in various positions will allow you to see your stroke from different angles. Use a chair or stool and position the camera so you can see the machine centered in the lens.

When you are reviewing a video, the slow motion and frame-by-frame features on a camera gives you a great deal of control for technical evaluation. Try to be systematic as you look at a videotape of yourself or another member of your crew. Use constructive criticism.

❧

Part Three
Principles of Technique

Basic Concepts

To move the boat through the water is the goal of each stroke we take. Whether sculling for recreation or training intensively for competition there are concepts that need to be applied to all styles. Rowing is founded on these axioms, which then help to form a model of the stroke. Details of how these technical points are executed can vary with personal sculling or coaching style. The purpose of the following section is to give a holistic picture of the technique, an overview that can be used as a platform for better understanding the dynamics of the stroke. The stroke is built on basics and will hold true overtime. How well you are able to understand and perform the skills will grow with correct practice.

The stroke cycle is fundamentally divided into four main parts: The *entry* is when the blade enters the water; the *drive* is when the blades are in the water for the forward propulsion; the *release* is the completion of the drive when the blades are taken out of the water; the *recovery* is the part of the stroke when the blades are over the water preparing to take the next entry. The *acceleration phase* of the stroke is from the entry through most of the drive and then when the blade is released from the water and the arms-body follow through. The *deceleration phase* of the stroke takes place during the remaining part of the recovery until the entry is taken. Correct timing and application of power contributes to the boat maintaining a given speed. The stroke cycle is fluid and rhythmical without any interruption of the movement.

Boat Movement

A boat should run smoothly in the water without noticeable checking or dunking, without irregularities in propulsion, and should not be adversely affected by changes in stroke rate or under difficult weather conditions. The hull needs to keep as level and as stable as possible while holding on course. Any vertical or radical movements will disrupt the run of the boat.

Bladework

Stability of the hull is evident by one's ability to keep the blades off the water during the recovery without touching the water. Contact with the water causes friction and retards the movement of the boat. During the drive the water reacts with the blade of the oar to do it's job in moving the boat forward. The blade is our tool for the application of work and is designed to naturally set its own depth in the water. Anchoring the blade in the water and moving past the point where the water holds the blade is the only indicator we have of the work being done. Executing clean effective entries and releases are paramount to the uninterrupted flow of the boat.

Hand Placement

The oar is the instrument we use to transmit our power and body weight to the boat. In order to use the oar properly, it must be held correctly. This is a technical priority. Improper hand placement will block the ability to use the body weight effectively and will unnecessarily complicate the feather and squaring motion of the blades.

The way the hands are placed on the handles does not represent a gripping action. In sculling, the handles are small and will rest in the fingers with the surface of the palm off the handle. Establish your hold with the blades square (vertical) in the water; this is the position the blade will be in during power application and is the reference point for placing the hands on the handle. Sitting at half slide with arms extended, square the blades letting them float in the water at their natural level, and then position your hands so your fingers curve over the handle in a hook grasp and your thumb is on the end of the handle. The base of the fingers, back of the hand, and wrist should be straight. As the hands draw towards the body the elbow/forearm complex moves to follow the arc of the handles to keep the hand/wrist/forearm level with the oarhandle. The hands transmit subtle lateral pressure into the oarlock is through core body strength. Acceleration of the body weight during the drive creates the momentum to release and feather the blade with a minimum of effort. Feathering and squaring is the result of small actions at the blade and handle that allow the sleeve to set the oar in the oarlock. The hands need not work to turn the handles but need to develop a lightness of touch that lets the natural impetus within the stroke initiate the movements by small changes of flexion and extension of the finger joints. This cannot happen unless the hand placement is correct to begin with.

Use of Body Weight

Rowing uses the muscles and body weight to move the boat. Rowing is not defined as a pulling action; a levering action to propel the boat forward would be more accurate. By learning how to use your body weight you will learn how to effectively move the boat. Body weight must be transferred to the footstretcher once the entry is taken, without disturbing the run of the boat. Leg power is the initiating force to employ the body weight. By keeping the feet firmly in contact with the footstretcher and pressure of the oar's collar against the oarlock, in the direction of the blade, the body weight can be applied through the drive to increase the speed of the boat. All power needs to be utilized for the forward propulsion of the boat without hindering its movement and the resulting energy from the drive will initiate the release with smooth flow into the recovery if the release is performed at the correct moment.

The length of one's stroke will be determined by the well-timed use of one's weight and posture. Moving a boat well involves tempo, correct timing entering the water and correct timing exiting the water. The release point is determined by the inability to maintain the body weight on the oars. With no further use of weight, effective work is not being done. The entry is the signal to simultaneously begin the drive with setting of the blade in the water. The length of one's stroke can increase with practice, improved stability or flexibility but should not try to be accomplished through random pulling at the release, overreaching at entry, or through the collapse of posture.

Posture

Sound upright posture or to use the Fairbairnism, "freely

erect" posture, is important for power and the proper application
of body weight. Posture allows the core trunk muscles to
support the body weight during release allowing the oarhandles
to rebound lively through the release. Keeping the head up
with the chin held level, eyes focused above the horizon, and
the rib cage lifted provide the stability the body needs to apply
weight on the oarhandles. Posture is of particular importance
at the entry and release, transition points of the stroke, when
the weight changes direction. Collapsing of posture at either
of these points drives the boat down into the water and this
vertical motion of the hull creates wakes slowing the boat,
disrupting the run.

Posture can be practiced out of the boat throughout the day
to be transferred into the boat during training sessions. Stand
and sit tall; correcting slumping or forward-head posture while
working on your computer or driving your car will improve your
posture in the boat. Specific strengthening exercises can also
be done using weights, calisthenics, or a therapy ball to develop
strength in weak postural muscles.

Rhythm

Taking good strokes relies on maintaining rhythm between
the acceleration and deceleration phases of the stroke to keep the
boat moving at a constant speed. Ratio between the time on the
drive and time spent on the recovery is usually one to two or one
to three; only at very high race cadences will the ratio be closer to
one to one. The rhythm of the stroke is fluid and uninterrupted.
It links an explosive drive with a relaxation phase on the recovery
after the hands and body are set. Relaxation is active and posture
needs to be comfortably maintained as the boat runs out from
under you. The boat approaches it's slowest speed as you near
the catch and it's fastest speed after the moment of release. So,
again, at these transition areas care needs to be taken to maintain
posture and rhythm to keep the hull steady by staying in touch
with the oarlocks to read the pace of the boat.

Rhythm is greatly aided by good breathing habits. To breathe fully the posture of the upper body needs to be raised so the diaphragm can act freely. As in weightlifting, work is performed with the breath held under pressure. Exhale at the release then breathe in during the recovery just before and during the entry. When racing your breathing rate is elevated and a second exhalation is needed on the recovery to expel additional carbon dioxide. Training at different paces and intensities will help accustom you to comfortable breathing patterns.

Balance and Stability

Without hull stability accurate execution of the stroke is unlikely. To maintain stability, the sculler must have contact with the pin in the direction of the blade at all times during the stroke. Symmetry of movements, proper use of body weight, and good bladework positively affect the balance of the boat. Balance is the result of all the elements of the stroke working together, allowing you to keep the blades above the water during the recovery and then use the boat as a platform for levering your weight. A smooth transition at the release will assist the stability of the boat. Fluidity will maintain stability just as abrupt, rough motions will disturb it. The balance of the boat is decisively important in competitive rowing especially under poor water conditions. Although an individual sense of equilibrium varies, it can be trained to learn correct righting reactions through drills such as: slow motion rowing, pause drills, or balancing the boat after several hard strokes, and by broadening your boat base by using the support of the oarlocks.

Sweep to Sculling: Sculling to Sweep

If you have the option, learn to scull before you row

in a sweep boat. The rationale for this is simple. Sculling is a symmetrical motion that incorporates equal learning on both sides of the body. The movements of the hands are finer and the balance of the single more delicate than any other hull size. By sculling you acquire watermanship, finesse, and a repertoire of skills that can later be applied to teamboat sculling or sweep rowing in a relatively short time. If you can row a single effectively, transitioning into a sweep boat is less complicated than the other way around. If you have only learned the gross motor movements of a sweep boat, your first outing in a single usually provides an interesting and tipsy experience. To transition into sweep rowing also has its challenges and to be part of high performance eight can be an exhilarating event. In the small boat class, rowing a pair rivals the intricacies of a single.

Differences in body position exist between sculling and sweep rowing. Because you row with one oar, in sweep rowing the body rotates towards its rigger during the recovery while preparing for the entry. The core body weight stays over the keel and the outside shoulder is higher than the inside shoulder, following the orientation of the oarhandle. The inside shoulder (side of the boat closest to your rigger) maintains the directional pressure into the pin. The outside arm is adjusting height and is between the knees at the entry versus sculling where both knees are between the arms. The basic principles of rowing agree with sculling in terms of the use of the body weight, acceleration, bladework, posture, and rhythm.

Each hand has a specific function when holding only one oar. The outside hand is responsible for extracting the blade at the release, placing the blade at the entry, and controlling the oarhandle height. The inside hand (nearest the rigger) is used to feather and square the blade and assists in keeping pressure on the pins. Exercises rowing with the outside hand only or inside hand only help learn these hand functions. Placement of the outside hand is at the end of the handle for good leverage;

the little finger should not fall off the handle and nearing the release the wrist/forearm complex rotates laterally to remain on the same plane with the handle as in sculling. Keep the oar in the hook of the fingers to avoid over-gripping. The inside hand initiates the turning of the handle, and then relaxes to complete the feather or square motion. The preparation of the blade for the entry (roll up) is a stylistic decision of the coach. Some coaches prefer an early gradual motion. Whatever the style, the entire crew needs to roll up together and place the blade simultaneously.

⚬◆⚬

Making the Transition from Water to Land

When you start transitioning your training from the water to land and using the indoor rower becomes your primary mode of training there are important points that you should bear in mind.

Stroke Awareness

Rowing indoors requires the same technical attentiveness as rowing in the boat does. Rowing incorrectly on the machine will only create poor motor patterns that will become unattractive additions to your water strokes. The machine does not replicate balance or the exact handle movements of a sweep or sculling oar but requires the similar use of body sequencing and core muscular patterns as in the natural on-water setting.

The machine is stationary on the floor and a boat is moving so how your weight acts is slightly different during the recovery. On the machine you move your mass, on the water the boat moves under you, as your mass generally remains stable. This is important to be aware of so you are careful with your body preparation and the posture you are rowing with indoors. When compressing, it is easy to overreach or dive the shoulders at the end of the recovery because the machine does not need to be balanced and flaws may go unnoticed; the boat does not tolerate this as well. A sliding frame for indoor rowing is now available and is gaining favorable reviews for feeling much more boat-like.

Hand Positions and Chain Level

When rowing, the chain connecting the handle to the flywheel moves through a guide on the front of the machine. This makes it easy for you to monitor the level of the chain on the drive and recovery. The chain should remain steady and level throughout the entire stroke cycle; there is no need or benefit to change the handle height when rowing indoors unless you want to intentionally mimic the handle pattern you use in the boat. Placing two pieces of tape, narrowing the size of the guide, can serve as a physical cue to keep the chain stable. The chain picks up tension with a minimum of slippage if the drive is started correctly. If you notice a lot of chain movement before you feel the resistance of the flywheel, correct your posture and work on a better initiation of the legs.

The hand placement on the handle is similar to that of a sculling grasp except that you are unable to put your thumbs on the end of the handle. Keep the handle in the hook of your fingers with the palm lifted off, thumbs gently wrapped under. The back of the hand, wrist, and forearm need to remain level with the handle. Allow the elbows to move laterally as the hands approach the body and keep the handle height at the level of your sternum.

Caution: Over-compression and Hyperextension

The ergometer seat travels on a long rail. Because there are no front stops, over-compression is easy to go unnoticed. Placing a piece of tape on the rail can subtly remind you to limit how far you want your seat rollers to go. The absence of a solid seat deck can be contributing to hyperextension of your knees at the end of the drive. Usually paying attention to this is enough to remedy it.

Rigging Your Rower

The adjustments of your erg are as important as the rigging of your boat for optimum performance. You can adjust the resistance level with the damper setting, heel cup height, and the performance monitor position. Drag factor is the indicator of resistance created by the flywheel; its importance is equivalent to the adjustment of workload in rigging a boat. The lower numbers represent lighter loads; higher numbers heavier loads. A general recommendation for steady state rowing is a drag factor of 100 to 115. The lower drag factor prevents the wheel from excessive deceleration between strokes and prevents unnecessary loading of the lumbar spine. Avoid doing short, low cadence power pieces with high drag factors. Drag factors over 130 to 140 place significant strain on the lumbar spine. Gravitate to the lightest setting that mimics the sensation of your boat speed.

Set your heel cups high enough so that you can compress comfortably but not so low that there is excessive sloping down of the legs. Try to get the same fit you have in your boat. The standard range of heel height in a boat is between 16 to 17 centimeters. Sliding your erg seat up to the footstretchers and measuring from the top of the seat vertical to the bottom of the heel cups can measure your heel height on the indoor rower.

The computer monitor is best set up at eye level or slightly above. Encourage yourself to keep your head steady and eyes focused forward. A low monitor screen will cause your head and eyes to drop negatively affecting your posture and application of power.

Feedback: Shadow Rowing, Mirrors, and Videotape

Feedback while rowing indoors is as important as when rowing outdoors to continue to make adjustments to your stroke cycle. Here are a few suggestions for making those long hours on the erg more interesting. Shadow rowing is one manner of technical training to solidify your technique and build uniformity in teamboats. Do not use the machine's handle but "row" using the same hand/arm motions that you would use in the sculling stroke to pattern new technical habits. You can develop better flow with your partner if you work one behind the other or side-by-side to match your movements. This can be a valuable exercise during winter months when you cannot be in the boat together. Shadow rowing can be used if you have a hand injury that prevents you from holding the handle or for mental training when conserving physical energy is important such as during tapering for races.

Technical feedback while rowing on the erg can be provided by setting up a series of mirrors in front, to the side, and at a 45-degree angle to your machine so you can see yourself. Videotaping yourself during practice can also be a great way to analyze your technique on the erg. The bottom line is when transitioning to your indoor training take as much care about your technique as you do in your single or in a team boat. Use the erg to positively improve your fitness and your on-water rowing throughout the off-season.

Performance Drills

Good technical skills are priceless: reducing risks of injuries, enhancing the aesthetic qualities of the sport, and developing efficient use of power. Drills allow you to concentrate on a small component of a complex movement and better understand the stroke cycle. The following drills outline different elements of the stroke When using performance drills select one or two relevant drills to be included at the beginning of your training session. Learn the movements and then improve your speed or pressure. Vary your choice of drills to make your workouts more interesting. Be creative and enjoy developing your skills.

Open Fingers On the Handle

While rowing continuously, recover with the fingers and thumb open (extended), not gripping the oarhandle. Relax the weight of the hands and forearms on the handles. Feel the weight of the oarhandle in your hands. Control the handles with the fingers and rotate the blade just before taking the entry. Be conscious of letting the sleeve rest flat in the sill of the oarlock during the recovery.

Two-finger Rowing

The purpose of this drill is to learn to relax the hands allowing them to feel the natural path of the oarhandles as dictated by the buoyancy of the blade in the water. Avoiding heavy gripping on the oarhandle will allow the blade to seek its own level in the water and provide perfect blade depth. This is a classic drill for learning a loose and relaxed hand placement on the oarhandle. The ease of letting the blades sit at the correct depth in the water is obvious and pleasant. Relaxation of the hands cannot be stressed enough to develop sensitive sculling skills.

- Row easy.
- During the recovery normal hand placement is used.
- Once the blade is placed in the water, lift the middle, ring, and little fingers off the oarhandle and draw through to the release using only the index finger and the thumb on the handle.

- Let the blades float in the water. There should be no tension in the hands, arms, or upper body during this drill. Relax and note how easy it is to keep the oars at the correct depth in the water.
- Perform continuously for 10 to 15 minutes when you include drills in your daily workout.

Pick Drill

One of the common drills used by scullers as a regular part of the warm-up. The pick drill sequentially builds the stroke up to a full slide stroke. It is important that each position has a technical focus. Row 40 strokes at each stage. As part of a race warm-up 15 acceleration strokes can be included at the end of 40 strokes.

- Arms-hands only. Keep handle height high enough to keep the blades buried. No body swing. Tall posture.
- Arms-back only. Pivot forward from the hip: timing of transfer of weight onto the footstretcher.
- One-quarter slide. Move just breaking the knees; timing the transition from the release to incorporating the slide.
- Half slide. Increase the distance the seat moves to half slide; maintain correct handle height and posture.
- Three-quarter slide. Prepare for the change of direction at the entry-head and body posture kept steady.
- Full slide. Complete the lower body compression; opening of the arms out for the entry. Full strokes.

Reverse Pick Drill

This drill is very effective for practicing the coordination of timing between the placement of the blade at the entry and the initiation of the drive. There should be a direct relationship between the commencement of the seat and handle movement. This drill emphasizes good connection between legs and back. Row 20 strokes at each station.

- Legs only. Row the first one-quarter slide of the drive keeping body position steady and arms extended.
- Legs-body only. Row full slide with the legs and body motions together keeping the arms straight.
- Add arms. Take full strokes with normal use of the arms.

Pause Drills

A pause of approximately two seconds interrupts the ordinary cycle of the stroke giving the opportunity to stop briefly and balance the boat with the blades off the water. It is also very useful for checking the position of the body at a designated point on the recovery. Pauses can be incorporated at arms-body away, one-quarter, half, or three-quarter slide. Arms-body away is an excellent way to focus on the acceleration phase of the stroke with a fluid release and complete body preparation. When the pause is broken the recovery can be continued by compressing the lower body and allowing the arms to open with the arc of the oarhandles.

Begin by pausing once every stroke for 20 strokes, than once every other stroke for 20 strokes, etc...up to five strokes continuous rowing one stroke pause. Relax. Balance the boat with the blades off the water. Take your time and let the hull slow down. An advanced sculler can pause with the blades square. Double pause drills incorporate two pauses during one recovery.

Placement Drills

Correct placement of the blade is a critical part of the rowing stroke. It requires precise timing, quickness, and relaxation combined. Placement drills teach you to put the blade in the water effectively without disturbing the boat. The entry is the final motion of the recovery; the blade must be set in the water before the drive begins.

Begin from the release position, the backstops, clear the blades from the water. Come forward on the recovery, stabilize into the oarlocks, opening the handle angle, and place the blades in the water as you compress at full slide. Do not initiate the leg drive. Take the blades out of the water and return to the release position. Repeat 10 to 15 times with precision and blending the recovery and entry into one fluid motion.

Feet-out Rowing

The purpose of this drill is to practice correct release timing of the blade from the water while keeping the body weight consistently behind the oarhandles. Feet-out rowing teaches to preserve the inertia of the drive in order to initiate an effortless flow into the recovery. While performing this drill, keep firm pressure through the handles and feel the pressure of the water on the face of the blade. This contact pressure into the oarlocks will assist you with a clean exit. Focus on achieving a sense of lightness at the release by learning correct timing, paying close attention to "freely erect" posture. This cannot be over-emphasized. Spend 10 to 15 minutes rowing feet-out two to three times per week until you integrate the tempo.

- Remove feet from the boat shoes and place feet on top of the shoes.
- Enforce good upright posture throughout the stroke, paying special attention to sitting up tall over the seat at the release. Allow your body's core strength to support the release with head up and shoulders still.
- Row continuously with firm pressure keeping the feet out. Maintain pressure with the collar into the oarlock in the direction of the blade at all times.

- Time and coordinate the release precisely with the completion of the leg drive in order to keep the body weight behind the handles and transition smoothly into the recovery.
- Poor execution of the change in oarhandle direction and follow through will allow the body weight to fall too far to the bow and the feet will come off the shoes.

Square Blade Rowing (SBR)

Square blade rowing is the top dog of drills. It demands and develops skill throughout several aspects of the stroke: balance, acceleration, bladework, blade depth, and relaxation of the hands. SBR involves continuous rowing with the blade vertical; no feathering motion is used. The emphasis is on clean entry and release of the blade from the water with uninterrupted movement of the oarhandles. Balancing the hull should be focused in the lower body with even weight on the seat and no wobble of the knees during the recovery phase. For the SBR inexperienced, you may angle the blades slightly on the recovery so as not to catch the surface of the water with the lower edge of the blade. Strive for a perfectly square blade. Doubles and quads may rotate one sculler out while the others row with square blades. Alternate every 20 strokes. Good SBR will take your sculling to the next level.

- Sit at the entry with the boat balanced and blades squared in the water.
- Establish your hand placement on the handles with the fingers in a hook grasp (as you would hold a suitcase handle) and with the palmar rise at the base of the finger gently weighted into the grip. The wrists are flat and the palm of the hand is off the handle.

- Begin the draw and emphasize a vertical release, enough to clear the lower edge of the blade. Be brisk without rushing and keep enough weight on the handles to keep the blade off the water. The hull needs to be kept stable using the oarlocks for support.
- Stay loose, work with the boat, and follow through to the arms-body away position. Compress on the slide and place the blade in at the entry without delay.
- Maintain constant pressure through the drive to assist the release and the balance.
- Begin by rowing five strokes with the feather, five strokes on the square. Progress to 20 with the feather, 20 strokes on the square.
- Gradually decrease the number of feathered strokes and build up to 15 to 20 minutes of continuous SBR.
- Variations for increased stability include: one-quarter, half, and three-quarter slide rowing on the square.

∾

Common Technical Errors and Corrections

Fault identification and correction is a normal part of technical training. Earlier in this chapter we discussed how we learn new movements, how to approach practice, and some causes of technical errors. Next, critical concepts were reviewed to present a holistic model of the sculling stroke along with drills to target some of the main elements to be practiced. In this final section about technical training, some common mistakes are identified with suggestions on corrective measures. Ideally, through proper learning, try to prevent a fault from taking seed in the first place.

Tips on Correcting Faults

- Identify the faults to be corrected, isolate the components of the stroke to be remedied.

- Prioritize the primary fault to be corrected.
- Give immediate attention to correction of the fault; an athlete needs to understand the implications of the fault.
- Work on one fault at a time.
- Once the fault is eliminated, the replacement element needs to be demonstrated and learned. The athlete needs a model to learn from.
- Practice the fault correction early in the practice, right after the warm-up so fatigue doesn't interfere with the learning process and concentration is better.
- Avoid working on fault correction late in a practice session when fatigue is present.

Overreaching

Presentation: In an attempt to get a longer stroke, the sculler tries to stretch too far to put the blade in and loses stability. The seat stops moving but the hands keep reaching. This severely compromises the strength of the upper body posture at the entry and weakens the link to the leg drive. The idea of reaching is an inaccurate attempt to gain stroke length too late in the recovery. Stroke length is accomplished by a combination of proper body preparation, correct lower body compression, greater opening of the oarhandle angle, rigging, and timing. You cannot row longer than your body dictates.

Correction: Once the body preparation is set by one-quarter slide on the recovery it does not change for the remainder of the recovery, keep the upper body position quiet and simply compress into the entry with the lower body allowing the oarhandles to open. Keep the eyes focused ahead and maintain posture. Practice the pick drill and placement drills.

Skying the Blade before the Entry

Presentation: Just before the blade enters the water, the

hands drop and the blades go high in the air causing water to be missed. This fault is deadly to your entry timing and causes missed water. It is often a result of overreaching, collapsed posture, poor balance, losing the stability of the pins, or the eyes looking down into the boat.

Correction: Practicing a correct recovery with a smooth transition between the last portion of the recovery and the initiation of the drive. This portion of the stroke is accomplished by the action of moving in and out of the entry. The levels of the head, eyes, and oarhandles need to remain steady through the transition. Practice placement drills, the pick drill, or square blade rowing.

Lifting Shoulders at the Entry

Presentation: The sculler attempts to place the blade in the water by throwing the shoulders towards the bow versus placing the blade with the hands and initiating the drive with the legs. This causes a great loss of power to the drive phase because the major muscles of the legs are not used. The sculler often thinks he feels stronger and is attempting to mimic a rowboat stroke not a sculling stroke by putting emphasis on an upper body stroke instead of a lower body generated stroke.

Correction: It is paramount to keep the level of the shoulders even from half slide on the recovery through approximately half slide on the drive. The lower body and the opening of the hands is the focus at the top end of the slide; the upper body remains steady and quiet as the hands open. The pick drill and the reverse pick drill are helpful.

Shooting the Slide

Presentation: The legs are applied too early before the blade is placed in the water. The seat moves but the upper body and blades do not move therefore the forward motion is impaired.

Correction: Improving timing between the placement and application of power. The seat and handle should initiate movement simultaneously. Shooting the slide can indicate lower back weakness or a heavy loaded rig as the body tries to take pressure off the lumbar spine. Improving back and lat strength can be indicated; practice the reverse pick drill.

Arms Breaking Early

Presentation: At the beginning of the drive, the sculler immediately bends the arms to attempt to pull the stroke. This is a serious flaw that negates the use of the body weight and in effect prevents a proper stroke from happening. Breaking the arms early also causes disruption to balance and problems with blade depth.

Correction: To use your body weight to row you need to develop a sense of relaxing between the points of the oarhandle, footstretcher, and pins. You need to allow the arms to be extended, yet connected, to be able to swing and accelerate your weight. Attempting to grab at the stroke produces an inconsistent and choppy stroke.

Lack of Acceleration

Presentation: Failure to accelerate right from the beginning of the drive is characterized by slow initiation of the legs. The boat will not pick up speed in a way that will assist stability or a clean release. It can be the result of weak legs, an incorrect mental concept of the drive, or lack of an explosive quality to the muscle contractions.

Correction: Execute a full and complete leg drive from the moment of initiation keeping constant pressure on the blade especially in the last one-quarter of the drive to preserve the momentum that has been built up. Leg strengthening or plyometric exercises may be needed to improve your ability to explode. Pausing with the arms-body away is an excellent drill to break the stroke into the acceleration and deceleration phases.

Breaking Wrists at the Release

Presentation: As the oarhandles approach the body, the wrists break attempting to release and feather the blade out of the water. This is usually accompanied by sagging posture, head droop, and the weight of the forearms drop below the oarhandles. As a result, the body weight is not optimally maintained on the drive and the release can be clumsy.

Correction: Proper acceleration of the weight needs to take place during the drive. If this happens, then there is enough momentum of the handles coming into the release to allow a clean exit if made early enough. This is accomplished by keeping the oarhandles in the fingers, letting the wrist/forearm/elbow complex stay level with the handle and moving laterally following the arc of the handles combined with quickness. The handles must be kept in front of the torso at all times. Handles pulling too far past the body make it difficult to keep weight on the blades. Half slide and one-quarter slide rowing are good exercises for working on flat wrists. The right release point must be met.

Improper Hand Placement

Presentation: The knuckles are white clutching the handle. The entire hand is gripped around the handle and there is excessive wrist motion to feather and square the blade. The arms in the stroke are consuming too much energy and the feeling of the blade is masked.

Correction: Establish your hold with the blades square

(vertical) in the water; this is the position the blade will be in during power application and is the reference point for placing the hands on the handle. Sitting at half slide with arms extended, square the blades letting them float in the water at their natural level, and then position your hands so they fingers curve over the handle in a hook grasp and your thumb is on the end of the handle. The back of the hand, and wrist should be straight. As the hands draw towards the body the elbow/forearm complex moves laterally following the arc of the handles to keep the hand/wrist/forearm level with the oarhandle. Subtle lateral pressure is applied into the oarlock. Practice two-finger rowing.

Collapsed Posture

Presentation: Chest and head are down at both the entry and the release causing checking of the boat. The torso does not effectively support the body weight. Overreaching and skying often result from poor posture. At the release, the body weight sags on the seat cause the bow to sink in the water.

Correction: Sit up tall with the rib cage lifted; chin level to the water, and eyes above the horizon. Throughout the stroke maintain this posture in a comfortable manner allowing your spine to support your torso. Do land exercises to strengthen the shoulder girdle (push ups, pull ups, bench pulls, bench presses), the abdominal muscles (various types of sit ups), and the lower back (prone extensions, back extensions). The use of a large therapy ball is excellent for doing stabilization and core strengthening exercises. Posture must be corrected in your daily activities as well.

Catching a Crab

Presentation: The blade is feathered under the water and is unable to be extracted. Catching a crab could cause one to be capsized or catapulted out of the shell.

Correction: Improve the release so the water assists in the clean exit of the blade. Practice the delayed feather drill, square blade rowing, and feet-out rowing.

Excessive Head Motion

Presentation: During the stroke there is excessive movement of the head up and down or side to side. This represents a loss of energy and disturbs the balance of the boat. It is often linked to weak posture, sagging body weight and poor body awareness.

Correction: Correct posture with an emphasis on keeping the gaze of the eyes above the horizon throughout the entire stroke. Avoid looking down in the boat or dropping the chin at the finish of the stroke.

Late Body Preparation

Presentation: At the completion of the leg drive, the hands sit in the bow too long before the recovery is initiated. The legs and slide begin to move before the body weight has been shifted out of the bow. The body is still upright with no pivot occurring at the hip. As the recovery progresses there is a lunge toward the entry to try to establish the body position at the last instance. Rhythm and stability are disrupted during the recovery. Poor flexibility can be a cause.

Correction: Completing the follow through of the stroke after the release but before beginning the slide motion on the recovery. Hold the knees down longer to allow the hands to pass the knees before the slide begins to move; the body weight must be shifted out of the bow. Focus on continuous handle movement to lead the body away. Doing pause drills with the arms/body away illustrates the motion.

Rushing the Slide

Presentation: Once the blade comes out of the water there is a rapid, uncontrolled movement on the slide to take the next stroke. The ratio is reversed and the oar is in the water longer than it is out of the water. There is no real rhythm or flow to the stroke.

Correction: Re-establish the ratio between the time on the drive and time spent on the recovery to one to two or one to three, only at very high race cadences will the ratio be closer to one to one. The rhythm of the stroke is fluid and uninterrupted. It links an explosive drive with a relaxation phase on the recovery after the hands and body are set. Let the boat run out from under you smoothly with legs relaxing near the top of the slide. Rowing at low stroke rates of 16 to 18 or exaggerating the time on the slide are good ways to practice the discipline of slide relaxation. Guide recovery speed by opening the oarhandles against the oarlocks. This is your reference for gauging boat speed. Stay neutral.

Incorrect Blade Depth

Presentation: The blade is too deep in the water making the boat feel unsteady. Much of the shaft of the oar is covered by water during the drive. There are a few potential causes: the oarhandle height does not travel level but lifts too high over the knees, the shoulders lift the blades in at the entry, or the hands raise too aggressively at the entry. Driving the blade deep causes the shaft to create turbulence and pull the hull down into the water.

Correction: Relax the hands and check that hand placement is correct. Allow the blade to float at its natural level in the water without exerting energy to try to control it. The top edge of the blade will be even with the surface of the water. Two-finger rowing and half-blade rowing will teach correct blade depth.

Faulty Bladework

Presentation: Incomplete squaring motion at the entry will cause the blade to knife into the water creating instability. Conversely, failure to keep weight on the blade until the release will cause the handles to drop and the blade washes out at the end of the drive. The release is made by pressing down on the handle while relaxing the tension of the hands on the handle.

Correction: The feather and squaring motions need to be complete motions. On the sleeve of the oar there is a flat surface. This surface rests against the pin of the oarlock when the blade is square and on the bottom sill of the oarlock when the blade is feathered. With minimal initiation, the blade will fall from one position to the other with the use of gravity. During the recovery, allowing the sleeve to sit supported on the sill of the oarlock allows for full relaxation of the hands. Once the blade is squared, due to the force of the water on the face of the blade and the sleeve against the pin, little is needed to hold it in the square position, thus the handle can be kept loosely in the fingers.

Correct washing out by maintaining handle height at the finish, correcting posture and practicing one-quarter and half slide rowing. Practice releases by bobbing the blades in an out of the water by pressing down on the handle and keeping the forearms level.

Short Strokes

Presentation: Full compression and full use of the body weight is not utilized giving the stroke a choppy appearance. The breakdown of any major component of the stroke will affect the length of the stroke. A sculler will guard opening up their handles at the entry due to instability.

Correction: Utilize all phases of the pick drill and reverse pick drill; complete hand motions, body preparation, and full use of the slide. Take care that blade depth is correct and release timing accurate. Practice relaxing the legs on the recovery to facilitate the opening of the oarhandle angle.

༄

Marlene Royle, OTR is a graduate in occupational therapy from Boston University's Sargent College of Allied Health Professions. She specializes in orthopedics and upper extremity rehabilitation. Her achievements as a competitive rower include a U.S. National Collegiate Championship, a U.S. National Championship in the lightweight quad, and in the year 2000 setting world indoor rowing records for the 30-minute and the 6000-meter row. Marlene competed on the elite level in sculling between the ages of 20 to 24 and 33 to 37.

CHAPTER 4

DRILLS, DRILLS

RELEASE. SQUARE BLADES. FEET-OUT. PAUSE. ENTRY.

BUILDING PRESSURE: RELEASE DRILL

This drill focuses on maintaining the resistance of the water against the face of the blade during the drive as the boat picks up speed. By combining different slide lengths and pressures this drill increases the pressure as the slide length decreases.

Row 10 strokes at each station:

- Full slide at no pressure.
- Three-quarter slide at half pressure.
- Half slide at three-quarter pressure.
- One-quarter slide at full pressure.

Sculling-specific: While practicing this exercise pay attention to the feeling of constant pressure of the water against the blade. Listen for feedback as you row-noise from the blade tearing through the water indicates a loss of power. Solid bladework is quiet and subtle.

Sweep-specific: This drill provides good practice for a crew to make slide length and power transitions together. Because of the rapid changes, every 10 strokes, the crew must have full attention focused on the correct execution of the drill. Encourage clean releases and correct blade depth during the exercise. For variety, try different stroke ratings.

BUILDING PRESSURE: SILENT PYRAMID

This drill develops rowing at full pressure while introducing elements of relaxation and concentration. Do at low ratings, 16 to 18 stroke per minute.

- Perform silently without the coxswain or bow-seat making calls.
- Row one stroke at full pressure followed by one stroke on the paddle.
- Row two strokes at full pressure followed by two strokes on the paddle.
- Continue up to 10 strokes at full pressure followed by 10 strokes on the paddle.
- Then reverse the pyramid back down to one stroke at full pressure followed by one stroke on the paddle.
- Total hard strokes: 100

Sculling-specific: Completely relax on the light strokes; maintain firm, powerful strokes during full pressure. Set the blades carefully avoiding tearing the blades through the water. A terrific exercise for workouts in doubles and quads

Sweep-specific: Excellent for developing concentration in a big boat, this drill will teach a crew to focus on the rhythm of the pressure transitions.

GENERAL PERFORMANCE: DELAYED FEATHER DRILL

The purpose of this drill is to practice a clean and silent release of the blade from the water eliminating a tendency to feather under water:

- Row at half pressure.
- Extract the blade from the water in the squared position.
- Emphasize a vertical release to clear the lower edge of the blade before feathering.
- The square blade release must be accomplished before the handles complete the turn.

Sculling-specific: During a steady row, alternate 20 strokes with the delayed feather followed by 20 continuous strokes. Repeat five times for a total of 100 strokes with the delayed feather. While performing this drill, keep lateral pressure into the oarlocks to assist you with a clean exit.

Sweep-specific: Perform the drill alternating stern-four and bow-four in an eight or stern-pair and bow-pair in a four. Each combination should row 20 strokes with the delayed feather while the boat is held steady by the non-rowing seats. Repeat the series three times.

GENERAL PERFORMANCE: FEET-OUT ROWING

The purpose of this drill is to practice the correct release point of the blade from the water while keeping the body weight behind the oarhandles. Feet-out rowing teaches to preserve the inertia of the drive in order to initiate an effortless flow into the recovery.

- Remove feet from the boat shoes and place feet on top of the shoes.
- Enforce good posture throughout the stroke, paying special attention to sitting up tall over the seat at the release. Allow your body's core strength to support the release.
- Row at a firm pressure keeping the feet out of the shoes. Maintain pressure of the collar into the oarlock in the direction of the blade.
- Coordinate the release with the completion of the leg drive in order to keep the body weight behind the handles and transition smoothly into the recovery.
- Incorrect timing of the change in oarhandle direction and follow through will allow the body weight to fall too far to the bow and the feet will come off the shoes.

Sculling-specific: While performing this drill, keep firm pressure through the oarlocks. This pressure will assist you with a clean exit. Focus on achieving a sense of lightness at the release by learning correct release timing. Pay close attention to posture. This cannot be over-emphasized. Spend 10 to 15 minutes rowing feet-out two to three times per week until you integrate the tempo.

Sweep-specific: Perform the drill with all members of the crew rowing feet-out together. This drill is very good to use with young crews as it provides a graphic demonstration of the negative effects of keeping the blade in the water too long. Use this drill to reinforce proper and uniform posture within the boat. This is an effective drill for a crew to do during steady rows.

GENERAL PERFORMANCE: SQUARE BLADE ROWING

Square blade rowing (SBR) is the kingpin of drills. It demands and develops skill throughout several aspects of the stroke: balance, acceleration, bladework, blade depth, and relaxation of the hands. SBR involves continuous rowing with the blade vertical; no feathering motion is used. The emphasis is on clean entry and release of the blade from the water with uninterrupted movement of the oarhandles. Stabilizing the hull should be achieved by even pressure into the oarlocks. The lower body should be relaxed with no wobble of the knees during the recovery phase.

- Sit at the entry position with the boat set and the blades squared in the water.
- Establish your hand placement on the handle with the fingers in a hook grasp, as you would hold a suitcase handle, and with the palmar rise at the base of the finger gently weighted into the grip. The wrists are flat and the palm of the hand is off the handle in sculling technique.
- Begin the draw and emphasize a vertical release, enough to clear the lower edge of the blade. Be brisk without rushing and keep enough weight on the handles to keep the blade off the water.
- Work with the boat, and follow through to the arms-body away position. Compress on the slide and place the blade in at the entry without delay.
- Maintain constant pressure through the drive then relax at the point of release.
- Begin by rowing five strokes with the feather followed by five strokes on the square. Then progress to 20

strokes with the feather followed by 20 strokes on the square.
- Gradually decrease the number of feathered strokes and build up to 15 to 20 minutes of continuous SBR.
- Variations for increased stability include one-quarter, half, and three-quarter slide rowing on the square.

Sculling-specific: For the SBR inexperienced, angle the blades slightly on the recovery so as not to catch the surface of the water with the lower edge of the blade but strive for a perfectly square blade. Doubles and quads may rotate one sculler out while the others row with square blades. Alternate scullers every 20 strokes. Good SBR will take your sculling to the next level.

Sweep-specific: Perform the drill alternating stern-four and bow-four in an eight or stern-pair and bow-pair in a four. Each rows for 20 strokes on the square while the non-rowing seats set the boat. Repeat the series three times then progress to stern-four, bow-four, all eight or stern-pair, bow-pair, all four. This is a challenging drill to do in a pair but well worth the effort to develop technical prowess and confidence.

GENERAL PERFORMANCE: TWO-FINGER ROWING

The purpose of this drill is to learn to relax the hands allowing them to feel the natural path of the oarhandles as dictated by the buoyancy of the blade in the water. Avoiding over-gripping on the oarhandle will allow the blade to seek its own level in the water and provide perfect blade depth.

- Row easy.
- During the recovery normal hand placement is used.
- Once the blade is placed in the water, lift the middle, ring, and little fingers off the oarhandle and draw through to the release using only the index finger and the thumb on the handle.
- Let the blades float in the water. There should be no tension in the hands, arms, or upper body during this drill. Relax and note how easy it is to keep the oars at the correct depth in the water.
- Perform continuously for 10 to 15 minutes when you include drills in your daily workout.

Sculling-specific: This is a classic drill for learning a relaxed hand placement on the oarhandle. The ease of letting the blades sit at the correct depth in the water is obvious and pleasant. This relaxation of the hands cannot be stressed enough to develop sensitive sculling skills.

Sweep-specific: Although with a larger handle than sculling, two-finger rowing teaches the development of light, relaxed hands and a perception of natural blade depth, which will help crews learn good rowing economy.

IMPLEMENTING THE PAUSE DRILL

A pause of approximately two seconds interrupts the ordinary cycle of the stroke giving the opportunity to stop briefly and balance the boat with the blades off the water. It is also very useful for checking the position of the body at designated points on the recovery. Pauses can be incorporated at several stations during the stroke:

- Arms away.
- Arms-body away.
- One-quarter slide.
- Half slide.
- Three-quarter slide.

Pause drills serve many purposes in technical training. Arms-body away, for example, is an excellent way to work on a fluid release and complete body preparation prior to the initiation of the slide. After the pause continue the recovery by compressing the lower body and opening the arms following the arc of the oarhandles until the blade is placed in.

Begin a pause drill session by pausing once every stroke for 20 strokes, then once every other stroke for 20 strokes, progress to five strokes of continuous rowing with one stroke pausing. Relax. Keep the blades off the water. Take your time and let the hull slow down. An advanced sculler or crew can pause with the blades square. Double pause drills incorporate two pauses during one recovery such as pausing at arms-body away and at half slide.

These drills are an effective way to isolate aspects of technical priority for a crew. They offer both single scullers and teamboats specifically designed exercises to develop uniformity in their stroke and master keeping the blades off the water. Pause drills are an excellent part of a warm-up routine.

SPECIFIC STRENGTH DRILLS

Rowing requires strength but it is sport-specific strength that can be transferred to the physical demands of the stroke cycle and racing distance that is most important for us. Maximum strength plays a determining role in developing sport-specific strength. Weight training with high loads between 85 to 100 percent and low repetitions of one to four per set, as part of your off-season training builds the foundation for power development as well as muscular-endurance to resist fatigue. This high load training improves strength by creating high tension in the muscle and activating a large number of fast twitch motor units. Untrained we use a little more than half the motor units available to us. One need not develop large muscles and high body mass to become significantly stronger. Once you have done your weight training on land, as you approach the racing season you need to put some fiber recruitment sessions into your water practice to prepare your stroke for higher power output. Such exercises also increase the coordination and synchronization of your muscle groups during high intensity stabilizing your drive phase and racing starts.

The bungee row is a means to perform resistive exercises while rowing in the boat. Wrapping an elastic bungee cord or a thick rope around the hull of the boat to the stern of the stroke's or sculler's feet will supply a substantial amount of drag to slow the hull speed way down during the recovery so you will be able to load the beginning of the drive. Once you have done a thorough warm-up, put the bungee cord on. Repeat four times 10 strokes at 10 strokes per minute applying maximum effort. Rest one minute between each 10-stroke piece. Then after the fourth, rest for five minutes. Repeat this series for a total of four times. The entire workout will take about 40 minutes. Rowing 10 strokes per minute is a challenge for balance and concentration.

In a single, you may need to insert a brief pause with arms-body away to maintain the correct rating. This drill can be performed in an eight and for added resistance alternate the stern-four and bow-four every 10 strokes. Rowing 10 strokes per minute can be a significant technical challenge in a pair, as well.

Another effective power workout using the bungee cord takes half an hour not counting warm-up and cool-down time. During the body of your practice, row for 30-seconds at racing effort then easy for 90 seconds; repeat this for a total of 30 minutes. You can vary the session by doing some from a moving five-stroke start and some by rowing into it.

For developing explosiveness on the drive combined with stabilizing your balance on the recovery continuous bungee rows are fun and productive. An example session is made up of four to six 10-minute pieces. For each piece start with the bungee cord on, row five minutes at a stroke rate of 14 at 85 to 90 percent effort, after five minutes, stop briefly, unhook one side of the bungee cord to remove it from the hull, tossing it in the boat, continue at a stroke rate of 18 for five minutes trying to maintain the same drive power that was required when the bungee cord was on. Rest for five to seven minutes between each piece. The boat will feel very light once the bungee cord comes off so you need to stay focused on loading the blade and keeping constant pressure against the water as the hull speeds up.

Using the bungee provides a precise type of resistance. Avoid rowing long miles with a bungee on with the thought that more is better because the firing of your muscle's motor units can be trained to react more slowly than what is needed for actual racing. Keep bungee pieces short and concentrated.

Another benefit of bungee rowing is that it will make you acutely aware of the transition from the entry to your leg drive application because of the slowed hull speed. Timing at the entry demands coordination of the hands, feet, hips, and shoulders plus the action of the blade to the water. When the blade placement is timed correctly the blade will lock onto the water and the hull will move forward as the leg drive takes over. At the entry, the boat is moving at its slowest so any hesitation getting the blades in the water will decrease the speed of the hull even more taking extra energy to build the speed again.

Pressure must be held firmly to the completion of the stroke through the legs and back. Learning to keep even pressure teaches crews to reach higher boat speeds. Once the stroke has started you do not have the ability to increase the pressure effectively and will tear the water if abruptly taking over with the arms and trying to work too hard. There are some very good team boat drills that can help develop good leg drive and the skill of applying even pressure through the water.

Rowing with only part of the crew at one time focuses the rowers' attention on leg drive and learning to react to hull speed. To feel the speed of the leg drive, start rowing in an eight with the bow pair only or in a quad with bow seat only. After 10 strokes, add in the three- and four-seat rowers in an eight or three-seat if in a quad. The boat velocity increases and those rowing have to sense this difference, adjusting their power application, in order to apply the same amount of leg drive. After 10 more strokes add in the next pair in an eight or seat in a quad until all positions are rowing together. When each pair adds to the speed, and each rower must adjust their leg speed or get left behind.

Another good team boat exercise is a drill to increase rower's awareness of holding pressure against the face of the blade as the boat increases more dramatically. This drill is done for one sculler at a time when sculling in a quad or for one pair when rowing in an eight. One sculler or pair begins rowing a sequence of easy paddle for 10 strokes; they then increase to 50 percent pressure for 10 strokes, and then to full pressure for 20 strokes. While the initial rowers are at full pressure, every

10 strokes, one sculler or pair joins in at 50 percent pressure until all for or eight are rowing. Every added pair or sculler will increase the travel of the hull and the rowers must react to the changing entry timing, application of the legs and keep the same pressure on the blade as the boat moves faster. The first pair or sculler's goal is to maintain the same resistance through the water felt when rowing alone even though the hull speed is increasing every 10 strokes when another joins in. In a double, the first sculler must keep the same full pressure resistance when the second sculler joins in. Repeat the drill for each seat or pair in the boat.

Lastly, half slide rowing is an excellent drill to improve the leg drive application. The motion of the boat is felt more immediately when the blades are perpendicular to the boat at mid-drive. Rowers and scullers will have to apply their legs faster than at normal catch position. Half slide rowing can be practiced in teamboats or singles.

START DRILLS: RACING STARTS

The purpose of this exercise is to practice a clean racing start. A standing start is the first five strokes of a race taken from a stationary position at the beginning of a 1,000-meter or 2,000-meter event. The main goal of the start is to pry the boat away from the starting line without kicking the boat sternward and accelerate the boat up to full speed as the initial short strokes are lengthened. A clean start can boost your confidence in the early phases of a race and being first off the line is for some an important tactic to place them in position to watch the other challenging boats. Crabs, missed strokes, and bad timing can put you way behind before you even get off the line.

Initially, perform starts at low stroke rates and power application to maintain relaxation. Start from the entry position, blades squared and set just below the surface of the water. Care and time should be taken to pattern the proper motions before progressing towards more intensity. Most importantly, concentrate on only one point at a time when working on starts and include a few at the end of every practice.

Start Sequence

- 5 x 1 stroke: three-quarter slide.
- 5 x 2 strokes: three-quarter slide, half slide.
- 5 x 3 strokes: three-quarter slide, half slide, three-quarter slide.
- 5 x 4 strokes: three-quarter slide, half slide, three-quarter slide, and full slide.
- 5 x 5 strokes: three-quarter slide, half slide, three-quarter slide, full slide, and full slide.
- 5 x 10 strokes: three-quarter slide, half slide, three-

quarter slide, full slide, full slide, then paddle five
strokes.

Sculling-specific: A start in the single requires a delicate
balance of relaxation and aggression to get away from the line
quickly and maintain a straight course. Practice keeping a quiet
upper body and loose hold on the handles to feel light and avoid
tension Single scullers may want to try a variation of three-
quarter slide, three-quarter slide, three-quarter slide, full slide,
and full slide for the first five strokes. Experiment to find that
start that is most effective for you and feels most stable.

Sweep-specific: Moving an eight or four effectively off the
starting line requires precise slide length timing between all
members of the crew. Spending time drilling a crew at half and
three-quarter slide rowing can benefit your starts as the crew
intuitively learns to interpret part-slide strokes in the same way.
Experiment with slide combinations of the first three strokes
to find the start that helps the boat move the right direction
off the line.

STARTS: FLYING STARTS

Flying starts provide a way to practice several starts consecutively without fatiguing a crew. In cooler weather, multiple flying starts can keep the crew warm, to avoid chilling down between starts from a stand still and risking injury.

- Row on the paddle, a flying start is done with the boat in motion.
- Take three strokes to build into a five-stroke start. You may use a standard three-quarter slide, half slide, three-quarter slide, full slide, and full slide or a sequence you prefer.
- After the fifth stroke continue to row for 20 strokes then repeat three strokes to build plus your five-stroke start.
- Repeat five times. Emphasize unity in timing, sharpness, and swing in the boat.

Sculling-specific: This drill will help the single sculler build confidence doing racing starts at higher ratings. Practice a few starts daily at the end of your row.

Sweep-specific: Familiarity with starts and frequent practice will give crews a mental edge going to the starting line. Crews will benefit from having fun doing starts and developing boat sense when it comes time to stay focused at the start of a race.

TECHNICAL DRILLS FOR SCULLING PERFORMANCE

Original text printed in 1996, revised in 2007.

Introduction

Good technical skills are priceless; reducing risks of injuries, enhancing the aesthetic qualities of the sport, and making boats go fast. The success and enjoyment of your sculling depends on the technique that you learn. Description of technique has to be given in terms of segments and separate phases. It is emphasized, however, that in practice each sculling stroke must form a complete, fluent cycle. All strokes must blend with one another consistently and with flow. Good technique develops economic and efficient use of power, as well as, greater chances of success in achieving your personal sculling goals.

Technical Drills for Sculling Performance presents drills related to five areas of sculling: General Performance, Drills to Build Pressure, Speedwork, Start Drills, and Drills for Teamboats. Outlining different elements of the stroke, these exercises are for use by scullers of all levels. Technical motor skills are basic elements of learning but even the elite sculler must constantly refine their body movements to maintain optimum ability.

When using this manual select one or two relevant drills to be included in your day's row. Progress at your own pace; learn the movements and then improve the speed or pressure. Vary your choice of drills to make your workouts more interesting. Be creative and enjoy developing your skills.

Technique training should be done at low stroke rates and power application so that you are able to devote attention to particular aspects of the stroke. High stroke rates and full pressure rowing introduced too early can have a detrimental effect on a novice's technique. The care and time should be taken to pattern the proper motions and then progress towards more intensive work. To maintain fitness while initially learning how to scull it may be necessary to continue with your usual training in other sports until your technique is sufficient to apply power. Most importantly, concentrate on only one point at a time. During a workout you may give attention to several details but address them individually and give yourself a moment of mental relaxation between exercises.

Section One

General Performance Drills

Pick Drill

A common drill used by scullers of all levels as a regular part of the rowing warm-up. The pick drill sequentially builds the stroke up to full slide strokes. It may be done with blades squared or feathered. Begin by sitting in the release position, hands near the rib cage.

Row 20 strokes at each station:

- Arms-hands only: shoulders stationary towards the bow.
- Arms-body: pivot forward from the hip a comfortable distance.
- One-quarter slide: just breaking the knees to add slide.
- Half slide: increase the distance the seat moves to half slide.
- Three-quarter slide: slightly shorter than full slide.
- Full slide: full slide strokes keeping the amount of body angle that was established at arms and body away.

Attention to clean bladework, entry, and exit, as well as, balance. This is a good drill for use in doubles and quads to develop uniformity.

Extended Pick Drill

The same drill as above except row 100 strokes at each station.

Delayed Feather Drill

To practice a clean and silent release of the blade from the water this drill is very beneficial. Row at half pressure, when you extract the blade from the water, emphasize a vertical exit before you feather. The point of the drill is to clear the lower edge of the blade to prevent feathering under the water and slowing the boat down. The square blade release must be accomplished quickly while the hands continue through the release turn and move away from the body.

Open Fingers On the Handle

While rowing continuously recover with the fingers and thumb open, not gripping the oarhandle, allowing the forearms and hands to relax, keeping weight over the oarhandles. Row on the paddle and control the handles with the area of the hand at the base of the fingers. Row 20 to 30 strokes then resume regular rowing continuing to hold the oars with a gentle grip.

Feet-out Rowing

The purpose of this drill is to practice correct release timing of the blade from the water while keeping the body weight consistently behind the oarhandles. Feet-out rowing teaches to preserve the inertia of the drive in order to initiate an effortless flow into the recovery. While performing this drill, keep firm pressure through the handles and feel the pressure of the water on the blade. This constant pressure into the oarlocks will assist you with a clean exit. Focus on achieving a sense of lightness at the release by learning correct timing. Pay close attention to maintaining your "freely erect" posture. This cannot be over-emphasized. Spend 10 to 15 minutes rowing feet-out two to three times per week until you integrate the tempo.

- Remove feet from the boat shoes and place feet on top of the shoes.

- Enforce good posture throughout the stroke, paying special attention to sitting up tall over the seat at the release. Allow your body's core strength to provide support into the oarlock, keep the head up and shoulders still.
- Row continuously with firm pressure keeping the feet out. Maintain pressure with the collar into the oarlock.
- Time and coordinate the release with the completion of the leg drive in order to keep the body weight applied to the handles and transition smoothly into the recovery.
- Incorrect execution of the change in oarhandle direction and follow through will allow the body weight to fall too far to the bow and the feet will come off the shoes.

Square Blade Rowing

Continuous rowing with the blade of the oar vertical in the squared position, no feather is used. The emphasis is on clean entry and release of the blade from the water, uninterrupted movement of the oarhandles around the release, and balance. Relax the grip on the oarhandles. Hold the oar with a hook grasp, as you would hold a suitcase handle, and with the palmar rise at the base of the fingers. Begin by rowing five strokes on the square then five strokes with the feather progressing up to 20 strokes on the square then 20 strokes with the feather.

As you improve, decrease the number of strokes on the feather to row continuously on the square for an extended length of time, 15 to 20 minutes. Beginners may angle the blades slightly on the recovery so as not to catch the surface of the water with the lower edge of the blade but strive for a perfectly square blade.

To start practicing this drill try rowing first with arms only then progress through the stages of the pick drill before reaching full slide rowing on the square. For success with this drill it is essential to keep the hands moving around the release.

Pause Drills

A pause of approximately two seconds interrupts the ordinary cycle of the stroke giving the sculler the opportunity to stop briefly and set the boat with the blades off the water. It also allows a chance to check the position of the body at a designated point of the recovery. Pauses are incorporated at the following recovery positions: hands-arms away, arm-/body away, half slide, or three-quarter slide.

Begin by pausing once every stroke for 20 strokes, then once every other stroke for 20 strokes, once every third stroke etc....up to five strokes regular rowing with one stroke pausing. Choose one position, i.e. arms-body away and pause there for the duration of the drill. Next time try another position.

Relax. Keep blades above the water. Maintain a stable upper body, an evenly weighted seat and keep collar pressure against the pins. Take your time and allow the hull to glide each stroke. An advanced sculler can pause with square blades.

Double Pause Drills

Same as the pause drill except two pauses are incorporated into each recovery. For example, pause one is at the hands-arms away position and pause two is with the arms-body away or at half slide. Hold each position for a short count.

Relax the upper body and hold on the oarhandles. The goal is to maintain the stability of the boat without the support of the oars on the water. This is a more advanced drill than the single pause drill.

Entry Drills

This drill is for stability and practice of direct entry of the blade into the water. The entry is the last motion of the recovery; the blades enter the water before the seat and handles reverse directions for the drive.

Begin from the release position, oars squared and buried just under the surface of the water, press the oarhandles so the blades come out of the water, feather, press into the oarlocks to move your hips through the level of the pins as you travel the slide, relax your legs, allow the handles to open up, and place the blades in the water. Stop there. Do not pull through the water. Repeat 10 to 15 times. Enter the water with precision, blades vertical without hesitation.

Entry Drill Detail

Sitting at the entry position, blades squared, boat stabilized; move the oarhandles up and down with slight pressure allowing them to dip in and out of the water. Focus the eyes ahead; the motion is a rising of the hands and arms. Upper back and shoulders are stationary though the shoulder joint allows the lever action of the arms. Notice how far you must raise the oarhandles to touch the blade's edge to the water's surface. Use this distance as a guide for changing the handle height during continuous rowing.

Release Guide Drill

Apply the same principles as in the *Entry Drill Detail* except perform from the release position. Square the blades in the water. Stabilize the boat by sitting evenly on the seat, keeping pressure into the pins, and holding the hands level. Bob the oarhandles up and down just enough to let the lower edges of the blades clear the water's surface. Then return. Move your oarhandles simultaneously and notice the distance you must press down to release the water. Use this distance as a guide for changing the handle height at the release during regular rowing. When rowing in rough water you will need to carry the blades higher above the water to clear the chop; adjust accordingly.

Row Eyes Closed

In a safe environment row 10 to 15 strokes with your eyes closed to feel the balance and movement of the hull through the water.

Time On the Slide

Row continuously. For 30 strokes exaggerate the slow slide forward on the recovery. Focus on releasing the tension in the legs on the slide and maintaining contact with the pins. Work to develop better core stability and body coordination on the slide. For variation incorporate into a steady state workout and row 30 strokes with *time on the slide* every 10 minutes.

Time On the Slide Variations

Row three very firm strokes, after the third stroke consciously slow the slide with relaxation and core stability. Practice for five minutes.

Section Two

Drills to Build Pressure

The following drills develop rowing at pressures varying from no pressure paddling to maximum. Full pressure is defined here as the exertion of the sculler's maximum effort during each stroke while maintaining good technique. As your sculling improves row at higher intensities but those that preserve the good technical habits that you have already mastered. The end result will be greater speed and efficiency.

Building Drill

Repeat the following sequence:

- Paddle five strokes.
- Row one-quarter pressure for five strokes.
- Row half pressure for five strokes.
- Row three-quarter pressure for five strokes.
- Row full pressure for five strokes.
- Total of 25 strokes; Repeat three times maintaining relaxation though the pressure increases.

Alternate Stroke Pressure

Row continuously; alternate one stroke at full pressure then one stroke no pressure on the paddle then one stroke at full pressure etc. for 50 strokes total. Paddle easy two to three minutes. Repeat.

Release Drill

This drill lets the sculler practice maintaining the

resistance of the water against the blade during the second half of the drive until the blades have released and the hands have completed the follow through out to the crossover of the oarhandles. By combining different slide lengths and pressures this drill increases the pressure of the stroke as it gets shorter and approaches the release.

Row 10 strokes at each station:

- Full slide at zero pressure.
- Three-quarter slide at half pressure.
- Half slide at three-quarter pressure.
- One-quarter slide at full pressure.

Varied Pressure: Entry to Release

An exercise to illustrate the feeling of staying connected to the water during the drive. Take the entry at a softer pressure and increase through to the release.

Row 20 strokes at each station:

- Zero pressure at the entry to half pressure at the release.
- Half pressure at the entry to three-quarter pressure at the release.
- Three-quarter pressure at the entry to full pressure at the release.

Strive for clean releases to keep the boat speed. Clear the lower edge of the blade from the water before feathering.

Full Strokes: Different Pressures

Adjust to rowing at different intensities. Row:

- 30 strokes at half pressure.
- 30 strokes at three-quarter pressure.
- 30 strokes at full pressure.
- 30 strokes at three-quarter pressure.
- 30 strokes at half pressure.
- Total of 150 strokes; Repeat the pyramid two times.

Build Slide and Pressure

Row a total of 30 strokes:

- 10 strokes at half slide, at half pressure.
- 10 strokes at three-quarter slide, at three-quarter pressure.
- 10 strokes at full slide, at full pressure.
- Paddle 10 strokes for relaxation; Repeat pyramid.

Silent Pyramid

Row one stroke at full pressure and one stroke paddle then two strokes at full pressure and two strokes paddle up to 10 strokes at full pressure and 10 strokes paddle. Then, reverse order back down the pyramid to one stroke at full pressure and one stroke paddle. This is an excellent drill for mental concentration in the boat.

Section Three

Speedwork Drills

Once a sculler has spent considerable time on the water and is able to row full pressure, in good form, an interest in racing can develops. A sculler must then train high-speed coordination and the ability to row at stroke rates higher than 30 strokes per minute. The following drills focus on stroke rate changes and increasing speed. To measure your own stroke rate put a stopwatch in your boat; count the number of strokes taken in 15 seconds, multiply by four. Therefore, if you count six entries it equals five strokes, thus, 20 strokes per minute. There are also commercially available stroke meters.

Acceleration-10

This is a 10-stroke piece. Build up to full pressure then increase the stroke rate one stroke per minute every other stroke for a total of 10. During a steady state workout take an Acceleration-10 every two minutes for a specific 10-minute period or use in warm-ups and short sprint workouts. For variety do Acceleration-10's at half slide or three-quarter slide.

Acceleration-20

This is a 20-stroke piece. Build to full pressure then increase the stroke rate one stroke per minute every five strokes for a total of 20 strokes.

Acceleration-25

Row 25 full pressure strokes. Five strokes at half slide, then five strokes at three-quarter slide, five strokes at full slide, five strokes at three-quarter slide, and five strokes at half slide.

Alternate Slide Length

Row one minute at half slide, with full pressure. Then one minute at full slide, with full pressure. Repeat each two-minute segment continuously for 10 minutes or as long as desired.

Stroke Transitions

Transitions are the changes from one stroke rate to another. They should be precise and happen in one designated stroke. To learn how to make good transitions define the leg drive to increase the speed of your hands moving away from your body at the release. This is a point of reference. The following are some varieties of transitions you can practice.

40-Stroke Pieces

- Full pressure for 20 strokes then up two strokes per minute for 20 strokes. Row at a base stroke for 20 strokes; Increase the rating by two strokes per minute for the last 20 strokes. Target rates: 24-26, 26-28, 28-30, 30-32, 32-34 strokes per minute.
- Full pressure for 20 strokes then down two strokes per minute for 20 strokes. Row at a higher stroke for 20 strokes; Settle the rating down two strokes per minute for 20 strokes. Target rates: 30-28, 32-30, 34-32 strokes per minute.
- Full pressure for 20 strokes then up two strokes per minute for 10 strokes then up two strokes per minute for 10 strokes. Row at a base stroke for 20 strokes; Increase the rate two strokes per minute for 10 strokes. Increase again two strokes per minute for 10 strokes. Target rates: 26-28-30, 28-30-32, 30-32-34 strokes per minute.
- Full pressure for 20 strokes high then down two strokes per minute for 10 strokes then down two strokes per minute for 10 strokes. Row at a higher rating for 20

strokes, settle rating two strokes per minute for 10 strokes, settle again for two strokes per minute for 10 strokes. Target rates: 34-32-30, 32-30-28, 30-28-26, 28-26-24 strokes per minute.

20-Stroke Pieces

- 10 high strokes then settle four strokes per minute for 10 strokes. Sprint for 10 strokes then take the stroke rate down four strokes per minute for 10 strokes. Target rates: 36-32, 34-30, 32-28 strokes per minute.
- Full pressure for 10 strokes then up two strokes per minute for 10 strokes. Row 10 strokes at a base rate increase the rate two strokes per minute for a second set of 10 strokes. Target rates: 30-32, 31-33, 32-34 stroke per minute.
- Full pressure for 10 strokes then an acceleration-10. Row full pressure at a lower base rate and then up one stroke per minute every other stroke for the second 10. Target base rates: 26-27, 28-29, 30-31 strokes per minute.

Race Warm-up

The full race warm-up includes Phase One and Phase Two.

Phase One

- Four minutes of easy paddle from the dock and then progress into the following series rowing 30 strokes comfortable pace then 15 strokes at maximum tempo for each segment. Give constant attention to clean bladework and correct blade depth, especially with the maximum tempo strokes. Strive for the 15 strokes high to be sharp.

- Arms only.
- Arms-body only.
- One-quarter slide.
- Half slide.
- Three-quarter slide.
- Full slide.

Phase Two

- This phase is to build up to your full slide race tempo. Do not overdo this phase but do make sure that you can reach the stroke rating that you want for the start.
- Row three 20-stroke pieces to building your stroke rate up to 36 to 40 strokes per minute. Paddle easy 20 to 30 strokes between to rest. If, by the third 20-stroke piece, you have not reached 36 strokes per minute or the highest rate you feel you can achieve do another one.
- Followed by three 10-stroke start sequences.
- Easy paddle and stay focused until the start.

Section Four

Start Drills

A start is the first five strokes of a race taken from either a stationary or moving position. It is usually followed by a sprint of 20 to 30 strokes and then a settle to a base rate that a sculler can maintain for the body of the race. The drills in this section focus on the first five strokes of the race from a stand still though moving starts are briefly addressed.

Practicing Starts

Starts are typically practiced by devoting attention to each stroke; thus, a sculler will practice repetitions of only the first stroke and then the first two strokes, building up to the first five strokes of the race and the initial sprint that follows. Starts are comprised of half slide, three-quarter slide, and full slide strokes. Most scullers experiment with their starts to find the one most suitable. An example of a five-stroke start is one stroke each at half slide, half slide, three-quarter slide, full slide, and full slide or three-quarter slide, half slide, three-quarter slide, full slide, and full slide. A great deal of care must be taken with the first stroke. In order to send the boat forward the sculler must apply force gradually, smoothly, yet firmly, to pry the boat away from the starting line. Since the boat is at a standstill extreme rapid force may kick the boat sternward.

Sit up at the top of the slide, the blades are squared and anchored below the surface of the water, while pressure is held against the pin in the direction of the blade. Row the first stroke with 90 percent pressure then go to full pressure. Practice the following:

Sequence One

- 5 x 1 stroke: Half slide.
- 5 x 2 strokes: Half slide, half slide.
- 5 x 3 strokes: Half slide, half slide, three-quarter slide.
- 5 x 4 strokes: Half slide, half slide, three-quarter slide, full slide.
- 5 x 5 strokes: Half slide, half slide, three-quarter slide, full slide, full slide.
- 5 x 10 strokes: Half slide, half slide, three-quarter slide, full slide, full slide, then paddle five strokes easy.

Sequence Two

- 5 x 1 stroke: Three-quarter slide.
- 5 x 2 strokes: Three-quarter slide, half slide.
- 5 x 3 strokes: Three-quarter slide, half slide, three-quarter slide.
- 5 x 4 strokes: Three-quarter slide, half slide, three-quarter slide, full slide.
- 5 x 5 strokes: Three-quarter slide, half slide, three-quarter slide, full slide, full slide.
- 5 x 10 strokes: Three-quarter slide, half slide, three-quarter slide, full slide, full slide, then paddle five strokes easy.

Initially, practice these sequences with no pressure. Decide which start seems to be more comfortable for you and then work up to half pressure, three-quarter pressure, and full pressure. Take your time. Develop the motions and then the speed. Relax and learn to be effective. Sharp bladework at the entry and release, smooth coordination, and quickness are the keys to successful starts.

Fly the Slide

Practice start sequences as previously described except

row no pressure through the water and race pace speed on the slide. This is a good drill to develop timing and coordination at the racing pace. The relaxation of pressure through the water allows you to repeat the starts several times without a great deal of fatigue keeping the focus on bladework.

Moving Starts

Moving starts are starts practiced from a paddle rather than a standstill. Row continuously, on the count of three, row into a five-stroke start, after the fifth stroke continue to paddle for 20 strokes and then repeat.

Variations of Start and Sprints

- 5-stroke start, 10 strokes high, and paddle.
- 5-stroke start, 10 strokes high, settle for 10 strokes, and paddle.
- 5-stroke start, 20 strokes high, settle for 10 strokes, and paddle.
- 5-stroke start, 20 strokes high, settle for 20 strokes, and paddle.
- 5-stroke start, 20 strokes high, settle for 10 strokes, down two strokes per minute for 10 strokes, and paddle.
- 5-stroke start, 10 strokes high, settle for 10 strokes, an acceleration-10, and paddle.
- 5-stroke start, 20 strokes high, settle for 20 strokes, an acceleration-20, paddle.

Section Five

Drills for Teamboats: Doubles and Quads

Row by Pairs

In a quad, the bow-pair rows, the stern-pair sets the boat. Alternate each pair every 20 strokes. Rowing by pairs allows those who are rowing to work on technique from a stable platform. It is particularly effective for work done with blades squared. In a double, alternate the bow and the stroke every 20 strokes.

Entry Drills

Repeat entry drills with one sculler sitting out and setting the boat. In a quad, rotate the non-rowing seat while the other three seats do the entry drill. In a double, either the bow-seat or the stroke-seat does the drill with the other setting the boat.

Balance Drills at the Release

All scullers sit at the release. On command, they push their handles down to their laps so the blades come up high above the water. Balance the boat a few seconds without letting the oars touch the water. Stabilize with even pressure on the pin, footstretchers, and the seat.

Acceleration Drill

This drill is done for one sculler at a time. In a quad, one sculler rows a sequence of:

- Paddle for five strokes.
- Half pressure for 10 strokes.
- Full pressure for 20 strokes.
- Full pressure for 30 strokes another sculler joins in every 10 strokes rowing at half pressure until all four are sculling.
- Total number of strokes = 65 (paddle five, half pressure for 10 strokes, and full pressure for 50 strokes).

The first sculler's goal is to maintain the same resistance through the water he felt when rowing alone even though the hull speed is increasing every 10 strokes when another sculler joins in. In a double, the first sculler must keep the same full pressure resistance when the second sculler joins in. Repeat the drill for each seat.

Rotation in Quads

During the warm up or a steady state piece, while rowing continuously, rotate one sculler out every 20 strokes to set the boat for the other three rowing.

Rotation in Doubles

Row 20 strokes bow-seat only then 20 strokes stroke-seat only then 20 strokes together. Repeat four times.

CHAPTER 5

DOING IT

RACE DAY. FAIRBAIRN. TESTING. ZEN. CHAMPIONS

BRIDGING SEASONS

Rowers can take part in multiple competitive seasons: the winter indoor rowing, spring scholastic racing, summer sprints, and fall head distances. Every annual training plan includes three phases: preparatory, competitive, and transition. The role of each training phase is the same regardless of having one cycle or repeating cycles through the year. Cycles needs to be carefully planned to include a defined transition period to ensure that you are rested and ready to start the next preparatory period.

When major competitions conclude we experience physiological and psychological tiredness. Muscular fatigue can disappear in a matter of days but central nervous system fatigue can last much longer. In *Periodization: Theory and Methodology of Training*, Bompa says, "The more intense the training and the greater the number of competitions, the higher the fatigue level. It is hard to believe that any athlete could immediately commence a new annual training cycle under these circumstances. Rest is necessary to refresh athletes physically and psychologically before training starts again. When the new preparatory phase begins, athletes should be completely regenerated and ready to train. In fact, athletes should feel a strong desire to train again after a successful transition phase."

The main goal of the transition phase is to remove central nervous system fatigue. Management of fatigue is a critical component of a program throughout the year but is paramount during transition periods. It is important to eliminate the stress of the previous season, particularly negative elements, so they do not carry into the new preparatory phase. Not really an off-season, this is a time to rest, relax, and maintain a basic level of physical activity that is 40 to 50 percent of the competitive phase. Transition phases should last three to four weeks and have two to four training sessions per week. Avoid the temptation of couch-potato syndrome (complete rest) because the sudden interruption of training and inactivity causes detraining; you'll lose much of your hard-earned shape. Insomnia, loss of appetite, and digestive system disturbances are also cited as possible side effects of suddenly shifting from intense work to passive rest. They are reversible if training resumes in a short time but can appear after two to three weeks: if the body has difficulty adapting to inactivity it is then susceptible to detraining syndrome.

Bompa devotes a significant passage to detraining syndrome that is worthy to take note of, "As a result of detraining, there is a marked decrease in the athlete's psychological well-being and work output. When training proceeds as planned, the body uses protein to build and repair damaged tissues. Disuse, however, causes the body to increase the process of protein degradation. It starts to breakdown some gains made during training and catabolize protein. Testosterone level, which is important for gains in strength, decreases as a result of detraining; this may have a diminished effect on the amount of protein synthesis. Psychic disturbances, such as headaches, insomnia, exhaustion, tension, mood disturbances, lack of appetite, and psychological depression, are among the usual symptoms associated with total abstinence from training. Each athlete may develop any of these symptoms or a combination of them. All these symptoms rise from lowered levels of testosterone and beta-endorphin, a neuroendocrine compound that causes euphoric post-exercise feelings." Other notable effects of detraining are decreases in muscle fiber cross-sectional area, early reduction in speed, loss of muscle power and endurance. Bompa says that the rate of strength loss per day can be as much as three to four percent for the first week and for endurance capacity seven percent in the first week to 12 days.

Passive rest can prevent you from starting your new training cycle at a higher level than before. So how to best plan your transition phase? Start right away with the first week after your last competition. Cut down the volume and intensity of training and do some cross training two to four times per week. Include activities that you do not normally do in training that are fun and interesting for you. Coaches of advanced athletes can let their athletes write their own transition phase programs and then go over it with them. This is a time of year when it is good for athletes to have a break from their coaches, routine, and spend time training on their own. This is a regeneration period for coaches as well. Changing your environment is refreshing. For rowers this can mean doing more on land such as running, hiking, cycling, playing soccer, or taking a yoga class. The beginning of the transition phase is the right time for coaches and their rowers to get together and review the past season while details are still fresh. Focus on what went well and discuss strategies for making improvements once specific training resumes. Remember to put it down on paper.

There are many body treatments, such as massage and hydrotherapies, to help you recover during the transition phase. Massage effectively assists the elimination of toxic substances from the tissues, stimulates circulation, and decreases muscle tension. There are over 300 massage modalities and techniques available. Sports massage is a good choice at anytime of the year because it precisely applies certain manual maneuvers at different times of your training schedule. Sessions done during this recovery period are body maintenance massages. They are targeted at injury prevention and restoration. A total body flush is defined by the type of superficial strokes used: jostling, compression, effleurage, and spreading which help to increase the elimination of lactic acid and other metabolic waste products.

Water therapies also help the mind and body rejuvenate during the transition phase but can be used throughout the year.

Hot showers and baths relax muscles, increase circulation, and improve the quality of sleep. Contrast showers that alternate hot and cold water stimulate blood flow and saunas allow for vasodilation and perspiration, which helps to eliminate toxins from the muscle cells. Toxins cause fatigue to linger and negatively affect central nervous system stimulation. Saunas taken weekly for a minimum of 15 minutes produce effects which would normally require two hours of rest to achieve. Cross-country skiers routinely build time for saunas into their training/recovery plans. A full session can consist of three 15 to 20 minute sessions. After each bout you immediately rinse in a cold-water shower blending it to warm to create a contrast effect. Once wrapped in a robe, relax and cool down for 10 to 15 minutes before the next round. Drinking lots of fresh water between sessions helps the cleansing process. Stay healthy and allow yourself some down time after racing season before you ramp up for the next one.

FOCUSING YOUR TRAINING

Making the step from a recreational rower to a competing rower is not always an easy one to manage. Once you decide to get more committed to training and racing a few things predictably happen. Your increase your total number of kilometers rowed each week, you try to practice on a more regular basis by adding more sessions per week, and you introduce more intensive work to your current program of steady rowing. Changing your training schedule too rapidly increases the likelihood of injury. Even if you realize the benefits of improved race results without any negative affects, you are in a higher risk category for setbacks if you continue an impulsive approach to training.

The guidance of a plan or a coach to confer with is vital. Reading about the training program of a recent Head of the Charles winner, with the idea that if you follow that same plan you too will be a future winner, is not the best way to embark on your personal goals. The fact that rowing and sculling require a high level of conditioning shouldn't pressure you to raise the stress of your training too rapidly. Everyone has strengths and weaknesses that need to be considered accordingly. Taking the time to evaluate the factors that contribute to your program will help you or your athletes train safely and more effectively.

A question that you have to ask regularly is, "what is the purpose of this workout?" You need to get to know yourself, as well as, your training needs while developing an understanding of the components of your program. There are some sound principles that apply to everyone and then there are some individual ways of doing things that work better than others. Based on a combination of the body's reactions to training and the environment, here are some guidelines that will serve as the basis for any system that you develop. Common sense and a willingness to experiment from time to time go a long way too.

Your body reacts to stress from exercise in two ways. The first is an acute reaction, such as hopping on the erg and rowing 5k. Heart rate speeds up, the stroke volume of blood pumped with each beat of the heart goes up, ventilation rate and depth of breathing increases, blood pressure rises, and your muscles feel fatigue. The second type of reaction is the training effect, which results from repeated exercise over time. Training produces changes throughout your body that allow you to cover that 5k distance with less discomfort and in less time. Muscles become stronger and the blood flow to them increases. Changes in the muscle provide more energy for the muscles and less lactic acid accumulates during a session of exercise. Resting heart rate lowers due to a stronger heart being able to pump more blood and needing fewer beats to delivery the blood. You benefit from lower resting blood pressure, lower body weight, and less fat under the skin.

Training has specificity; the system that is stressed is the one that benefits from the stress. To improve your performance you must practice doing the specific activities that are part of performing and give thought to every aspect of training. To be a better single sculler you need to spend more time in a single. To build endurance you need to row long distances. Be aware of what your routine is doing for you. Just as training benefits those body systems that are properly stressed by exercise, overtraining has a negative impact on the systems that are overstressed. One overstressed system can affect activities other than the one that caused the damage. For example, a rib stress fracture, brought on by faulty rowing, can prevent you from doing other activities that stress the injured area. We need to care for our bodies especially we when depend on everything going right to get to our goals.

It seems common sense; a specific stress produces a specific result. Benefits that you expect from doing three 20-minute pieces at a 2:15 split with seven minutes rest between each, three times per week, are specific to that frequency, amount, intensity, and recovery. Over time your will become proficient at this work then adding a new level of stress on top of your current training will be needed to increase your fitness. You can increase the frequency from three to four days per week, the amount of training from 60 to 80 minutes per session, the length of each piece 20 to 25 minutes or the pace 2:15 to 2:12. You can also increase the recovery time between pieces. Any change in frequency, duration, intensity, recovery, or in combination will affect the result of your program, leading to a new level of fitness.

The rate of achieving benefits of a training program is rapid at first and then tapers off. Most benefits of a particular phase are realized in six weeks. If you then want to increase the load, after six weeks is a good marker to make a small jump. Changing your phase too soon will prevent you from achieving the maximum benefit of that phase and the danger of increasing too fast escalates the risk of injury and overstress by doing too much too fast. You won't get a sense of what a training load is doing for you if you change too fast. Individuals reach various degrees of success, which is greatly defined by their unique limits. Few people actually really reach their true limits and improvement is possible for any athlete. If you increased the difficulty of your program, started to feel tired in your workouts, and then raced at what you feel is a sub par performance, your reaction might be, "I need to train harder." when in fact you may have simply reached your limit for the season and next season your performance will improve again to a new limit.

As training increases in duration and intensity, the return from the training decreases. This effect of diminishing return does not mean that increases decrease fitness but that increases do not have as great a result as earlier in training. For example, you row 50k per week, double the volume to 100k, and then double again to 200k. Regardless of how gradual the process is, the benefits from 200k per week are not double those from 100k per week. Adding more kilometers to your weekly training does not produce equal percentages of improvement in competitive fitness. That is why novices make fast improvements in their fitness compared to more developed elites. The principle of diminishing return also applies to increasing the amount of faster, intensive training that you do.

Low levels of training produce fewer setbacks: injury, illness, or lack of interest in training. The harder the training, the greater the risk of experiencing a setback; increasing your training stress raises your chances of injury or illness. A setback should be avoided at all costs so you stay healthy. The maintenance principle applies to the ease of maintaining a certain level of competitive ability. This can be physiologically or psychologically. In long-term planning this is important because it allows you to change your emphasis from one system to another and still maintain the other systems; you are better able to improve a system and then maintain as you build up another. For instance, you shift from emphasis on the development of the cellular adaptations needed for low intensity rowing to another system, such as speed work to develop efficiency at race pace, and you are able to retain the cellular benefits you have though you are doing fewer long rows.

When you are planning your own or an athlete's program, there are important points to consider. Here are some of the questions you should ask to help problem solve issues that are part of moving towards a more focused training program: What is the rower's current level of fitness? How ready is he or she for training and competing? How many weeks do you have for a season's best performance? How much time per day is available for training? What are the strengths and weakness with regard to speed, endurance, aerobic capacity, and volume of training? What types of training do you or your athletes respond well to?

For what specific event are you getting ready? What does the potential racing schedule look like? What are the conditions and facilities available?

Formal training is a means of education. Education is a process as is the potential for improvement. Learn by asking other coaches or athletes about ideas how to improve your training. Stay flexible with your program and make adjustments when you have to especially if it means staying healthy and avoiding setbacks.

GETTING TOUGHER

How tough are you? Have you ever thought to yourself, it's never over until it's over or never give up? Or said, "I could have rowed faster if I had stayed concentrated in the second half of the race; I wasn't thinking clearly." Building mental and emotional strength, an essential ingredient for success in rowing and sculling, is what James Loehr's book; *The New Toughness Training for Sports* is all about. Loehr's classic book covers issues related to recovery, understanding the language of emotion, signs of overtraining, the performer-self versus real-self, balancing stress and recovery, as well as the role of awareness in the mental toughening process. Loehr describes toughness training as, "the art and science of understanding your ability to handle all kinds of stress-physical, mental, and emotional-so that you'll be a more effective competitor." It is a method of perfecting your sport skills while minimizing the risk of physical injuries and emotional setbacks that can result from overtraining. Loehr explains that a key element of toughness training is improving the routines used for recovery from stress during practices and between competitions to maximize an athlete's potential so that the mind, body, and emotions will become more flexible, resilient, and strong.

Common words that we associate with toughness; cold, mean, insensitive, or heartless, are not those included in the definition of toughness here. Phrases such as responsive under pressure, resilient, and flexible rise to the surface. Loehr describes four indicators of toughness. First is emotional flexibility, which is, "the ability to absorb unexpected emotional turns and remain supple, non-defensive, and balanced, to be able to summon a wide range of positive emotions (fun, joy, fighting spirit, humor) to the competitive battle." Second is emotional responsiveness, "the ability to remain emotionally alive, engaged, and connected under pressure. Responsive competitors are not calloused, withdrawn, or lifeless as the battle rages." The third aspect is emotional strength, "the ability to exert and resist great force emotionally under pressure, to sustain a powerful fighting spirit against impossible odds." Fourth, emotional resiliency, "the ability to take a punch emotionally and bounce back quickly, to recover quickly from disappointments, mistakes, and missed opportunities and jump back into the battle fully ready to resume the fight." Simply defined, it "is the ability to consistently perform towards the upper range of your talent and skill regardless of competitive circumstances."

There are many athletic situations when the way that you really feel isn't the way that you know you need to feel to perform at your best level. The way that you really feel is referred to as your real-self and the way you need to feel to perform at peak is referred to as your performer-self. Positive and negative emotions are constantly intertwined in our daily feelings. Positive emotions relate to balance and health, negative ones typically point to unmet needs. Every feeling serves a purpose and you will become a better athlete when you can respond to negative messages in ways that are appropriate versus blocking them out. To perform consistently under pressures at a high level requires that you have enough food, rest, sleep, and water. You must develop the capacity to move from the real-self to the performer-self on demand, which calls for precise thinking and acting skills. You also must be fundamentally physically fit. If your tolerance for physical stress is low your battle may be lost before it begins.

Performer skills include disciplined thinking and imaging skills that keep your emotions focused. In addition, physical acting skills that help you act the way you want to feel to achieve your ideal performance state. This is your body language. The way you move intensifying whatever emotion you are feeling. Lastly, you have to learn new emotional responses to old problems. Just as your muscles need time and stimulation to grow, so do your emotional responses. You need to practice putting yourself into situations that help you train your reactions. For racing this is why doing time trials and scrimmage races can be critical to improving your performances; you have the opportunity to practice new reactions. You can use words and images to control your performance state. Learn how to tell yourself to hang in there, that is tough but you are tougher, that you can do what you want to achieve. Avoid showing weakness on the outside and let yourself know that you are right where you want to be so you stay passionate and fight no matter the circumstances.

Balancing stress and recovery is a major focus of Loehr's book. He writes, "Stress is anything that causes energy to be expended; it occurs physically, mentally, and emotionally. Recovery is anything that causes energy to be recaptured; it occurs physically, mentally, and emotionally. Unfulfilled needs represent forms of stress. Fulfillment of needs is recovery. In order to fight great battles in competition, your energy deposits should be roughly equal to your energy withdrawals. Your goal should be to enter battle fully recovered whenever possible. Balancing stress and recovery is fundamental to becoming a tough competitor." Like balancing your checkbook, these factors need to be kept in line. For example, when you are going through difficult emotional times be sure to include some fun into your day. To get tougher you need to "jump into the fire and jump out before you get burned" taking risks in life and competition is a natural part of developing strength. Talking or writing provides powerful relief for dealing with emotional pain or turmoil. Spend time talking with your coaches, friends, or family about your problems or keep a training journal to help sort out your thoughts.

Work hard but recover equally as hard. Sharpen your saw regularly. Your recovery schedule should receive as much attention as your training plan does. Sleep ranks number one when it comes to recovery methods. Get eight to 10 hours of sleep every night, go to bed and get up within 30 minutes of your normal sleep times, learn to take short naps of 15 to 20 minutes whenever you can, and track your amount of sleep. Eat a healthy well-balanced diet with adequate amounts of water and nutritious food. Enjoy both passive and active rest activities. Active rest can include walking, yoga, flexibility exercises, or easy outdoor games. Passive rest activities do not involve body movement; examples are laughing, meditating, getting a massage, watching television, having a whirlpool bath, or taking a nap. On a final note, the application of stress is the stimulus for growth but recovery is when you grow.

ORGANIZING YOUR RACE DAY

With summer racing season underway you spend time doing your training and mentally getting ready for each event. However, there are many logistics involved in going to a regatta that need to be taken care of when you compete in order to have your race day run smoothly. Being organized before the day of the race and staying organized at a regatta decreases stress making that sure you have created the best situation to concentrate on rowing. The degree to which you need to plan will vary; a single sculler has one level of need, a coach overseeing a large squad another. Staying focused on your racing is easier if you do not have to spend extra energy on unexpected details. In fact, you should prepare for the unexpected to happen.

It is wise to make a seasonal plan for multiple races, gathering your entry information, when you must submit your entry fees, and travel dates. Then develop a list that you use to prepare for each regatta. Include collecting any information that you need to know about the race site in advance, maps, arranging accommodations, renting a car, setting up boat transportation, and estimating travel time. Make sure to plan adequate travel time so you have a chance to rest and relax before you race. If you are flying and changing time zones, ideally, allow one day at the site for every hour of change. One week before your race, make a list if what you need to get done and when. Include errands to do before you go away, confirming hotel reservations or boat transportation, and making important phone calls. If you are changing the rigging on your boat be sure to allow some time to row with new adjustments before you race.

Having a pre-regatta routine supports your race preparation. The ritual of a routine eases you into the mindset of getting ready for competition. The day before your race get everything together that you'll need. So pack your things; take your racing suit, tights, wind shirt, wind pants, rain gear, warm up clothes, jacket, a complete dry change of clothes, dry shoes, a hat, sunglasses, and your lucky charm. Folding clothes is a more thoughtful process than heaping it all in a bag. Coaches should give to their athletes a list to ensure they have proper gear with them at all times.

Make any repairs to your equipment before you leave home. Double-check your equipment list so you don't find yourself without a seat. Set aside your car rack, boat rack, boat cover, boat, seat, riggers, footstretchers, oars, slings, and tie downs. If you have many boats label all seats and riggers. Have your SpeedCoach, bow markers, toolbox, boat towel, seat pad, duct tape, plus an extra fin and collars.

Go shopping and take enough food with you that you like to eat so you can have something familiar. Eating the foods that you are used to helps you feel more comfortable when you are in a different setting. Load up on snacks and drinks so that when you are on the road you have an option to eat your own food and have calories on hand when you need them. Not having available food will cause you to lose energy. Staying well hydrated on a hot summer race day is a priority to performing well.

When you arrive at the race site there is usually much more activity going on around you than at home in your daily practice. To focus on racing and minimizing distractions develop a pre-race routine and stick to it even if you have to ask a friend to remind you to do certain things. It might include when you eat, weigh-in, warm-up time, mental preparation, time to be alone, or what music you choose to listen to. It should be a routine that works well for you and that you practice no matter what site you are at. At a crowded race course it may not always be easy to do this. You have to keep track of time, avoiding chatting too much with friends, make sure not to skip part of your warm-up at the last minute. Save socializing until after you race and adhere to your plan before the start.

Going to a new location is exciting but you need to be able to tune in quickly to the different surroundings so that daily logistics do not distract from your racing or practice sessions. As soon as you arrive on site find out the essentials: Who do you ask questions of? Where should equipment be stored? Where are the restrooms? What is the traffic pattern on the course? Which docks are for launching and coming in? Are there obstacles you should be aware of? Then take the time to row the course a bit so you become familiar with the water, background noises, level of boat traffic, and important landmarks.

Recently I rowed at the club VK Smichov in Prague. I was aware of the number of fine points you have to attend to whenever you come to a new venue. The Voltava River is wide, slow, and long. Once launched off the dock, the physical expanse of the river itself was an adjustment. There are several bridges to go under as you row through the old city with small rapids at either end of the eight-kilometer stretch so it was important to know the traffic pattern. There is a festive clatter of streetcars and trains on the bridges, restaurant boats playing music, cars along the shore, and a barge-size bottle of *Staropramen* beer sailing along. At any new place the activity level will eventually become familiar but the more you can feel at home away from home, enjoying the atmosphere, the better you are likely to perform.

LOOKING BACK TO MOVE FORWARD

To set clear objectives for your upcoming year you need to dedicate some time to look at your past season. For masters and club rowers, November and December are the transitional months from the conclusion of the summer and fall competitive seasons into the preparatory phase for the following year. Scholastic rowers will want to review last spring's season but some can have the added advantage of having raced in the summer or autumn head races to give more perspective to the whole picture. To adequately analyze your performance characteristics you must look a your response to a variety of training factors to determine your level of success. An honest analysis of what you achieved and what your limitations were plus setting goals based on those observations provides a valuable tool for establishing new objectives for the upcoming season.

You need to first look at how well you were prepared physically. Did you build adequate stroke power, aerobic endurance, and speed to perform at the level that you had intended to? Review your races to identify areas that you improved on and others that need further development. For example, you might note that your final sprints were more effective this season so your anaerobic speed was better but you still need to improve your endurance for the third 500-meter segment of the race because in every race you slowed considerably at that point. Review your logbook for consistency of training sessions and track your weekly training volume. Look at what type of workouts you thrived on and which ones you avoided. Ask yourself what type of workouts helped your fitness and racing capacity the most and what didn't you do enough of?

When reviewing your technical preparedness examine individual elements of the stroke- your entry, drive, release, recovery. Consider the quality of your bladework, your ability to row at varied stroke rates, or hold form at under high stress. To what extent do you feel that your technical abilities affected your overall performances? Catching a boat-stopping crab with 100 meters to go in a semi-final, knocking you out of the final, because you were over-gripping and your forearms locked up, is one of those situations when better skill would have advanced you to the next race because fitness may not have been the limiting factor. If you made technical changes in your training were they positive or negative? Prioritize the technical elements that you feel will improve your standard of rowing or sculling.

Evaluate how you were able to handle the problems and challenges of actual racing. This includes steering, race plan execution, racing strategy, and your psychological preparation for competition. These represent tactical areas that you can improve. If you were racing your single and you rowed out of your lane in every race, causing you to go many extra meters, you need to put time into correcting your steering so you are not rowing farther than everyone else in the race and disrupting your speed by having to correct your course multiple times. For the races that you would rate as peak performances, where you were in a state of flow and everything came together, write a one-page description of how the race felt and what were the positive factors that you think contributed to such a great race. How were each of these factors reflected in your best races of the year?

Once you have listed your strengths and weaknesses, you need to set new goals to work towards. Your goals can be stated in simple language and be based on your past performances, rate of improvement, competition dates, and priority of training factors such as physical, technical, tactical, or psychological elements. Coaches will want to determine goals for their teams, as well as, helping athletes set individual goals.

Set both subjective and objective goals. Subjective goals are more open by nature such as: becoming more aware of pressure into the pins throughout the entire stroke, developing a better sense of swing at higher stroke rates, improving the ability to keep the shoulders relaxed in the second half of the race, or gaining more confidence for the start of a sprint race. Objective goals are measurable such as: place in the finals at the USRowing Masters Nationals, qualify for an automatic entry for next year's Head of the Charles, improve anaerobic threshold demonstrated by improving 6k erg score from 1:45 per 500 meters to 1:43 per 500 meters in three months, or train five days per week for 90 percent of the weeks from December to April.

Write your goals down in your logbook stating three main subjective goals and three main objective goals for the upcoming season. Always begin your goal with a verb. Then spend time to draw up a plan. You need to make a road map of how you will get from where you are today to where you want to be next season. Setting short-term weekly or monthly goals will help break your goals into achievable steps. Review each goal and determine what you need to accomplish it. Set yourself up for success at each stage in order to build confidence to reach your long-term goal. You cannot row a 2k erg score in 1:59 per 500 meters unless you have accomplished 2:00 per 500 meters. Take small steps.

Make sure that you collaborate with a coach. A good coach can give you valuable advice along with informed perspective. Helping you to determine realistic goals and outlining a plan together are benefits of good coaching. Be flexible throughout the year. After you outline a plan, keep in mind that it is just an outline. There will be times when outside stresses interfere with your plans or your response to training may indicate that you need to adjust. You will have to incorporate more rest or more work depending on whether or not you are adapting positively to your training.

It is important to make wise daily decisions that are based on your goals. You must prioritize training elements especially when juggling the demands of school, work, family, and friends. Spend time on those elements that improve your rowing the most and keep you motivated to do better.

NEXT YEAR'S TRAINING PLAN... ALREADY?

The conclusion of head racing season is the perfect time to analyze your performances of the past year and start planning for next season. To set realistic objectives for the upcoming year, you must first consider your level of success or reasons for under-achieving in recent racing. Here are some aspects of your performance that you will want to look at to identify areas where you made progress and those that need work. Being honest with yourself will help you formulate your next step or give information to a coach to help in designing the next annual cycle for you.

How Fit Were You?

Did you build adequate strength, aerobic endurance, and anaerobic capabilities to perform at the level that you intended? Review your races of this past year to identify areas that you improved on and others that need further development. Read your training log for consistency of training sessions and average weekly training volume. Identify what type of workouts you thrived on and which ones you avoided. What type of workouts helped your fitness and racing capacity the most? What didn't you do enough of?

How Well Did You Row?

Analyzing your technique should focus on the precision of stroke elements and to what extent your technical abilities affected your overall performance. If you made technical changes in the past year's training were those changes positive or negative? Prioritize the parts of your stroke that you feel will improve your rowing or sculling.

How Well Did You Execute?

Evaluate how you were able to handle the problems and challenges of actual racing. This includes steering, race plan implementation, race strategy, and psychological preparation for competition. How were each of these factors reflected in your peak performance of the year; what went well and what didn't?

Tips for Setting Goals

A candid look your performance is a valuable tool for establishing new objectives. Your goals can be stated in simple language and be based on your past performances, rate of improvement, competition dates and priority of training factors (physical, technical, tactical, or psychological fundamentals). Set both subjective goals and objective goals.

- Subjective goals are more open:
    1) Feel the boat run better during the recovery.
    2) Develop better rhythm at higher stroke rates.
    3) Increase the ability to concentrate on one stroke at a time.
- Objective goals are measurable such as:
    1) Improve 2k erg score from 7:20 to 7:15 by the CRASH-B Sprints
    2) Decrease body fat percentage from 17 to 15 percent in four months.
    3) Place in the top five percent in the Head of the Charles men's club single
- Write your goals down in your logbook. State three subjective goals and three objective goals for the upcoming season. Always begin your goal with a verb.
- Draw up a plan. You need to make a road map, generally and specifically, how you will get from where you are today to where you want to be next season. Setting short-term weekly or monthly goals will help

you break your goals down into achievable steps. Review each goal and determine what you need for each. Set yourself up for success at each stage to build confidence in reaching your long-term goal. You can't row a 2k erg in 7:15 until you have accomplished 7:19, 7:18, or 7:16. Put one foot in front of the other at every stage.

• Collaborate with a training consultant or coach who can give you valuable objective advice combined with a more informed perspective. Helping you determine realistic goals and outlining a plan together are other benefits of working with a coach. Written materials and the Internet provide good training information but may not be specifically tailored to meet your needs or adequately explain the rationale behind certain workouts. Having a professional design your sessions for you is a worthwhile investment to insure you are training smart. On-water coaching sessions are key to getting feedback on how to improve your stroke.

Be flexible. After you outline a plan realize that it is simply that-an outline. Outside stresses may interfere with your plan or your response to the volume of training may be different that you anticipate necessitating modifications. You might need to incorporate more rest or more work depending on whether you are making positive adaptations to your training. Make wise daily decisions based on your goals. Many of you have limited time schedules and must prioritize your training elements; spend time on the ones that improve your rowing.

STEVE FAIRBAIRN: FINDING GOOD STROKES

It's the thickest rowing book I own; in size it rivals the 1,223 paper-thin pages of *Lonely Planet's Europe on a Shoestring*. A hearty two inches thick, *The Complete Steve Fairbairn On Rowing* stands as an essential classic. Inside the jacket reads, "Steve Fairbairn is generally regarded as the most inspiring and innovative rowing coach of the last 150 years. His glory days were in the 1920s, when he coached Jesus College, Cambridge and Thames and London Rowing to an extraordinary succession of regatta victories. Wherever they went, Fairbairn's 'disciples' lifted standards of performance to undreamed heights." Fairbairn, who lived from 1862 until 1938, is called the father of modern rowing.

During his lifetime, the Australian wrote six definitive works: *Rowing Notes, Some Secrets of Successful Rowing, Chats on Rowing, Rowing in a Nutshell, Don't Exaggerate, and The Endless Chain Movement*. Originally published in 1951 and then reprinted in 1990, *The Complete Steve Fairbairn On Rowing* is a collection of these pieces. I particularly like Fairbairn's rowing chats. There are 15 in total and each one has its own slant. Steve writes in a conversational manner explaining his concepts, not mincing his words. Chats range from *The Rhythm of Rowing, Lateral Pressure and Turns* of *the Oar*, to *Unscrew the Tension Nut*.

Chat Five is about initiative. The word *initiative* is defined as the power of acting independently. Physical talent aside, having initiative and being responsible is a key component of becoming a better rower or sculler. Fairbairn has good words on the subject that, if internalized, improve every stroke you take and keeps an eye on the big picture. First, he writes, "concentrate on working the blade: rowing is merely doing your best to work your oar to move the boat every stroke. If a man realizes that he has to take charge of his own rowing, he will then learn to concentrate properly and to feel what his blade is doing, and he will try to do better next stroke. The next stroke is really the race, and the race is only an illustration of how the crew rowed the next stroke. So every man should be ready and determined to do his very best the next stroke to propel the boat the best he can. As he does that, he will row each stroke better than the previous one."

The second point: "continual improvement possible by concentration: rowing is really like climbing a high mountain, if one concentrates. As one climbs one sees a peak ahead, and thinks that is the top. When he arrives there, another peak appears and so on *ad infinitum*. So in rowing, as one concentrates on working the oar to move the boat, he feels a fresh power come in, and he thinks he has reached the top. But again he feels an improvement come in and so on. There are always heights in the distance to be found out by working the oar and sensing and feeling that one is doing his best to move the boat. New feelings of increased power and ease keep coming in, and so one climbs the heights of the rowing mountain. He never reaches the top; as he reaches height after height he realizes there are more heights to climb. I fancy the same principle applies right through everything in this world and a good solid religion is, whatever your hand finds to do, be sure you are going to do your best, next stroke."

Fairbairn touches on hard work, firm grip with elastic spring, as well as, the art of coaching but emphasizes that, "The oarsman must sense this feeling of what his blade is doing with the water and what the water is doing with the blade. That is the beginning and end of learning to row. As he senses this feeling, his rowing will improve. But to think about holding or moving his body in certain positions takes away from his capacity to work the oar to drive the water away and get the reaction of the water to drive the boat. By working the oar to move the boat, the body moves easily and elastically, smoothly and continuously." Fairbairn adds, "I do not coach for any movement of the body. That has all got to come from inside you, laddie, and it comes unconsciously through the subjective mind's unconscious action. I coach entirely to work the oar to move the boat. Everyone has moved their bodies unconsciously all through their lives. Becoming body conscious is the first step towards locomotor ataxy." He advises that oarsman can learn a lot by reading rowing notes, reading intelligently as if he were rowing and going through the motions all the time. He encourages rowers to read, criticize, and test out new points in their rowing. He tells his rowers to watch their blade to find out what it is doing and to shut their eyes and learn to sense what it does. Fairbairn believed that rowing with the eyes closed opened the eyes to rowing more than anything else.

Finally, *Chat Five* reminds, "no careless strokes; do your best every stroke. A careless stroke reflects through the crew and does harm; a careless stroke does harm to you and your crew and your club and college. The harm of a careless stroke will reflect through the ages, doing harm, just as a good stroke will do good." Fairbairn concludes, " Enjoy every stroke-only done by concentration and doing your best."

TESTING FOR IMPROVED TRAINING

If training for competition and high performance, regular testing of physical condition is a necessary part of exercise plan design and revision. Testing and time trials play a variety of roles in a training protocol depending on the setting. On the collegiate and national team level, ergometer testing, seat racing, and speed order trials in small boats are an important part of the evaluation of an athlete to identify physically and psychologically fit rowers. For masters athletes in club programs, ergometer tests also serve as a way to identify more competitive individuals for boat selections. Those who train on their own should also have a way to measure their progress and set personal fitness goals.

In order to identify the strengths and weaknesses of an individual or team's performance, athletes must be subject to conditions or stressors requiring efforts that resemble race conditions. Based on the results of a time trial, a coach can assess what an athlete or boat does well and where more development is needed in the current physical or psychological preparation for competition. Individuals learn how they handle the demands for performance and learn the process of how to work at maximal efforts. Good trial results give you information about your current state of fitness and provide a reference for setting appropriate training speeds and goals based on your known capabilities at the moment.

The volume and timing of testing will vary during the year depending on the phase of the annual cycle and the purpose of the test. Progress checks are often scheduled at the end of a macro-cycle, a phase of training two to six weeks long, and during a recovery micro-cycle, approximately one week. Trial results will then help to structure the next macro-cycle to improve weaknesses. On occasion, coaches will schedule trials after a period of intense training to expose the athletes to stress under conditions of high fatigue and to facilitate psychological adaptation to such situations. Preparing for tests should be taken seriously with the same importance as getting ready for a competition. These are opportunities to learn how to perform well under race conditions and to build confidence in your ability to push your limits.

Tips to Approach Tests and Trials

- Prepare yourself psychologically to do your best effort.
- Being rested will help you physically and mentally deal with the pain of an intense test.
- Set realistic goals that help you achieve your best speed on the given day.
- Prepare a race plan or goal for each segment of the trial to help you keep your mind on performing well each stroke with good form.
- Keep your long-term goals in mind and realize that becoming a good competitor requires practice.
- Keep the results of your trial in proper perspective. Few row a personal best every time they sit down on the erg but consistency of performance and the ability to put forth your best in every testing situation is a quality that is important for individual and team performance.
- Use the trial to identify strengths and weaknesses physically and mentally in order to revise your plan.

Achieving your goals in trials will help you build competitive confidence for racing. Managing adrenaline or nervousness by practicing staying in the present each stroke and focusing on the process of doing well during the event will yield good results each step of your competitive development.

THE BEGINNER'S MIND

There is a mist of excitement added to a competitive season by Olympic racing that trickles down to regattas of every level. I can remember during the 1984 season when our college and summer racing seemed injected with an extra dimension that was charged and focused. At the Royal Canadian Henley Regatta or USRowing Masters Nationals, there is a level of inspiration and intensity that is palpable on the shores, as well as, on the course. Olympic rowers each have a story about what got them into the boat this season. Then there are the athletes who didn't win a seat to the penultimate event who are outstanding and responsible for pushing the envelope hard, therefore raising everyone else's performance level. They have all taken risks and applied themselves fully to be among the best. It is very commendable to say the least.

I have been thinking a lot about patience this season. While coaching single scullers, I have been impressed by the large numbers of scullers keen to get into racing or to race better but have also noticed what a task it is to get some of the most competitive ones to slow down enough to have the staying power to do the technical work that will give them a faster moving boat. Elite rowers spend many hours of training going slow, meaning rowing low stroke rates to work on details. They then raise rates gradually to preserve improvements. The best athletes are constantly looking for ways to improve subtle details and will spend hours or an entire season to perfect an element or part of a race. Refinement is a constant process that requires patience and repetition. Staying in the frame of mind of the beginner allows highly skilled athletes to continually develop for years. I encourage the rowers that I coach to approach their training with a beginners mind no matter their level of experience. Basic skills are extremely important and though they may seem mundane at times, to race successfully you need to be able to perform those basics at high rates of striking. Life in the shell takes on a new dimension when you go above 32 strokes per minute.

In rowing we do both part-stroke and whole-stroke practice. We break the stroke down into steps (entry, drive, release, recovery) or phases (acceleration, deceleration). We are taught separate tasks within the stroke such as when we do drills like pausing arms-body away or time-on-the-slide to row slow motion. The stroke is also being practiced in the context of a whole; rowing steady and focusing on an element within the stroke cycle, i.e. releasing the blade cleanly. The goal of part-stroke practice is to transfer the skills learned to the performance of the whole skill and is very effective if the steps are progressively integrated with the practice of the whole-task. In a continuous skill like rowing it is reasonable and beneficial to practice component parts (drills) and the whole cycle (full strokes) during the same session. Therein lies the benefit of drills.

Feedback is needed during all stages of learning and is termed intrinsic or extrinsic. Intrinsic feedback is the information you receive from your sensory systems such as vision when you can see your blade is washing out at the release, proprioception when you can feel that you are dropping your wrists at the release, and cognition when you can judge how you need to adjust your handle height to place the blade in the water. Kinesthetic feedback is internal information that your body gives about its position in space and motion. This and feedback about balance is generated by the vestibular system, visual system, as well as, special stretch sensors called muscle spindles located within the muscle fibers and golgi tendon organs which are found near the junctions of tendons with muscles. Intrinsic feedback is significant for learning the rowing stroke due to the need for balance combined with the accurate timing of bladework that is essential for good performance.

Extrinsic feedback is information that comes to you from external sources. This could be from a human coach or non-human environment like the water or boat. Frequent extrinsic feedback is needed for learning new skills but should gradually become intermittent in order to enhance performance. The feedback you receive may focus on information regarding the result or outcome of the movement, "You came off the starting line at 45 strokes per minute." This type of information is termed knowledge of result. Verbal or non-verbal feedback that focuses on the position or movement pattern used is termed knowledge of performance, "Your hands were too high at the entry; keep your wrists level at the release." Knowledge of performance is a more beneficial form of feedback for motor learning and motor teaching, but the combination of information is better than one or the other in isolation. Proper and frequent feedback can have a highly motivating effect, supplying information required to detect and correct errors, as well as, providing positive reinforcement for good execution of the stroke. Take the time to be patient with your technical training. Allow yourself the freedom and the time to work on the subtlest elements and consistently refine.

THE ELEMENT OF ANXIETY

Concentration, confidence, control, and commitment are components to rowing or coxing a good race. Knowing how to manage stress before an event or erg test can eliminate worry or nervousness that can interfere with reaching your goals. Stress can be a beneficial element, but when you don't have power over it, it has a negative impact on performance.

In *Preparation for Success: A Rower's Guide to Mental Training*, Sandra Stroope Dupcak writes, "Each athlete has their own optimal level of arousal, but it is easy to become under- or over-aroused. The typical signs of being under-aroused are feeling flat, bored, or not focused. Hyperactivity and inability to block out irrelevant sensory information are signs of over-arousal." Dupcak describes that a large component of arousal is anxiety. Anxiety can take the form of worry such as thinking you won't make it through the third 500-meters at your target split or it can manifest itself physically as butterflies in the stomach, sweaty palms, feeling fatigued, or a racing heart beat. Anxiety is strictly internal and does not exist outside of the athlete's head. One is not required to become anxious in a race situation.

"People are anxious, situations are not." Dupcak writes that you become anxious when you interpret a situation to be overwhelming or when you become overly concerned with the outcome or consequences of an event. All the thoughts and feelings that flood your mind before a race can severely inhibit your ability to concentrate on the appropriate cues in the environment. An apprehensive coxswain can project a tone that exacerbates a crew's existing nervousness. With rowing you must take one stroke at a time. It does you little good to think about the power 10 you will take in the third 500 meters when you are in the middle of your start and settle sequence. You have to learn to trust that you are well trained. Be confident that you know and can execute the race plan.

"Performance enhancement is one area of specialization for sport psychologists. Athletes who work with a sport psychologist to address their performance anxiety can benefit from learning the mental training skills that help them move out the anxiety or use it. Performance anxiety can be useful information for an athlete and sport psychologists are trained to help athletes work with it in ways that potentially enable them to release it, move beyond it, and at times, transform it into positive energy for their athletic performance. Athletes learn mental training skills that allow them to gain control of things within their control and to achieve a readiness for those aspects of athletic competition that are outside of their control. Each athlete is unique in how they use mental training skills. A sport psychologist helps athletes individualize their mental training plan to successfully manage performance anxiety," says Dr. Susan Hess of Team Concepts in Amherst, Massachusetts

Hess has been working with athletic teams, individual athletes, and coaches since 1990. Also a recreational sculler, Dr. Hess says that performance anxiety is a common issue with many of the athletes she consults with. Athletes often describe pre-race or pre-test anxiety in terms of not having full access to their physical strengths and skills. They describe their bodies as feeling restricted or having feeling of panic that keep them from being fully present. She explains, " Some report of fear of failure, fear of injury, and fear of disappointing others. There may be stressors outside of sport that inhibit athletic performance. Together, we identify what's getting in the way."

I asked Dr. Hess what are the steps in treatment the she generally follows to help an athlete work through their anxiety and what are some of the most difficult issues to address. Her response was, "Initially I want to get a good sense of how their anxiety presents. I then teach the athlete relaxation skills so I know their continuum that moves from anxiety to relaxation. The idea is that anxiety and complete relaxation can't co-exist, so the athlete needs to find their individual optimal level of arousal for their sport and competition. Athletes might interpret an arousal state as anxiety rather than excitement that can be used for athletic performance. I also introduce the use of visualization to reinforce physical and mental toughness skills. A cognitive-behavioral approach works to identify and shift negative thought patterns that inhibit athletic performance. Cue words and other positive self-talk can reinforce changes in perception and performance enhancing behaviors. In considering the most difficult issues to address, I would say that the athletes with whom I've worked have been highly motivated for change, and in turn have worked very hard and efficiently to successfully address many different and difficult issues. We naturally start with the information to which we have direct access. The determining factor seems to be the athlete's readiness for change rather than the presenting issues."

Offering advice to rowers who find it difficult to manage their mental preparation for races or tests, Hess is encouraging, "Athletes who experience performance anxiety have the opportunity to integrate their mind, body and spirit in ways that release anxiety on a cellular level. Let the anxiety inform you, as you are open to exploring it. The great news is that athletes have successfully managed performance anxiety by incorporating mental training skills. You want to practice these skills as you would your physical skills. With intention, you can work on your behalf to bring out your best performance. I tell athletes that ideally they work me out of a job as they learn the skills necessary to use themselves as a resource in addressing their performance anxiety." A winning boat needs positive power, clear focus, and swing. In conclusion, Dr. Hess says taking decisive steps to learn to express yourself through your rowing in the boat rather than through your performance anxiety will allow you to achieve the goals you have set for the season.

WHY SHOULD I RACE?

Racing is hard work. It requires discipline, dedication, risk-taking, and mental toughness. There are many reasons why athletes and coaches race or engage in performance-oriented training. Knowing why you race is part of setting goals and better prepares you for achieving those goals. Here are a few reasons you may want to consider if you are making a decision whether or not to compete or coach a competitive crew.

- Racing can be very satisfying. The more effort you have put into preparing for an event, the greater rewards you receive for rowing a well-executed race.
- Effort equals achievement. In rowing, if you work hard, train wisely, and stay healthy you will improve and get faster.
- Racing is fun. Being part of the racing scene is an ideal way to enjoy camaraderie with other rowers your age. Although competition is often fierce, rowers and coaches share great respect for one another.
- Testing the unknown. Unless you enter a race and go down the course you won't know your potential. When you sit at the starting line, you never know exactly what's going to happen between the start and the finish. You have to row the race to find out and gain the experience.
- Finding your personal limits and striving to do your absolute best.

Setting Goals

You must have an overall plan and an idea how you are going to achieve what you want. Your goals and visions are what fuel you during those tough moments in training or a race when you have to push your limits. Your goals can be stated in simple language and be based on your past performances, rate of improvement, competition dates and priority of training factors such as physical, technical, tactical, or psychological elements. You may set subjective goals and objective goals.

Subjective goals are more open by nature: feel acceleration of bodyweight through the entire stroke, develop a better sense of rhythm at higher stroke rates, increase the crew's ability to focus on one stroke at a time.

Objective goals are measurable such as: improve 2k erg score from 7:20 to 7:15 by March 01, decrease body fat percentage from 17 to 15 percent in four months, Place in the top three in the varsity women's eight at the Dad Vail Regatta.

- Write your goals down in your logbook. State three subjective goals and three objective goals for the upcoming season. Always begin your goal with a verb.
- Draw up a plan. Make a road map, generally and specifically, how you will get from where you are today to where you want to be. Setting short-term weekly or monthly goals will help you break your goals down into achievable steps. Review your goals and determine what you need to do for each. Set yourself up for success at each stage to build confidence and reach your long-term goal. You can't row a 2k erg in 7:15 until you have accomplished 7:19, 7:18, or 7:16. Put one foot in front of the other at every stage.
- Collaborate with a coach or advisor. A good coach can give you valuable objective advice combined with an informed perspective. Helping you determine realistic goals and outlining a plan together are benefits of coaching. Written materials and the Internet provide training information but may not be specifically tailored to meet your needs.

- Be flexible. After you outline a plan realize that it is simply that-an outline. Outside stresses may interfere with your plan or your response to the volume of training may be different that you anticipate necessitating modifications. You may need to incorporate more rest or more work depending on whether you are making positive adaptations to your training.
- Make wise daily decisions based on your goals. If you have limited time schedules and you must prioritize your training elements. Spend time on the ones that improve your rowing.

ZEN AND THE ART OF BOAT RACING

Like a dancer, there is the moment when you need to step up on the stage and perform. We go to the start never knowing exactly what will unfold on the course. Racing is a personal experience; one that exposes our vulnerabilities yet rewards us for our strengths. Racers are risk-takers by nature. There is little chance to win without putting yourself into the mix to see where you rank against others. The challenge exists to row well from within, amidst the excitement, and in situations that are different than practice. You learn something from every racing experience. After the race, it is important for you and your crew to know what worked, as well as, what didn't work. Spending time to write down the details of a race is a valuable resource to prepare for your next peak event.

When you write your performance evaluation record the date, event and result. Then, be more subjective and write down how you perceived your performance, when did you feel your best and worst, what was your goal for the event, and did you achieve it? You should also look at how focused you were, how confident, and did you stay concentrated during the event? Noting other factors such as your warm-up routine plus, your physical, technical, and mental strengths and weaknesses will help you to decide what to improve on for the next contest. Discuss your race with your coach to get another important perspective on your row and how it fits into your long-term picture.

Setting realistic goals is perhaps one of the most difficult parts of race planning. This is where your competitive experience and athletic history merge together. Knowing your capabilities yet being ready to seize opportunity or bounce back from unexpected arrows will keep you getting better.

Chance favors a prepared mind. Great patience is required to improve your technical skill, clock the endurance miles, and learn deeper concentration under pressure. If you know that your erg score is equal to one of your competitors but you are much slower on the water, you need to look at your skill level and application of power in the boat. When you know that you row your practice pieces more effectively than in a competition, start a more structured mental training program to learn to be more grounded during your events. Losing time with poor tactics and steering can be improved with experience. The Head of the Charles is a good example of racers rowing good times on the course but losing places because of inexperience and accumulating time penalties. Whatever your weak points, you can turn them into strengths with attention and correct practice. Be critical of your performance, but also be your own best friend giving yourself credit for being out there putting it all on the line.

LEARNING FROM CHAMPIONS

Long, slow distance work takes as much concentration as it does time. One might view rowing thousands of kilometers at 18 strokes per minute as a boring process, but it is a vital component of strengthening your aerobic base for next year. To be a better competitor in the upcoming season you have to stick to your winter training program and put in your meters. The off-season is not the time to slack off. To stay motivated is key and it can be very tough when the days are short and most of your sessions are done before the sun comes up or after the sun goes down. When you are feeling low, find a source of inspiration away from the erg monitor to give yourself a boost. Read books by athletes and coaches from various sports who share their experiences. Insight into the lives of champions is a great way to gain knowledge and perspective that you can apply to your own career path. Two Olympians whose accomplishments can only hearten you to embrace your polar night stadium run are Lasse Viren and Pertti Karppinen. Here are a few words devoted to them.

Lasse Viren is the only distance runner in history to have won Olympic gold in the 5,000 and 10,000 meters twice, 1972 and 1976. Friend, Eino Romppanen, offers this description of Viren, in Micheal Sandrock's book, *Running with the Legends*, "There is a quality that Finns have that makes them think that they can overcome incredible odds. That "something" is *sisu*, the most Finnish of words that is also the most difficult to define for outsiders, but which best explains Viren's and the Finnish character. It is the ability to persevere under the most adverse conditions, when others have quit; it is something Viren had that made him special...it means to believe in yourself and have the guts to do it, and have the resistance and craziness to endure. But we don't like to talk about it so much."

In *Top Distance Runners of the Century-Motivation, Pain, Success: World-class Athletes Tell*, by Seppo Luhtala, Viren recalls, "I really cannot say defeats have troubled me very much. I have been beaten by better runners on the day, and that's it. I never have let defeats depress me. I have always enjoyed running even without winning. I was coached by former international runner Rolf Haikkola for almost the whole of my career. I never had any other coach...the most important thing is in the relationship between and athlete and a coach is to have complete faith. An athlete has to believe in what the coach says. On the other hand, a coach must make an athlete believe that these are the correct systems to do." Viren continues, "As to self-confidence, I suppose it equals being sure of what you are doing. A big race is a very hard thing mentally, and if you have problems with self-confidence, at that last moment you may lose it all. It is like being a building contractor. If you are planning to build a 10-floor house, you have to be sure of being able to do it. Self-confidence is developed only by hard work, step by step, by succeeding in what you are doing. I have met 14-year old boys who tell me they are going to be Olympic champions. That is fine, but they have to realize what it takes and that only very few people are able to make it. I very seldom had thoughts of dropping out of a race. Sometimes you are feeling real bad, but you have to remember that so is everybody else in the race. It was a very unusual thing for me not to finish a race. It may become a habit of which it is very difficult to get rid of. I have seen runners who have spoiled their chances by having the completely wrong mental attitude towards a race. I tried to think as little as possible of the upcoming competition. If you let yourself sail with your thoughts-what it will be like to win the Olympic final etc.-it takes away from your energy which will be needed in the actual race."

A short article by Melissa Bray in the 2005 summer edition of *World Rowing Magazine*, features the Finnish single sculler, Pertti Karppinen. Defined as, "the rowers' hero" Karppinen won three Olympic gold medals in the men's single: 1976, 1980, and

1984. Only one other, former Soviet sculler, Vyachesla Ivanov, has won three gold medals in the men's single. Bray quotes a more recent Olympian, Matthew Pinsent, from his website talking about his heroes saying both he and Steve Redgrave looked up to Karppinen, "The ability to win only one race in four years that matters is staggering, added to which his inability to speak English made him a silent god as far as I was concerned," Bray's article continues, "Karpinnen can also be found on the list of top 100 athletes of the twentieth century and can be credited for forcing Steve Redgrave to give up the single and try another event." In the same issue a photo by Dominik Keller, son of the late FISA President Thomas Keller, is published. About his favorite photo, Keller says "This photo shows the moment when Finn Karpinnen passed the German Kolbe in the singles final at the Olympic Games in Los Angeles. In the look they exchanged, I believe we can see that Kolbe cracked. One needs luck, patience, and a bit of anticipation to get such a shot-I never got another like it." In 2004, at the age of 51, Karpinnen rowed 5:52 at the Finnish Indoor Rowing Championships and set a record for his age group; *sisu* at work. When winter training gets tough and you need some fresh input, head to bookstore for some inspiration and espresso.

CHAPTER 6

RACE PACE

STARTS. STEERING. PLANS. RATES. THE UNEXPECTED.

RACING STARTS

A good start feels fast, sharp, and light. When you get off the line on the right foot it's the boost you want to row an aggressive race. Missing the first stroke or catching a crab before you ever really get going is a major setback in your sprint race. The shorter the race the more critical a clean start is. Confident racing starts take repetition. Including elements of your start in your daily workouts will make them more predictable and successful. Racing starts depend on good balance, stability, coordination, and bladework combined with speed.

First, address the issue of practicing balancing the boat. Sit in your boat, press the handles down to your lap so they come high off the water and learn to balance the hull. Coach Fairbairn, wrote in *The Complete Steve Fairbairn on Rowing-Chat XIII,* that this is the best exercise to learn how to balance in the boat. In *Rowing Faster*, Volker Nolte writes, "Balance allows rowers to keep their blades off the water, keep the boat from rolling, and cost the least amount of work." Sit in the release position with the blades buried and bob the handles lightly so the blades move in and out of the water. When you get comfortable press the handles down and balance as long as you can with the blades off the water. When the boat gets tipsy set the blades back in the water. Pay attention to what it feels like to relax tension on the handle so the blades set naturally in the water. Keep pressure against the pin at all times by pushing outward to increase stability by the elbows pressing laterally, avoid pulling the handles into the body like a straight ergometer handle which decreases stability. Next you can let the blades sit in the water and lightly lift your hands off the handles and balance. Then move to half slide position and do the same until your balance gets to the point you can keep the hull stable.

Another static balance drill is to develop comfort sitting at the entry with your blades buried in the water. Initially, try doing this for a few minutes at a time. Learn to maintain pressure into the pin, stabilize your upper body, and let the blades set quietly in the water-breath, relax, settle. When you get confident sitting here start lifting the blades out of the water and balancing. When you get really good at it, sit at the top of the slide with the blades in the water and lift your hands off the handles and keep level.

Improving your high-speed coordination will help your starts. There are a number of ways you can train your bladework and movements to react faster. To begin with, add in 20-stroke accelerations at one-quarter slide and then half slide every five minutes during your steady state rows. Push the envelope on these short pieces to aim for high stroke rates over 50 strokes per minute during half slide, over 60 strokes per minute during one-quarter slide, and focus on developing clean bladework. Learn to keep the handle moving allowing speed without tension and keeping the blade depth precise. Another drill you can do during a steady row is a flying or moving start. The boat is already moving and you go directly into your start sequence such as half slide, half slide, three-quarters slide, full slide, full slide or the slide length combination that you use. Flying starts allow you to practice multiple starts without becoming fatigued from sitting up for long periods of time as you would when doing standing starts only. You can keep rowing without interruption and they are fun to do. Starts can also be worked on by doing some reverse ratio work. For example, go slow motion through the water with no pressure then race pace on the recovery. This unorthodox rhythm gives you a chance to repeat the coordination of the race pace recovery and then to relax any tension when the blade is supported in the water.

A standing start is the first five strokes of a race taken from a stationary position at the beginning of a dash, 1,000-meter or 2,000-meter event. The goal of the start is to pry the boat away from the starting line without kicking the boat sternward and accelerate the boat up to full speed as the initial short strokes are lengthened. A clean start boosts your confidence in the early phases of a race and being first off the line is an important tactic for some to place them in the position to watch other challenging boats. There is a saying though, "You don't win the race at the start but you can certainly lose it, " meaning crabs, missed strokes, and bad timing can put you way behind before you even get very far. Initially, perform starts at low stroke rates and power application to maintain relaxation. Start from the entry position, collars pressing against the pin, blades squared, and anchored just below the surface of the water. Care and time should be taken to pattern the proper motions before progressing the intensity. Most importantly, concentrate on only one point at a time.

Practice the following start sequences on the water: Five times the first stroke at three-quarter slide; five times the first two strokes at three-quarter slide and half slide; five times the first three strokes at three-quarter slide, half slide, and three-quarter slide; five times the first four strokes at three-quarter slide, half slide, three-quarter slide, and full slide; five times five strokes at three-quarter slide, half slide, three-quarter slide, full slide, and full slide; five times 10 strokes at three-quarter slide, half slide, three-quarter slide, full slide, full slide, and paddle five strokes.

A start in the single requires a delicate combination of relaxation and aggression to get away from the line quickly and maintain a straight course. Practice keeping a quiet upper body and loose hold on the handles to feel the water and avoid tension. Single scullers should try a variation of three strokes at three-quarter slide, full slide, and full slide for the first five strokes. Experiment to find that start that is most productive for you and feels most stable. In a sweep boat, moving an eight or four effectively off the starting line requires precise slide length timing between all members of the crew. Spending time drilling a crew at half slide and three-quarter slide rowing can positively rub off on your start timing as the crew intuitively learns to interpret part-slide strokes in the same way. Try out various slide combinations for the first three strokes to find the start that helps the boat move effectively off the line.

For the start of your race it is important to learn how to deal with your nervousness. Five-time Olympic gold medalist, Steven Redgrave shares with us, "When you feel over-anxious and out of control, take a moment to reassure yourself that it is normal and good to feel nervous. It shows that your body is preparing to race. Now, focus your mind on the present: anxiety is the gap between now and the future. You are over-anxious about a race before you have even stepped into the boat. There are many things that you must do before you get into the boat; focusing on the present and the immediate things you must do is often sufficient to overcome your over-anxious state. Take a deep breathe and slowly exhale to help you ease the tension from your muscles and to help you make the step towards your warm-up routine and you will have no need to feel anxious about the start of the race. You can have control over your anxiety by taking one step at a time."

It is wise to incorporate starts into your practices throughout the year so they become familiar to you. When you begin a training piece do a start to get going and when you are doing intervals settle to your target stroke rate after a start. Sometimes during a long row a flying start is just the thing to get your head back into the boat and stay sharp. When the sprint season is here it will pay off.

PLANNING YOUR RACE

Your success on the race course is the result of your decision about what you want to achieve, how you will achieve it, and being willing to pay the price required. Your race plan is your design for getting from start to finish in the best possible way given your skill, fitness, and mental preparedness on the day. Your tactics will give you the best chance of winning the race. For instance, against strong competition you may need to row close to your limits to win the race so flawed tactics such as going out too hard at the start of the race could mean that you develop high levels of fatigue early on in the event only to slow later on.

Sir Steven Redgrave, five-time Olympic gold medalist offers his insights towards approaching a race in his book, *Steven Redgrave's Complete Book of Rowing,* "Try to obtain as much information as possible about the crews you are going to race against: What are their usual race methods? When do they push? Do they have a particular fade pattern? What is their weakness? The race plan is an imagined line of the course that the race will take. It should not be looked upon as a scheme of bursts, for with anticipated bursts the tendency is to soften off prior to the burst-and there is no overall gain in speed. Race plans are designed to guide the crew through an expected situation, but the cox and/or stroke may have to take the initiative to alter the race plan if the opposition appraisals have been incorrect. It is essential to remain flexible." Redgrave continues to relate that the crew and coach should discuss the race plan a couple days before the event so the crew has time to mentally register it and visualize it. He advises discussing all eventualities, possible changes that may have to be made, to stay alert in the race, and respond appropriately. Redgrave concludes, "A race may be won or lost by the 'race intellect' of the crew. Above all else, keep the race plan simple but positive, be confident in your own abilities but be realistic."

How you prepare to execute a race needs to be practiced in advance. Know what your focus will be for each segment of the race in order to maximize your potential in the competitive situation. Consider certain factors to provide insight before you draw up your plan such as what are your strengths and weaknesses physiologically, psychologically, and technically. Address your weaknesses so you find the aspects of your race you need to improve. If you have a poor start, give the first 250 meters more attention in practice. If you have a weak final 500 meters, devise a plan to boost your motivation and speed during the race. Your race plan must work within your present level of capability. Know your times for 500-meter, 1,000-meter, and 2,000-meter time trials to find your base speed. Be realistic and plan a race dependent on your demonstrated abilities. Practice race pace tempo during your workouts, learn what your maximum cruising speed is, and the stroke rating is for the body of the race over the set distance you will be racing. Your target base speed for 2,000 meters is your average split per 500 meters in good conditions. You also want to know your maximum boat speed by clocking your all-out speed for 20 strokes so you have a sense of your reserves.

The most efficient way to cover the race course is by rowing close to the same time each 500 meters versus by varying boat speed up and down during the race. Paul Thompson has coached world champion crews for Australia and Great Britain; his crews have won medals at three Olympic Games and he oversaw the British women's rowing team that came back with three medal-winning boats from the 2004 Olympic Games. Thompson's chapter, *Mental Skills and Racing Strategies*, in the publication, *Sculling Training, Technique, and Performance*, explains, "When assessing race strategies, an effective method is to calculate the average speed and review each 500-meter split time, above or below the average race speed. To compare across boat categories and weather conditions, the time can be expressed as a percentage above or below the average speed."

Thompson illustrates the race strategy used in the final of the 2004 Olympic Games in the women's quadruple scull final, where Germany won the gold and Great Britain the silver. Compared to their average speed, the German crew rowed +2.77 percent the first 500 meters, -0.26 percent the second 500 meters, -1.29 percent the third 500 meters, and—1.22 percent the fourth 500 meters. The Great Britain crew's values were +2.80 percent the first 500 meters, -1.27 percent the second 500 meters, -0.89 percent the third 500 meters, and—0.64 percent the fourth 500 meters. " Using this assessment," Thompson says, "you can see how the German crew stayed closer to their average speed throughout the second 500 meters, a strategy that gave them a clear lead. The British crew closed the gap the second 1,000 meters and raced much closer to their average speed than the Germans; however, the could not overcome the deficit from the second 500 meters."

Thompson refers to the work of Dr. Valery Kleshnev, an Olympic silver medalist from 1980, a rowing biomechanist at the Australian Institute of Sport in Canberra, who assessed a total of 977 world cup, world championship, and Olympic races between 1993 and 2001. Winners were found to be faster relative to their average speed in the first part of the race compared to the second and third place finishers, who were faster in the last part of the race. During these years deviation has decreased and crews raced closer to their average speed changing from 2.7 percent in 1993 to 1.7 percent in 2001.

When it comes time to make a plan for your single's race or for your crew, work it out on paper. Determine if you need a structured plan, stroke by stroke, or simply a few points of technical focus at key points of the race. Remember all members of a crew need to know what to expect and coxswains need to work closely with the coach and crew to put the plan into action. Approach your race plan in 250-meter or 500-meter segments. Count how many strokes it take to cover a 500-meter distance. Decide where you need major focal points such as, clean releases or body swing. Know what command will identify important transitions. A simple word 'up' can be a command to start your final sprint in a coxless boat or a sharp 'now' may signify settling two beats to your cruising stroke rate. Expressions such as 'rhythm', 'length', or 'power' all generate reactions rehearsed in practice. Your crew needs to concentrate to row well as they row strong.

A race plan for 2,000 meters can have short reminders every 250 meters. The cox calls 'lengthen', 'blade depth', 'legs', 'releases', 'rhythm' etc. based on what the crew needs. Or it could be more detailed: Five-stroke start, 25 high with quick legs, lengthen 20, tempo for 20. At the 500-meter mark: 10 for sharpness, tempo for 20, 10 for sharpness, catches for 20. At the 1,000-meter mark: 30 strokes for long leg drive, tempo for 20 strokes, 20 strokes to prepare for final 500 meters. Final 500 meters: concentration 10, tempo for 20 strokes, acceleration 10 to raise stroke rate two strokes per minute, then increase one stroke per minute every 10 to the finish.

Whatever plan you work out for your singles race or for your boat write it clearly on a paper and copy it for each rower in the boat. Every rower needs to know the planned sequence of the race and be able to rehearse it mentally before practices and in the evenings. Use simulation pieces in practices to refine each part of the race. Use your race plan to ground your concentration at a busy regatta course.

Your plan reflects your commitment to your goal and what you have decided will be the best way to get to it. Richard Burnell leaves us with this note in the classic text, *The Complete Sculler*, "A man comes to the start of a race with just so much strength and energy to expend. Perhaps, psychologically, he can squeeze out a little more than he realized he possessed. But he cannot squeeze out more than he actually possessed. If he races himself to a standstill, and is beaten, that is that. And it ought to be a matter for congratulation, not for condolence. For no man can do more…how much better to have 'had a go', while there was still time, and sleep easily that night, in the knowledge that he was beaten by a faster sculler, rather than by himself."

RACE CHOREOGRAPHY: PART ONE

This article addresses the race plan design of a head race. These races are four to six kilometers long and run in time trial format from a moving start. The most common distance is five kilometers or three miles. How you prepare to execute your distance race needs to be planned and practiced well in advance of the actual race day, especially if there is a race you will peak for. You must know what your focus will be for specific segments of the race in order to maximize your potential in a given competitive situation. Initially, you must consider certain factors before you can draw up an effective race plan. The following considerations will provide you with insight towards designing a race plan that will fit both your personality and physical attributes. Approach your race plan with honest considerations about your own expectations and abilities so you may maximize your positive outcomes and achieve your goals.

What are Your Strengths and Weaknesses?

Physiological

*   How high is your level of aerobic power or anaerobic threshold?
*   Do you have a sense of maintaining constant speed over the entire course?
*   Are you quick in the first half but lose speed the second half?
*   Does your leg drive remain strong the entire race?
*   Are you too fast or slow across the starting line or the finish line?
*   Can you row a competitive stroke rate in the body of the race?
*   Review each one-kilometer or one-mile section of the

race and identify your strong points and your weak points to determine your typical patterns and identify areas you need to work on.

Psychological

- What is your personal reason for rowing in a particular event?
- What is your level of motivation to succeed: High/ Medium/ Low?
- What price are you willing to pay to reach your goals?
- Are you confident sprinting to catch up to a boat that started before you?
- Do you give in when another boat passes you or do you hold them off?
- Do you have the confidence you need to row from behind to catch another boat?
- How aggressive are you while racing?
- What ideas motivate you to race better?
- Can you visualize the race before it happens?
- Can you see yourself winning?
- Do you believe in your training program?
- What is the most difficult segment of the race: What can you do in training to improve this?
- What is your favorite part of the race?

Technical

- Do you need to work on your steering?
- Do you know the turns and currents of the course?
- Are you strong into a head wind but unable to hold it together to row well in a tail wind?
- Do you have difficulty raising your rate to a racing beat?
- Do you lose your technique/posture when you get tired?

- Are you able to keep your hands and upper body relaxed?
- Do you have good bladework throughout the race?
- Do you get tense?
- Are you confident in your technical abilities?
- What can you remind yourself of during the race to help you row better?

Address Your Weaknesses

Determine the aspects of your race you need to improve. For example, if you have a poor second half, learn better pacing during the first half to keep your speed even. Include technical reminders during the race such as "10 strokes for the drive" or "10 strokes for clean releases," focus on the elements that you need to pay attention to.

Know Your Performance Capability

Your race plan must work within your present level of capability. Know your times for five-kilometer and three-mile trials to determine your base speed. Be realistic and plan a race dependent on your demonstrated abilities. You need to practice race pace tempo during your workouts.

Determine Your Base Speed

You must learn what your maximum cruising speed is for the body of a race over the set distance you will be racing. Your base speed for five kilometers or three miles is your average split per 500 meters that you can maintain evenly in good conditions. Time trials need to be rowed periodically to help you determine your optimum stroke rating and pace over the same distance. If you do not use a speed device in your boat use a determined distance near your boathouse, which you can easily repeat and time. Ideally, the most efficient way to cover the race course is by rowing even splits rather than varying boat speed up and down during the race.

You can have successful or disappointing performances but knowing your strengths and weaknesses will help you prepare a race plan that supports your talents, meets your goals, and focuses on improving inconsistent areas of your race. At the end of the day, a race well rowed will leave you with a sense of accomplishment that will further build up your skill and confidence.

Sculling-specific: Head race planning for single scullers relies heavily on your individual preferences. Do you need a structured plan breaking down sections of the race or simply a few points of technical focus during the race? Determine your need for more structure or less specificity. If simply focusing on keeping a certain stroke rating through the middle portion of the race helps you, identify that. In doubles and quads, you must experiment with different race plans as a team and to see what maximizes your potential and motivation. All scullers need to know what to expect during the race and be prepared for key moves as you jostle for position with others. Practicing steering and passing can also be of the utmost importance. Remember to experiment with your race plan during time trials and less important races as you prepare for your peak event of the season.

Sweep-specific: Coxswains must work closely with both the crew and the coach to help the entire crew execute a predetermined race plan. A crew must practice stroke transitions in addition to the technical focal points that will take place throughout the race. Practice every section of the race so the crew knows what to expect from the coxswain's signal. Coxswains need to practice steering the sharpest direct course and knowing how to maneuver turns at top boat speed gives a crew great advantage. A coxswain that can take a solid race plan, adding intuitive calls to match the crew's needs and determination is an asset to any boat.

RACE CHOREOGRAPHY: PART TWO

This is the second installment of the discussion about effective race planning. There are several ways to win or lose a race but knowing your strengths and weaknesses will help you to design a race plan that supports your talents and focuses on improving your inconsistent areas of the race. Here are some tips:

- Approach the race plan in 250-meter or 500-meter segments.
- Count how many strokes it takes you to cover 500 meters.
- Decide where you need to make your major moves.
- Determine your technical focal points: For example: clean releases, keeping your head up, strong legs etc.
- Know what key words or commands will identify important transitions. A simple "up" may be a command to start your final sprint in a coxless boat or "lengthen" may signify settling to your base rate. You must determine what works best for you.

Sample Race Plan: 2,000 meters

Start to 500 meters:
5-stroke start
25 strokes high, quick legs, limited body swing
20 strokes to lengthen, rhythm is determined
20 strokes to maintain tempo

501 meters to 1,000 meters:
Focus 10 strokes for clean releases
20 strokes for focus on rhythm
Focus 10 strokes for breathing

20 strokes to focus on entries

1,001 meters to 1,500 meters:
Power 30 to move, respond, and hold other crews off
20 strokes for rhythm and tempo
20 strokes to prepare for the final 500 meters

1,501 meters to 2,000 meters:
Focus 10 through the 1,500-meter mark to check steering
20 strokes for rhythm and tempo
Acceleration 10 to raise stroke rate two strokes
Increase one stroke per minute every 10 to the finish

Sample Race Plan: 1,000 meters

Start to 500 meters:
5-stroke start-be very short and quick on the first three strokes
15 strokes at high stroke rating
20 strokes for rhythm and settle to base speed
Focus 10 for breathing
5 strokes to check steering
Power 10 to move through the 500-meter mark

501 meters to 1,000 meters:
20 strokes for good entries
5 strokes to bring focus into the boat and prepare for the sprint
20 strokes-take the stroke rate up one stroke per minute
10 strokes-take the stroke rate up one stroke per minute
10 strokes-final dash to line

Sculling-specific: Determine your need for structure or simplicity. If simply focusing on keeping a certain stroke rating through the middle portion of the race helps you, identify that. Know thyself. Remember to practice and experiment with your race plan during time trials and less important races as you prepare for your peak event of the season.

Sweep-specific: Practice every section of the race so the crew knows what to expect from the coxswain's signal.

THE VIRTUES OF THE START

Nailing those first few strokes of the start sends a bit of jet fuel through your veins. It feels fast, clean, and light. It's the boost you want to row an aggressive race. Nothing can rattle you more than missing the first stroke or crabbing before you ever really get going. A confident racing start takes repetition. Including elements of your start in your daily workouts will make them more predictable and successful.

Getting comfortable with high-speed coordination can help your starts improve. There are a number of ways you can train your reactions to be faster in terms of bladework and body movement. To begin, add in 20-stroke accelerations at one-quarter slide and then half slide every five minutes during your steady state rows. Push the envelope on these short pieces to aim for high stroke rates over 50 strokes per minute during half slide and over 60 strokes per minute during one-quarter slide. Focus on developing clean bladework. Learn to keep the speed of the handle moving and the blade depth accurate. Another drill you can do during a steady row is flying or moving starts. The boat is already moving and you go directly into your start sequence such as half slide, half slide, three-quarters slide, full slide, full slide or the slide lengths that you prefer. Flying starts give you the chance to practice multiple starts without becoming fatigued from sitting up for long periods of time like you would when doing standing starts only. You can keep rowing without interruption.

Starts can also be worked on by doing some reverse ratio work. For example, go slow motion through the water with no pressure then race pace on the recovery. This unorthodox rhythm give you a chance to repeat the coordination of the race pace recovery and then to relax any tension when the blade is supported in the water. When you progress to standing starts at race pace repeat sequences of the initial strokes until you feel each stroke of your start is effective. Do a series of 10 times the first stroke, followed by 10 times the first two strokes and progress up to all five. Use the first stroke to get the boat moving with clean bladework and a good course and build your power from there. Blade depth is very important so take extra care not to be too deep or get stuck.

Incorporate starts into your rowing all year long so they become familiar to you. When you begin a training piece do a start to get going and when you are doing intervals settle to your target stroke rate after a start. Sometimes during a long row a flying start is just the thing to stay sharp.

RAISING THE RATE

During a race there is a point where you need to increase your stroke rate to increase your speed; it often comes in the final sprint of the race. For example, in the final 500 meters of a 2,000-meter event your race plan may call for 20 strokes at your base pace, up two strokes per minute for 20 strokes, up two strokes per minute for 10 strokes, then up two stroke per minute every five strokes until you cross the finish line. Each increase will have a stroke where one makes a definitely shift in the rating. We call these transition strokes. Transitions are changes from one stroke rate to another-up or down. In these drills the focus is on raising the rating. A transition stroke should be precise and happen in one designated stroke. You must commit to it. To learn good transitions use the emphasis of a strong leg drive to define your rating shift and carry the speed of your hands away from your body as you complete the release. You can practice these all year long at various rates.

The following 40-stroke pieces are some of the stroke varieties you can practice in racing season:

- Row at a base stroke rate for 20 strokes then increase the rating two strokes per minute for the last 20: Target rates: 26-28, 28-30, 30-32, 32-34.
- Row at a base stroke rate for 20 strokes the increase the rating two strokes per minute for 10, then again two strokes per minute for 10:Target rates: 26-28-30, 28-30-32, 30-32-34, 32-34-36.
- Row at a base stroke rate for 10 strokes then increase the rating two strokes per minute every 10th stroke for a total of 40 strokes: Target rates: 26-28-30-32, 28-30-32-34, 30-32-34-36, 32-34-36-38.

- Row at a base stroke rate for 20 strokes then increase the rating two strokes per minute every fifth strokes for a total of 40: Target rates: 28-30-32-34-36, 30-32-34-36-38, 32-34-36-38-40.

Sculling-specific: In a single, practicing your rating shifts can help you find that extra gear when you need it in a race. Focus on clean bladework and correct blade depth as the rating comes up. Learning what works best for you and making rating changes purposeful will give you more confidence to follow and execute your race plan.

Sweep-specific: Having crews learn to focus on the coxswain's call and the stroke's lead will teach the crew to act with precision and decisiveness, building confidence in the ability of the boat. It is important to train the crew to be very attentive to solid technique on a transition up so the increase in rating increases the speed of the boat.

FALL BACK INTO HEAD SEASON

Sprint season has wrapped up and the long distance events dotting the race calendar are coming. Late August and early September is the time to return to some foundation work to get ready for your headraces. Taking a moment to review your strengths and weaknesses of the summer will help you prioritize what you need to focus on before the fall events begin. Here are some important workouts that you should include as part of your fall preparation.

Basic aerobic conditioning and your anaerobic threshold are big determining factors in long distance racing if you want to row your best possible pace without hitting the wall midway through your event. Now is the time to add in a distance row each week, perhaps over the weekend when you have more time. Your distance row should be your longest row of the week by time or kilometers. If you practice 60 minutes daily, your long row might be from 75 to 90 minutes. Building up to a two-hour row once a week is a good goal. The emphasis of these outings should be low intensity, high volume, with a focus on good technique. Only stop briefly about every 15 minutes to drink or turn around. If you will be rowing for more than an hour take a bottle of sports drink with you, as well as, water so you can take in two to three hundred calories in the second hour of your session. Keep your stroke rates low between 18 to 20 strokes per minute and your effort should be conversational. If you are breathless you are rowing too hard for this type of session. These rows will help your body learn to burn fat more efficiently, increase your capillary density for better blood flow to your muscles, develop good concentration, and work the bugs out of your technique because you are moving relatively slowly. You can include occasional drills during this row such as inserting one minute of pause drills every five minutes, doing square blades for 10 strokes on/10 strokes off for five-minute segments, or rowing the entire session feet-out changing slide lengths, especially one-quarter and half slide. The variety will make the kilometers pass by quickly and your skills will get finer.

Anaerobic threshold work needs precise attention too. I would rate this intensity of rowing as comfortably hard. You are breathless but the pace is doable; it is by no means race pace but is still substantial work. Do one or two anaerobic threshold workouts per week spaced at least two days apart in order to let your glycogen stores to recover. You may also want to place your rest day between your long row and before your threshold work. Plan for 30 to 60 minutes of work at this intensity keeping strokes rates in the range of 24 to 26 strokes per minute. Some examples of continuous sessions are two to three times 20 minutes with seven minutes rest between, four times 10 minutes with five minutes rest between, or one 30-minute row at set stroke rate 24 where each week you try to increase your distance. For more variety you can work above and below your anaerobic threshold to get the net training effect that you want such as spending 40 to 60 minutes alternating five minutes at head race pace with five minutes at steady state. There is still time to boost your fitness before the races start this fall. The training you do will pay off with more consistent speed, mental toughness, and the ability to catch up with the boat that started just ahead of you.

HEAD RACING RHYTHM

Unlike sprint events where you are lined up and start from standing, headraces clock you crossing the line already at pace. In distance races your start is important to get you into your racing beat as soon as possible. Having swing from the beginning of your race will help spread your effort more carefully so you can maintain a consistent pace and avoid slowing down in the second half of the event because of fatigue. Spend some time working on the tempo of your rowing and striving for a rhythm that has a sense of lightness and boat run. Working on your ability to have contrast each stroke between the application of work during the drive and momentary relaxation on the recovery go far to improve your efficiency.

When you are preparing for your fall races develop an idea of what your stroke rate will be. You will want to target a pace that is aggressive yet allows you to row well. In practice you then want to begin building up to that rating while rowing clean. For example, we can look at the goal of rowing a single at 30 strokes per minute over five kilometers. During your steady state rows you will want to begin to interject short segments where you increase the rates. If you are rowing at a base rate of 20 strokes per minute for four minutes, over several practices increase your stroke rate to 26, 28, and then 30 for one-minute bursts during the row. The emphasis should be on quickness to achieve the rate comfortably without trying to muscle the action, keeping the oarhandle in constant motion at the entry and release, and your focus of power should remain in the legs. Making sure that you really complete the leg drive will help you keep the momentum of the handle making it easier to keep the boat feeling light.

When you start to be able to achieve 30 strokes per minute you'll want to expand the time you can row at that rating. Next, you can do a workout where your goal is to stay at 30 strokes per minutes though the pressure is a bit relaxed. Row three times 3,000 meters at 30 strokes per minute with seven minutes rest between. Concentrate on the tempo of the rating and settling into this swing at a firm but comfortable effort. This workout teaches your nervous system to get used to a slightly faster speed and adapt to it. Then progressing towards racing conditions will become important. You can add a time trial into your program once a week at your target stroke rate so you begin to work on keeping your flow when you begin to fatigue or do some longer rows such as 60 minutes alternating 20 minutes at 18, 20, and 22 strokes per minutes followed by a final 20 minutes at 30 strokes per minute. As the season comes closer plan how you want to approach your racing pace and what you need to do to be competitive in your class. Select paces that match your current ability and dedicate some practices to boost them up for your peak event.

HOW TO AVOID THE UNEXPECTED

With roughly 600 strokes to execute your peak head race plan, now is the time to map out the final details of your main event off the water, as well as, on the water. At big events such as the Head of the Charles Regatta, the Head of the Lake Regatta, or the Head of the Trent Regatta, there is a sense of excitement at the course that we don't always experience in our daily training. This is what makes going to competitions festive events but it can also cause us to forget important details or become distracted. Spend time before your regattas to work out the fine points of what you will do to get ready to race. If you are a single sculler you are solely responsible to have everything you need. If you are a team coach you are concerned with each rower having what they need in addition to your equipment.

Make a checklist ahead of time for racing days so you take all supplies with you to put your boat in the water. Your equipment includes your car rack, boat cover, boat, seat, foot stretchers, oars, slings, tie down straps, SpeedCoach or Cox Box, tools, towels, extra fin, spare parts, and duct tape. Make sure you have your racing suit, tights, wind shirt, wind pants, rain gear, dry clothes, a change of shoes, and a warm jacket for after the race. Take your entry information, hotel confirmation, mobile phone, map to the site, food, sunscreen, sunglasses, water bottle, a blanket for stretching, and some extra cash for the unexpected. Arrive at the course early enough to get your equipment ready without rushing and to check carefully for breakage. Take some quiet time away from the crowds before you need to get in your boat to race. Starting your warm-up on land with easy jogging can be beneficial if your time is limited or less time than you are accustomed to. Launch in time to go through a routine that you are familiar with and gets you comfortable in your boat.

Once you've made your way to the starting line, find the bow marker of the boat that will be ahead of you, listen carefully for instructions from the starting officials, and get your boat pointed in the direction you want to go. Bring your focus into your own boat and try to minimize distractions as you prepare to start. Once you are on the course, steering, conditioning, technique, and mental preparation have to come together during your performance. Keep your technical reminders in a positive tone and use key words that will help you row better. Target elements that will improve each stroke such as posture, relaxed hands, or blade depth. Stay in the present and carry out your strokes one at a time. Stringing together a successful chain of attentive, well-executed strokes will give you the best chance of performing at the level that you are capable of.

STEERING THE HEAD SEASON

Steering, head races present very different challenges than racing 1,000 or 2,000 meters. Sprint racing is conducted in buoyed lanes necessitating a straight course but head races vary from race to race and often include considerations such as: current strength, turns, and wind direction. In a head race situation a good course will get you to the finish line without rowing extra distance or being slowed by current.

- Ideally, arrive at the racecourse in time to row over the course, otherwise study the course map carefully to be aware of curves or snags in the course.
- Study where the markers are placed and determine the shortest course for the race. Markers may not always represent the best course and are placed simply to designate course boundaries.
- Inquire about places where the current of the river can vary. Aim to have current help you pick up speed rather than rowing against it.
- Look for important landmarks to line up your stern for various sections of a race course in order to point the bow in the correct direction.
- Make steering corrections when the blades are in the water. Scullers can change their course by altering the handles at the front end. Slightly lengthening the arc of one oarhandle will allow the boat to turn to the opposite direction at the initiation of the drive. This will keep disturbance of the drive phase to a minimum. If you are using a rudder make corrections during the drive.
- Check your course by glancing over your shoulder during the drive if you are in a sculling boat. Some scullers also prefer using a mirror mounted on a hat or

headband. Practice alternating looking over your right and left shoulders for 10 to 20 strokes during steady rows to get comfortable with this. In a race situation, look out of the boat only as much as you need to for safety, steering, and passing other boats. Excessive steering decreases your boat speed.

Sculling-specific: Practicing steering is part of ongoing skill development for a single sculler. A variety of asymmetries during the stroke can cause deviations in your course. Be attentive to precise bilateral entry and release timing with the blades, as well as, stabilizing the hull and equal movement of the opening of the oarhandles. As your skill improves so will your ability to steer straight.

Sweep-specific: Head races offer many creative opportunities for coxswain's to shave seconds off their crew's time. Turning and curve tactics should be practiced during the pre-competitive season. Have a crew get familiar with alternating pressures on either port or starboard so the boat is able to make adjustments and keep its swing. Another technique that can be practiced for long turns in a course is to drop out either the bow-seat or two-seat, whichever is on the inside of the turn, so the remaining crew members can keep racing pressure. Combined with skillful use of the rudder, this can be a very effective way to hug the buoys on the inside of a turn.

NEW ADVENTURES IN RACING

Hippos don't usually share rivers with rowing shells and neither do crocodiles. So my interest was caught when BBC World television reported on the 2004 Zambezi Centenary Regatta in Zambia featuring, Oxford, Cambridge, and South African eights racing by these extraordinary spectators. Set on the Zambezi River, the regatta was part of the centenary celebrations for the town of Livingstone and was hosted by the 99-year old Zambezi Boat Club. Races for men and women included 500-meter sprints and 2,000-meter races. Later this year, Livingstone will commemorate the World Professional Sculling Championships held in 1910 as one of its landmark events. My first response to all this was rowing just keeps getting more adventurous. Though many of us are addicted to our more common racing distances, 1k, 2k, or 5k, I decided to see what else was going on out there. After all, everybody isn't the perfect slow-twitch/fast-twitch muscle fiber combination to conquer these tough middle distances of four, eight or even 20 minutes.

The Hamburg Speedrows are an example of a short-course regatta designed to test skill and speed. The 500-meter course in downtown Hamburg, Germany was a pretty bumpy course to go down this year but proved great entertainment for the many spectators lining the riverbank. Races were held in various boat classes for elite, senior, and junior rowers. Eurosport, the European sport channel, televised the events held on September 25th. The coverage was a bonus to the post-Olympic rowing schedule. Like the new sprint format for Nordic skiing events, these fast races have popular appeal and help boost the amount of television coverage of the sport. For more information and to watch a video clip of the Speedrows featuring even Peter-Micheal Kolbe racing Pertti Karppinen, go to www.speedrows.

de/start. For those of you who are more on the fast-twitch side
of life, consider doing the 500-meter dash events at USRowing
National Championships or the Royal Canadian Henley Regatta
next season.

Long distance open water events abound, but flat-water
courses longer than five kilometers are on the rise. These
are great events if you are a slow-twitch type, like to work at
anaerobic threshold level for long periods of time, and enjoy
some post-event festivities. If you decide to combine some
travel with rowing, consider going to some of these races in
Europe and the United States.

Riverside Boat Club's coach, Karen Chenausky, calls
this race, "great." Held early in September, the Meguniticook
Mini-Marathon is in the seaside town of Camden, Maine. The
Maine Rowing Association site, www.rowmaine.org, has this
description, "With its sparsely populated shoreline and the
surrounding Camden Hills, this lake is a truly beautiful row. This
unique event starts at the foot of the cliffs of Mt. Megunticook.
The start is in waves of five to seven rowers grouped by age and
sex approximately 30 seconds apart. The 10-mile race threads
its competitors down through the narrow passages of the lake's
coves and islands, leading to the motto of the race "Not just a
race...an adventure." The rowing conditions are generally well
protected. The superb choice of lobster restaurants in town
after the race also makes the trip well worth it.

The Skiff Regatta, "for all racing rowers, challenge rowers,
and pleasure seeking rowers" is held mid-October in Klagenfurt,
Austria. The 16-kilometer mass start event goes from Lake
Worthersee West Bay to Lake Worthersee East Bay. Scullers
are taken to the start by coach and race back to the Albatros
Rowing Club boathouse. The event includes a sparkling wine
reception and a guided tour through the old city of Klagenfurt.
For more information go to www.rv-albatros.at and click on the
link for Rose Vom Worthersee.

Promoted as, "a single scull long distance race over nine kilometers with a mass start" the classic BKW-Armada Cup held late October in Bern, Switzerland is hosted at the Rowing Club Bern. There are world-class scullers at the starting line, as well as, many recreational enthusiasts. The top male and female scullers are awarded 1500 Swiss francs. Their website, www.bkw-armadacup.ch, promises, "after the race you can enjoy a glass of wine and some good food in a nice atmosphere." Then, if you wish to travel south to Torino, Italy, the Silverskiff Regatta, www.silverskiff.org, is an 11k international endurance race in mid-November rowed on the Po River. You'll scull by castles, under classical bridges, eventually catching sight of the range of mountains that includes the Massif of Grand Paradiso and Levanna.

The Marathon Rowing Championships is one of the few continuous 26-mile rowing regattas anywhere. Held in Natchitoches, Louisiana, nearly 350 competitors gather on the Cane River in mid-November to race the course in different boat classes. The regatta promises a challenge "a little out of the ordinary" and to test your limits of rowing endurance. The average time it takes to complete the course is three to four hours and the 2004 regatta marks the 15th anniversary of the regatta. Go to www.regattacentral.com for more information.

No description of rowing endurance races would be complete without the talking about the CPR. The Corvallis to Portland Regatta is a 115-mile race held over two days on the Willamette River in Oregon. Starting south of Corvallis, the first day is an 85-mile leg ending at Champoeg Park with a campfire and Buster's Texas Barbeque dinner. You provide your own tent for the night. The second day includes a 19-mile row to the Willamette Fall Locks, a 30-minute rest while you descend 45 feet to the lower Willamette, followed by an "11-mile sprint" to the finish. Few scullers have tackled this in singles but Tiff Wood and Rob Slocum are out there setting the examples on the men's side and Gia DeAngelis on the women's. The CPR is held in late May or early June. You'll need some heavy-duty volume on the erg this winter to get ready for this event. If you are up for the challenge visit www.newworldrowing.com/cpr.

A CHANGE OF RACE PACE

If you are seeking some adventures this season that are outside of traditional racing lanes, adding a long distance event to your annual calendar could be just what you are looking for. Today's opportunities range from flat-water marathons and open water challenges to multiple-day events. Successful scullers share their experience in these pursuits giving us advice how to approach long distances and avoid pitfalls.

Representing Rocky Mountain Rowing Club, Darin Hayden, won the women's single in the C division at the 2004 Marathon Rowing Championships in Natchitoches, Louisiana. For Hayden, the marathon tests both her endurance and mental toughness, "The longer the race is the better indicator of whether or not you can move a boat consistently over time and it is less impacted by a missed stroke or rogue wave." For a first-time marathoner Darin recommends training on the water and the erg at long distances not only for the consistent rowing and time in the seat but to be comfortable about what you take with you in the boat to maintain your strength. She adds, "Too little water can get you into trouble quickly. Mentally, if you are at home on the erg and your water bottle is just a reach to the floor, you don't get the same feeling as you get when you are two hours out on a three-hour row without access to water or other types of nutrition." Besides the training time, Darin credits her success to the encouragement given by her teammates on the course and a good support crew on land to provide transportation to the start or finish along with pre- and post-race nutrition.

Open water racing demands different strategies than flat-water racing. In 2006, over a 7.6-mile course of rough chop, Dan Gorriarian of Rhode Island, won the men's single event by one second at the first North American Open Water Rowing Championship. The championship was held in conjunction with The Great Cross Sound Race at Bainbridge Island, Washington. In 2007 it will be in combination with the Blackburn Challenge, a 20-mile open water circumnavigation of Cape Ann, Massachusetts. A repeat performance could be in the cards for Gorriarian as he is a three-time Blackburn Challenge winner of the sliding seat racing single category.

Why take on these extreme conditions? Dan replied, "I've raced flat water forever. There is limited strategy to racing 1,000 meters. In open water racing there are so many variables. I find the longer the race the more strategy plays a role. This is why I find the Blackburn Challenge fascinating. The fastest guy doesn't always win, the strongest guy doesn't always win, the guy who rows best in rough water doesn't always win but it's the guy that can do it all pretty well that usually prevails." Gorriarian continues, "Mental preparation is vitally important. To me, the Blackburn has been a death-defying event. The first year I won I was terrified. I am afraid of the ocean so suddenly being in front of the race with no one around me for over 90 minutes of racing was unnerving but it also made me race harder. I started hallucinating badly over the last two miles from lack of fluids. I have learned in subsequent races to calm down, eat, drink, focus, and row smoothly. I always visualize the entire race before hand." For scullers beginning to do such events Dan shares his know-how. He cautions to start out at a reasonable stroke rate because pacing is key. Study your map and use a GPS because conditions can change quickly. Eat well before the event plus take food and fluids with you. Relax in rough water. Study the direction of the waves to figure out when you can pull hard and when you can cruise. Have complete safety equipment and an exit strategy if the conditions deteriorate. Lastly, "You can get in a lot of trouble out there so respect the environment."

Rob Slocum is the indoor rowing world record holder for the 100-kilometer and marathon for ages 50 to 59. According to Slocum, deciding to row the 115-mile, two-day Corvallis to Portland Regatta was a natural choice. Rob won the double in 2003 and raced his single in 2004. For this ultra-distance event Rob says, "To avoid blisters, slather your hands in Vaseline and put batting gloves on. Reapply the Vaseline every stop-three hours or more often. Work on what to eat during the event. Avoid going out too hard. CPR is a steady state pace. I felt so good after the first three hours in my first year that I decided to take it up for the next stretch and paid for it. Cramps in the legs; just felt horrible." Slocum says he views this as a race rather than taking the trekking-suffering-survival approach, "I recommend doing a mileage binge for a month leading up to the event ending two weeks before CPR. I did a million miles total water and erg (80 percent water) my second year." Be prepared and work out the details.

For sightseeing, Cape Cod resident, Carol Lyall, recommends the annual FISA Rowing Tour, "I love to row, travel, meet people from all over the world, and speak broken English." The Douro River in Portugal was one of her favorites because it her first and was the hardest. To get ready for covering 200 kilometers in five days, Carol recommends, "Make a point of rowing long distances to get your back in shape, your hands calloused, and your patience tested. These tours are not aerobic challenges so sprint and fast training paces aren't part of the picture. Avoid thinking these tours are a piece of cake. There are plenty of toughing-it-out situations. They are what make the row really worthwhile." The 2007 FISA Rowing Tour will be held on the Connecticut River, in Long Island Sound, and around Manhattan.

CHAPTER 7

RIGGING UP

PINS. PITCH. HEIGHT. SPAN. DIGGING.

HOW TO RIG YOUR SINGLE: GETTING STARTED

When one mentions rigging one of two things usually occurs: either your friend starts running out the door as fast as possible claiming a sudden appointment or a broad smile comes across his face as he rubs his hands together preparing to dig into his toolbox. Like the cross-country skier who spends more time waxing skis than skiing on them, we too have that type of character in our sport-the rigging fanatic. This extremist will not hesitate to tinker and move *something* on his single almost daily. The unconfident rigger though, will avoid touching any nut or bolt at any cost, afraid of opening up Pandora's box and sliding into an irreversible state of chaos. Needless to say, a happy, healthy, balanced medium can be reached when it comes to knowledge of rigging. Approaching rigging your single in a calm, organized fashion can help you learn about an important technical aspect of sculling that you might even find enjoyable. This mini-series will attempt to clarify how to rig your single and give you a systematic approach to doing so.

Getting Started

Rigging is the art and science of adjusting a boat and oars to meet your individual needs. The hardware of a boat such as: riggers, pins, oarlocks, footstretchers, seat, and tracks can be set to optimize your biomechanical position in the boat in conjunction with your chosen oar dimensions and blade type. The make of your boat will dictate the amount of adjustability available to you. Generally, performance singles have the widest range of possibilities to customize your rig. Before you begin you will need to get organized:

- Keep a logbook of all your rigging activities. Record the date and current measurements so you can retrace your steps if you need to.
- Have the correct tools ready: Hex keys, wrenches, a pitch meter, a long carpenter's level, and a tape measure with centimeters.
- Put your boat up on slings in a quiet place away from the distractions and curiosity of other scullers willing to give you lots of advice.
- Take your time and write everything down.
- Complete one step at a time.
- Once you measure, measure again.
- If you get tired, take a break. Keep your sense of humor.

Setting Up Your Boat

Before you start to take measurements or change the dimensions of your rigging, you need to set your boat up in a way that will make it easy for you to work on it. Since a third hand is not always easy to come by, here is a suggested way.

- Set your boat on slings of the same size. To stabilize your boat, take a rod or stick (like a broomstick) and place it vertical next to one of the riggers. Using a large spring clamp;-secure the rigger to the stick to prevent the boat from tipping.
- Level the boat end-to-end. Place the carpenter's level along a flat part of the boat such as the base of the gunnel; do not use the seat deck because there is a slight angle from bow to stern. If needed, fold and prop a towel between the boat and sling to level the boat.

- Level the boat side-to-side. Place the carpenter's level across the gunnels. When the bubble is centered, adjust the clamped rigger with the vertical stick to hold the boat level.
- Strap or tie your boat to the slings to further stabilize it.
- Bring your toolbox close. Now you are ready to start.

HOW TO RIG YOUR SINGLE: BASIC TERMS

When you rig your single you are setting the dimensions of the riggers and oars to maximize your biomechanical efficiency and comfort in the boat. As we know, rigging is not an exact science as there is a fair amount of art and touch mixed in. There are some basic rules and references that need to be adhered to and serve as a platform to fine-tune your boat for you. Your rigging needs can also change over time. As elements of your technique improve, rigging details can be adapted to support those improvements.

Keep in mind that you are working multi-dimensionally when you rig your boat. You are balancing horizontal, vertical, angled, and diagonal measurements to create a leverage system that allows you to move the boat effectively. When you make one change to your rigging it affects the entire system and small alterations can produce large effects. Once you alter your rig you need to row with it several times to get accustomed to a new feel to decide whether the change was positive or not. A speed device such as a SpeedCoach that can measure meters per second, distance, and 500-meter split times is useful for objectively observing whether a rigging change makes you go faster or not. Having a stretch of flat water without current is valuable for testing rigging changes over 500-meter or 1,000-meter repeats. Before we start measuring, the following descriptions of the terms "through the pin" and "load" will give you an overview of important aspects of rigging.

Through the Pin

The pin is the vertical axle the oarlock rotates around that extends upward from the end of the rigger. In rigging, the pin serves as a reference point for positioning yourself in the boat. The terms "through the pin" and "work through" refer to where the centerline of the hip joint is relative to the location of the pin. The hip joint axis may be behind, equal to, or astern of the pin at the entry position. Drawing an imaginary line from pin to pin provides a standard for the hip joint axis to reach in full compression when ready for the entry. In a performance single be at least at zero, or equal, with the pin. In a faster moving boat you may work more through the pin. Your flexibility, skill level, and boat type can all affect your ability to get up through the pin, but the point here is to identify the pin as a reference. Being centered in the boat and around the "work" helps to produce increased angle of the oar at the entry and the release when combined with proper oar inboard adjustments.

Load

Load is the term that defines the resultant energy relationship of the distance between the pins, inboard/outboard settings of the oars, blade size, and a sculler's physical dimensions. On a rowing ergometer, the concept of load is illustrated by setting the damper resistance high at "10" or low at "1" and is expressed as drag factor. Unfortunately, in the boat, there is no clear-cut way for the average person to define drag factor and measure the load of their rigging system. Rigging charts exist; however, there are reasonable parameters to follow as we continue our discussion of rigging.

Keep in mind that more is not necessarily better when it comes to load. It can be too heavy producing stress on the lumbar spine, creating excessively large arcs in the water, and making it a strain to increase your stroke rate during a race. On the contrary, too light is a bit like trying to pedal a bike down a hill while spinning on your large chain ring; you need to take too many strokes to maintain the desired speed. Your individual body dimensions, strength, and race pace stroke rating, play a role in how much load you can optimally row with. Boatbuilder,

Ted Van Dusen, of Concord, Massachusetts, advised to, "Rig for the end of your race," meaning set a load that is adequate to maintain efficient race tempo yet light enough that you can increase the stroke rate for the final sprint when you are in a fatigued state.

HOW TO RIG YOUR SINGLE: SPAN

Approaching rigging in an orderly, systematic way will make it easier for you to detect problems and make adjustments. If you are rigging your boat for the first time, get all your measurements within a reasonable range. Once the boat is rigged, then make only one change at a time so you can assess the effect. Remember to write your measurements in a logbook.

Step 1: Setting the Span

The span is the distance between the two oarlock pins. This is a major measurement of your gearing system that will combine with your oar settings to determine the load of your rig. Measure from the center of the top of the pin to the center of the top of the other pin. To make it easier, you may have another person to hold one end of the tape measure for you. Record the number of centimeters.

The range for setting the span is usually between 158 to 164 centimeters. An average starting point is 160 centimeters. If you are a smaller sculler a span of 158 centimeters may be appropriate, and if you are a larger sculler, 162 centimeters may be more comfortable. Moving the span in creates a heavier load and larger arc through the water. Moving the span wider lightens the load, creating a smaller arc in the water. You need to feel that you are comfortable to open your hands along a horizontal plane well over the gunnels as the blade is prepared for the entry. This happens in conjunction with other factors but setting the span is the initial consideration.

It is of the utmost importance to make sure that the pins are set an equal distance from the centerline of the boat.

Measure across the gunnels of the boat, take half the number of centimeters, and then measure from that point to the pin. For example, if gunnel to gunnel is 46 centimeters, half of 46 is 23, locate the 23-centimeter mark on your tape measure, place it on the gunnel nearest the pin you are measuring, and measure the remaining distance to the pin. It should read 57 centimeters if your overall span is 160 centimeters; One half of 160 centimeters=80 centimeters). Another method to check if the pins are equidistant is to measure from the outside of the opposite track to the base of the pin and check that both sides are the same. You can use this method because the seat tracks should be set centered in the boat. Once you have finished setting the span. Measure it again. Do not change your span casually once you have it set, you can use oar adjustments to make smaller gearing changes.

Step 2: Determining Inboard

Setting the inboard on your oars is another rigging step that relates to overall load. The inboard is the measurement that is defined as the distance from the end of the handle to the blade-side face of the collar. The inboard setting is dependent on the overall spread and the amount of overlap of the oarhandles or crossover. Take one half your span and add eight centimeters for a good initial setting of your inboard. Thus, if your span was 160 centimeters, you inboard setting would be 88 centimeters. The inboard measurement serves as a way to fine-tune your load as you can move the collar in small increments to affect the load. Moving the collar towards the handle creates a shorter inboard lever and makes the load heavier. Conversely, moving the collar towards the blade, makes the inboard lever longer and lighter. Measurements between 87 to 89 centimeters allow a great deal of adjustment. If you need a setting such as 86 centimeters or less, you also may need to select a shorter overall length of the oar to avoid a heavy load.

Step 3: Oar Length

The third factor in determining load is the overall length of your oars. Your size, strength, and blade design will affect what length oar you choose to scull with. A shorter oar lightens the load; a longer oar increases the load due to the longer outboard. Outboard is the measurement from the blade-side face of the collar to the tip of the blade. A standard overall length for a Macon blade is 298 centimeters. Hatchet-shaped blades come in many sizes with adjustable lengths ranging from 278 to 290 centimeters depending on the blade type. Every oar manufacturer has recommended rigging specifications for each blade type. Larger-sized blades have shorter oar lengths. A heavyweight man may increase the length and a lightweight woman sculler may decrease the length according to their needs.

Some experimentation is needed in your sculling to set the overall length. Your needs may change as your personal style of sculling develops, you race at higher rates, or gain strength. You may find that you prefer a lighter load if you tend to be quicker and more reactive versus someone who prefers a heavier, power stroke. Remember that span, inboard, oar length, and personal attributes must work together. There is no sense to row with excessively heavy loads to impress others. If anything lean towards lighter loads to protect overstressing the lumbar spine.

HOW TO RIG YOUR SINGLE: HEIGHT AND PITCH

Reminder: Approaching rigging in an orderly, systematic way will make it easier for you to detect problems and make adjustments. If you are rigging your boat for the first time, get all your measurements within a reasonable range. Once the boat is rigged, make only one change at a time so you can assess the effect. Remember to write your measurements in a logbook.

Step 4: Oarlock Height

When you sit in a boat, the first thing that you usually notice is where the handle height is. If you row club boats, you know that some boat feel high and others low. This can be due both to the size of the boat relative to your weight and to the height set at the oarlock. If you row a hull that is too big for you, you do not sink the boat to the proper water line and you will generally feel too high in the boat; as if the oarhandles come up to your chest. Rowing with the correct height is a one reason to row the right hull size for your weight. Accurate oarlock height allows you to clear your blade from the water on the recovery and lets you to apply your body weight properly during the drive.

Due to the crossover, in sculling there is a slight height differential between the starboard and port oarlocks of one to two centimeters allowing the sculler to row left hand leading right hand. This difference in the height setting gives room for the hands to nest together at the crossover and keep the boat level. The differential setting can be a personal setting, as some scullers may like a little more and some a little less. The important point is that the boat stays on keel at the point of crossover.

Standard oarlock height runs between 13 to 18 centimeters. At the release, sitting with good posture, and blades buried, your thumbs on the handles should just brush your middle ribs at the level of your sternum. You do not want to feel that your handles are in your lap or up near your neck but right at the level of your center of gravity.

To measure height, use a long level placed across the gunnels. Set one end through the center of the oarlock and hang the other end over the seat. Use a tape measure to establish the distance from the bottom edge of the long level, to the bottom of the oarlock, and the top of the seat. Every time you measure height make sure to put your level in the same place and measure to the same point on the seat and oarlock to keep the references consistent.

Sliding the oarlock off the pin and changing the number of washers above and below the oarlock suffices to change height in most boats. Note: When you purchase a boat ask the builder if the height differential is set in the rigger construction or needs to be set at the oarlock; if you row in a boat with a wing rigger check whether the starboard side of the wing is shimmed higher than the port. Some European clubs row right over left, in which case you need to reverse the standard height differential to raise the port side.

Step 5: Sternward Pitch

Sternward pitch is the angle of the blade away from perpendicular during the pull through of the stroke. A small amount of pitch, four to six degrees, is enough to help the blade stay buried at the proper depth through the water. If a blade has too much pitch, more than seven degrees, the blade will wash out at the end of the drive; too little pitch, less than four degrees, causes the blade too dive deep. Sternward pitch is a fore-and-aft measurement usually taken at the oarlock but it must be kept in mind that it is the angle of the blade that we are concerned with, so knowing the pitch of the pins and the oars has to be taken into final consideration. The pitch of the blade = the pitch of the pin + the pitch of the oarlock + the pitch built into the blade.

Measuring the pitch will begin with checking the pin. Ideally, if the pin is set at zero degrees it makes it easy to calculate your oarlock pitch. Unless you check it you don't know what the reference is. A commercially available pitch meter or a simple level can be used. With your boat set up level in slings, slide the oarlock off taking care to count the washers setting the height. Place a vertical level against the sternward face of the pin and see if it zeros out. If it does the pin is at zero degrees, if not, you may be able to shim your pin to get it to zero degrees, otherwise use your pitch meter to determine how many degrees you are plus or minus zero.

Adjust your pitch meter on a level portion of the gunnel. Put the pointer on zero and then center the bubble on the level. Tighten the level so it is firmly in place. Place the squared surface of the pitch meter against the face of the pin and move the pointer until the level's bubble is centered. Record the number of degrees the pointer reads in that pin.

Next, put the round pitch inserts into your oarlock with the number of degrees you want and check that the top and bottom shims are in the right orientation (read your oarlock owner's manual). Slide the oarlock back on the pin. For example: If your pin is at zero degrees and you want plus five degrees put in the five-degree shim. However, if your pin is plus one degree you need a four-degree shim to give your oarlock five. Once you have put the oarlock back on the pin and secured the top bolt, measure the pitch in the oarlock. Hold the oarlock at the mid-drive position (with the gate closed and nut pointing towards the stern) parallel to the midline of the boat. Zero your pitch meter and then place the squared surface of the pitch meter against the back plate of the oarlock. A spring clamp can be handy for this. Make sure the surfaces are flush to get an accurate reading. Your measurement should agree with the sum of the degrees in the pin plus the inserts. If not, try again until you get the desired degrees. Five degrees is the most common setting, six may give you a little more bite at the entry and four a little less lift to the boat. Whatever amount of pitch you choose, make sure that both sides measure the same.

HOW TO RIG YOUR SINGLE: PITCH

Reminder: Approaching rigging in an orderly, systematic way will make it easier for you to detect problems and make adjustments accordingly. If you are rigging your boat for the first time, get all your measurements within a reasonable range. Once the boat is rigged, make only one change at a time so you can assess the effect. Remember to write your measurements in a logbook.

Step 6: Outward Pitch

Outward or lateral pitch is the tilt of the pin away from the centerline of the hull. The standard zero to two degrees assists the tracking of the blade in the water. You can measure it by placing your pitch meter on the lateral aspect of the pin and measuring. You can also see the effect of lateral pitch in the oarlock. With the pitch meter in place against the back plate of the oarlock, check your reading of degrees at mid-drive, swing the oarlock to the entry position and you should see the sternward pitch increase. Then swing the oarlock to the release position and you should see the degrees diminish to assist the release of the blade. Your readings should look like: entry-six degrees, perpendicular-five, and release-four. If you have the inverse relationship, your pins could have negative lateral pitch and require creative shimming to rectify.

Step 7: Pitch in Oars

In North America, the majority of oars are built with zero degrees of pitch, meaning that the position of the blade is level with the wear plate surface on the sleeve. If you row with unknown or wooden oars you may have to measure your oars at the blade to determine if there is pitch built into the blades and take those degrees into consideration when setting the pitch at the oarlock. You can do this by setting your oar on a bench with a level block, as wide as the blade, supporting the blade and another support block under the handle. Place the blade face down on the block with one inch of the tip off the edge of the block if you are measuring a Macon blade or with the short side corner radius of the blade just off the edge of the block for hatchet-shaped blades. The put your level across the wear plate surface to see whether it is at zero degrees. Shimming to get the level zeroed, Concept2 advises that .025 of an inch equals approximately one degree of pitch. If it is necessary to measure your oars check with your manufacturer for specific instructions because there are variations depending on blade type.

HOW TO RIG YOUR SINGLE: COCKPIT ADJUSTMENTS

This is the final installment of our discussion about rigging. Learning about your boat is an important way to develop an understanding of the technical side of sculling and can be fun. Rigging should be done with care and once you arrive at a good general rig that works for you, spend time rowing it before you begin to make too many readjustments. When you need to make changes only do one thing at a time so you can observe the effect of the change. Rigging supports your ability to row with good technique; it is not a substitute for it.

Step 8: Footstretcher Adjustment

The footstretcher adjustment should be placed so that you are both able to get up through the pin at the entry and have about the width of a fist between the handles at the release comfortably in front of your body. Avoid feeling crowded by your oarhandles at the release forcing unnecessary lay back and eliminate excessive room that allows the handles to swing past the plane of the body losing the weight off the handles.

Step 9: Heel Height

Heel height is another measurement that can facilitate easier compression into the entry. The standard range is 16 to 18 centimeters from the top of the seat to the bottom of the heels. Many boats have adjustable footboards making this easy to change. If your boat has clogs, you may be able to re-drill and lower the heel cups to get a better setting.

Step 10: Rake of the Footboard

The angle of the footboard can be measured with a protractor or a goniometer (like those used in physical therapy clinics). Standard measurements fall between 39 to 42 degrees. If you have poor ankle flexibility, it may be necessary to flatten the footboard to get into a more comfortable position at the entry. If you have good ankle flexibility, 40 to 42 degrees is a desired setting to assist the leg drive in using the entire surface of the foot. Many performance boats have this adjustable feature; otherwise you will have to reposition the footboard and its attachments.

Step 11: Setting the Tracks

Once you have set your rigging dimensions and footstretchers, you need to set the seat tracks so you do not touch either end and have freedom of seat movement. Most tracks are quite long giving lots of room for adjustability. Reaching inside the hull and loosening the small wing nuts that hold the track allow you to move the tracks. Do not take the wing nuts off; just loosen enough to slide the tracks fore-and-aft. Set the front stops to the stern of the pin far enough to allow you to get up through the pin in full compression but not so far as to hit the back of your calves in an uncomfortable way. If your boat does not have adjustable tracks you must try to get the best possible position within the dimensions available to you or replace your fixed tracks with adjustable ones.

Step 12: Wing Rigger Adjustments

Boats with wing riggers offer additional adjustability to get through the pin and set oarlock height. Some care needs to be taken to position the wing in a way that maintains the trim of the boat and does not shift weight too far to either to the stern or bow. Your boat builder is the best person to discuss the rigging of the wing of a particular type of hull.

What is rigging? Art? Science? It is both. As you work on your boat you will get better at it. On one final note, once you have measured; measure again.

DETECTING PROBLEMS IN YOUR RIGGING

Once you have your boat rigged you should feel comfortable rowing it. No matter how careful you are with your boat, adjustments do get bumped or moved occasionally. Here are some signs of rigging defects:

- If your blade dives deep in the water, check that you are not under-pitched at the oarlock.
- If your blade is washing out of the water, check that you are not over-pitched at the oarlock.
- If the blade does not feel stable in the water, check your lateral pitch measurement.
- If you do not feel you can get your bodyweight applied at the entry without lifting, you may be rigged too low. Raise your oarlock height.
- If your hands are down in your lap at the release or you cannot adequately clear the water, you may be rigged too low. Raise your oarlock height.
- If you cannot get your hips in line with the pin at the entry you may need to move your footstretchers and tracks sternward or lower the heels of your shoes.
- If the load feels too heavy, you may need to increase the span, increase the inboard of the oar, or decrease the oar length.
- If the bow or stern are diving in the water during the stroke, you may have to adjust the trim of the boat or the wing setting to center your weight in the boat. The boat also could be too small for you.
- If you cannot get your heels down on the footboard during the drive, the rake of the footboard may be too steep.

These are just a few examples of rigging abnormalities you may detect. When rigged well the oars and boat should handle in an easy, balanced way.

CHAPTER 8

THE ERG

DRILLS. DRAG FACTOR. REPETITIONS. SPEED. SCORE.

ERG AWARENESS

Indoor rowing is a major part of our land training for rowing especially in the cold season. You can do sport-specific testing, workout at home in case you can't get to the boathouse, or train as a team when you don't have access to rowing tanks. The competitive world of indoor races has raised the number of races rowers can participate in and has stimulated the development of ultra-distance events. If the erg is part of your exercise regime, here are some basic technical considerations to keep in mind when putting on the meters this winter.

Be aware of the strokes you take. Rowing indoors requires the same technical attention as rowing in the boat does. Erging reinforces motor patterns that will transfer to your water strokes. The machine does not replicate balance or the exact handle movements of a sweep or sculling oar but the body sequencing and core muscular patterns can be trained as in the natural setting. With the use of mirrors or videotaping you can effectively improve your technique on the erg if you pay attention to the same details you do on the water and during time trials.

Machines are stationary on the floor and a boat is moving, your weight acts differently during the recovery phase. On the machine your mass is moving, on the water the boat moves under you, as your mass remains more stable. This understanding is important so you are careful with your body preparation, posture, and slide speed. When moving your mass forward it is easy to compress too quickly or to overreach because the machine does not need to be balanced; the boat does not tolerate this as well. A sliding frame for the Concept2 indoor rower is now available and is gaining favorable reviews for feeling much more boat-like.

The chain connecting the handle to the flywheel moves through a guide on the front of the machine making it easy for you to visually monitor the chain level on the drive and recovery. The chain should remain steady and level throughout the entire stroke cycle, there is no need to change the handle height when rowing indoors. The chain picks up tension with a minimum of slippage if the drive is initiated correctly. If you notice a lot of chain movement before you feel the resistance of the flywheel, correct your posture and work on a better connection between the legs and back.

The hand placement on the handle is like that of a sculling grasp except that you are unable to put your thumbs on the end of the handle. Keep the handle hooked in your fingers with the palm lifted off and thumbs gently wrapped under. The back of the hand, wrist, and forearm should remain level with the handle throughout the cycle. Allow your elbows to move out as hands approach the body keeping the handle height at the level of your sternum. Avoid over-gripping and focus on relaxed hands on the recovery as you would if manipulating an oar.

The ergometer seat travels on a long rail. Because there are no front stops, over-compression at the end of the recovery can easily occur. Placing a piece of tape on the rail can subtly remind you to limit how far you want your seat rollers to go. Because of the absence of a solid seat deck, hyperextension of your knees at the end of the drive sometimes occurs. Usually paying attention to this is enough to remedy it.

Your erg's settings are as important as the rigging of your boat for optimum performance. You can adjust the resistance level with the damper setting, heel cup height, and the performance monitor position. Drag factor is the indicator of resistance created by the flywheel, equivalent to the adjustment of load in rigging a boat. The lower numbers represent lighter loads; higher numbers heavier loads. A safe guideline for steady state rowing is a drag factor of 100 to 115. The lower drag factor prevents the wheel from excessive deceleration between strokes and limits unnecessary loading of the lumbar spine. Extreme care should be taken when doing short, low cadence power pieces with high drag factors. Drag factors over 130 to 140 place significant strain on the lumbar spine so this type of session should be done sparingly. Gravitate to the lightest setting that simulates the sensation of your boat speed.

Set your heel cups high enough so that you can compress properly with your shins near vertical but not so low that there is excessive sloping down of the legs at the end of the drive. Aim for the same fit that you have in your boat. The standard range of heel height in a boat is 16 to 17 centimeters. If you have poor flexibility lowering your heels cups will help you reach full compression better. Sliding your erg seat up to the footstretchers and measuring from the top of the seat vertical to the bottom of the heel cups can measure your heel height on the indoor rower.

As a final important point, keep your head steady and eyes focused forward when erging. Correct positioning of the head and eyes influences the body's response to posture, breathing, and power application. The computer monitor is best set up at eye level or slightly above. Keeping the eyes and head up reinforces good technique, breathing, and that does matter when you want to row better.

KEY DRILLS FOR BETTER ERGING

I arrived at Club La Santa Sport, on Lanzarote, one of the seven volcanic Canary Islands, just in time to watch the weekly Concept2 rowing challenge. This center is the home of the *Lanzarote Ironman Canarias*, which is the European qualifying competition for Hawaii's Ironman triathlon so the participants in this week's 2k competition were predominantly swimmers, cyclists, and runners. Though, perhaps not what one would consider a major event on the world indoor calendar, the trial is an important part of a guest's completion of the center's all-round fitness test. Some rowers from Denmark strolled in just as the race was getting started and together we enjoyed the spirit, as well as, some colorful variations of technique on the machine. After things quieted down, I figured I better do a row so I sat down, put the lever on three leaving my feet out. In a few minutes, Andre Schenk, a German instructor, sat down next to me and asked, "Why don't you put your feet in the straps?" We started talking about the purpose of the drill, one question lead to another and the next day he arranged for me to meet with their sports instructors. Meeting in the fitness room we talked about ways to row better on the erg. Here what our conversation was about:

We started talking about posture, keeping the trunk stable and the lower back firmly connected to the legs. This means putting the monitor up at eye-level and keeping the body "freely erect" without slumping or collapsing the lower back at any point of the stroke. All the instructors teach weight lifting and Swiss ball classes so they could immediately see the similarity between the posture needed for proper lifting technique and the connection of the upper body to the flywheel without slippage occurring in the lower back at the beginning of the leg drive. To get to the correct upper body position for the beginning of the drive, though I had to go to the release position and start from there.

Sitting at the release position, head and rib cage up, I kept my weight over the seat. I showed them rowing with the feet out of the footstretchers as a natural way to learn where the end of the leg drive is without falling too far off the back of seat.

Drill #1: Rowing Feet-out

The purpose of this drill is to practice correct release timing while keeping the body weight consistently behind the handle. Feet-out rowing teaches you to preserve the inertia of the drive in order to initiate an effortless flow into the recovery.

Place your feet on top of the straps. Pay attention to good posture throughout the stroke, sitting up tall over the seat at the release. Allow your body's core strength to support the release with head up and shoulders still. One rows continuously with firm pressure keeping the feet out. Time and coordinate the release precisely with the completion of the leg drive in order to keep the body weight behind the handle and transition smoothly into the recovery. Incorrect execution of the change in handle direction and follow through will allow the body weight to fall too far to the "bow" and the feet will come off the shoes. During the winter do most of your steady rowing with feet-out.

The most misunderstood part of the stroke was the recovery. How to transition your bodyweight? How to get ready for the drive? How to set a rhythm? Next, we talked about how could they easily show their athletes to keep the flow of acceleration then prepare for the next stroke? The reference point I gave them for completing each stroke was getting to the position of arms-body away. My advice was to use the arms-body away position as the indicator of one stroke ending and the next beginning. This way you avoid a back and forth motion in the stroke and eliminate hesitation at the end of the leg drive. The importance of taking the time to set the body plays a big part in keeping the three to one ratio of the recovery compared to the drive. This allows the flywheel to decelerate and makes it easier to row at lower drag factors avoiding the heavier settings that place stress on the lumbar spine in order to feel resistance.

Drill #2: Pausing Arms-body Away

This pause drill serves many purposes in technical training. Arms-body away is an excellent way to work on the stroke focusing both on a fluid release and complete body preparation prior to the initiation of the slide. When the pause is broken the recovery can be continued by compressing only the lower body, keeping the torso stable, head up and allowing the arms to guide the handle evenly.

Begin a pause drill session by pausing once every stroke for 20 strokes, then once every other stroke for 20 strokes, etc…up to five strokes continuous rowing one stroke pause. Relax. Take your time. Let the flywheel slow down. Double pause drills incorporate two pauses during one recovery such as pausing at arms-body away and at half slide.

With a reference established on the recovery for the upper body, we then worked on isolating the compression of the lower body without changing the shoulder or handle height; keeping the correct posture. We worked on a drill from the beginning of the drive to learn to connect to legs and pick up the tension of the flywheel without the lower back flexing or slipping.

Drill #3: Reverse Pick Drill

This drill is very effective for practicing the coordination of timing between the pick-up of the flywheel and the initiation of the drive. There should be a direct relationship between the commencement of the seat and handle movement. This drill emphasizes good connection between legs and back.

Row 20 strokes at each station.

- Legs only. Row the first one-quarter of the drive keeping body position steady and arms extended.
- Legs-body only. Row the full slide with the legs and body motions together keeping the arms straight.
- Add arms. Take full strokes with normal use of the arms.

We wrapped up our talk with how to get a sense of applying body weight between the feet and the handles to use the acceleration of mass, avoiding the temptation of simply trying to muscle the flywheel. This brought us back to where we started: posture, core strength, and good connection between the legs and lower back. For those of you in colder climates, the winter is upon you. Incorporate drills you do on the water into your erg sessions, row well on the erg, and keep it interesting. The best advice one can offer about the erg is summed up in this quotation from Canadian coach, Volker Nolte, given during a Craftsbury Sculling Camp lecture one summer: "Love your erg-it's all a state of mind."

ADDING IN SPEED

There comes a time in every plan when you need to start picking up the pace to train your body and mind to go faster for racing. For the 2,000-meter indoor rowing season, the late months of the year are the time to introduce yourself to some speed work. With long intervals further down the line in your program, approximately eight to 10 weeks from your competition, a gradual move to the more intensive side of things will help you maintain good quality later on.

Repetition training is an important type of training geared more towards stroke mechanics and anaerobic metabolism than with aerobic training. The intensity of rowing repetitions generates stress on your body to supply energy anaerobically, which then produces positive changes in anaerobic metabolism, where fuel is converted to energy in the absence of adequate oxygen. By practicing repetitions you will learn to row faster in a relaxed manner, so actual race pace becomes more known and comfortable. The specific muscle fibers you need to row economically are recruited during these types of sessions, allowing your muscle cells to adapt to the new speeds and not waste energy. The key to doing good repetition workouts is to practice rowing at your 2,000-meter race pace or just faster while paying attention to proper technique and getting plenty of recovery.

Rest time during repetition training is not very structured as compared to pure interval sessions where it is clearly defined. You decide subjectively the type and amount of rest following each bout of work. You should wait until you feel that you can do the next piece as well as you did the one before. If you need to paddle five minutes easy after rowing a 90-second piece then that is fine. The goal is to maintain high quality strokes, so there is no sense to rush into the next piece if you are still tired. You must always keep in mind that the purpose of these pieces is to improve speed and economy; to do that you need to row fast in good form several times over and be 100 percent ready for the next one. A general guideline is to take it easy about four times longer than you work. So after one minute at race pace you row slow for four minutes. Part of each recovery period should include easy rowing. The down side of this type of workout is that if the recovery time is too long you could cool down too much between efforts or the workout could be too time consuming on a day when your schedule is tight. But whatever it takes to get you ready to begin each piece and row at the correct pace is the right recovery for you; each set of strokes has to be treated as if it will be your best of the day.

Repetition work bouts are shorter than most intervals; they are generally less than two minutes but could be slightly longer. The pace will be faster than your long interval pace but will vary depending on the race distance you train for; a 1,000-meter race pace is higher than a 2,000-meter or head race pace. Aim to work at your current race pace or one that is about two to three seconds per 500 meters slower than your target 500-meter pace for the end of the season if you are focusing on 2k.

Quality rowing at this pace is demanding so do not overdo this intensity in your weekly schedule. Total meters per week should stay below 5,000; this amount of meters could be spread over two sessions three to four days apart or can be done in one session as well.

Example sessions include: 10 sets of 250 meters for a total of 2,500 meters, four sets of the following series (2 x 250 meters + 1 x 500 meters) alternating every other week with four sets of (2 x 250 meters + 1 x 750 meters), or 10 sets of 30 strokes gradually building to 10 sets of 50 strokes over the course of a month. You can also do reps by time such as 10 sets of one minute then 75-

seconds, 90-seconds or decide that you will row for a total 40 minutes and include short race pace pieces within that time.

Another interesting variant is called *fartlek training* and is even a little more open-ended. This Swedish term common in running and cross-country skiing in pronounced "fart-lake" and is translated as *speed play*. Fartlek workouts mix easy rowing with race pace work in one session; there is no need to necessarily achieve specific splits but you alternate between your low intensity steady speed and a perceived race pace. You can do a long session such as an hour or a short session for 30 minutes. A fun way to do this alternating type of speed work is to do a pyramid starting with 10 strokes at race pace, then paddle 10 strokes, 20 strokes at race pace, then paddle 20 strokes up to 50 strokes and then back down again. You can also choose a set distance and row 10 kilometers doing race pace bursts whenever you feel like it. This helps you build up to speed in an easy manner so you learn to stay relaxed as your stroke rates climb. Fartlek training is also a good way to prepare your body to handle accelerations within a race when you make a move and pass someone, because whenever you shift up, you will require some anaerobic energy to increase your speed. You need to be able to handle that metabolically. Even though in a time trial format rowing even splits are the more economical way to cover a set distance in the best time, physiologically, when you want to win your race you need to put up a good challenge or at least make the other guy work pretty hard to beat you.

You must learn to row fast but still be in control of your technique, stroke output, and feeling that you have another gear to call on if you need it. Having a high aerobic capacity certainly pays off in your 2,000-meter erg trial but by including repetition training you can prepare yourself to dip into those anaerobic reserves during the late stages of your event while holding your form.

NAILING YOUR ERG SCORE

A maximum 2,000-meter piece on the erg takes you through a fierce adventure. For days ahead your mind and body know it's coming. You do your race pace intervals faithfully, tune your warm-up, but eventually, the moment comes when you have to sit down on the machine, take the handle, and get ready to go. The clock ticks, and even though you're ready, you feel like you're going to fall into the abyss.

Time trials are different animals than races. Live on the water, you have competitors with strategies that they will use to try to beat you to the finish line. There are elements that can help one rower win over another besides sheer physical strength. Head races are great examples of situations where a savvy cox can shave seconds off a course or a sculler who knows where to catch the faster current on the river can gain speed. When you time trial you focus on what will make you go the fastest over the distance. On the erg this means from start to 2,000 meters. Conquering your approach to erg tests is a way to score better, learn to push your limits, and become better at racing in the boat.

The first place to start designing your piece is to know what your target 500-meter split is. As an example, we'll use an average 1:45 per 500 meters aiming for a total time of seven minutes. There are a number of ways to achieve this result. You can do your start then immediately settle into a rhythm that gives you even splits of 1:45 for each 500-meter segment. This is the most economical way to cover the distance from a physiological point of view if you know you can stay at this pace without variation. Another way is to precisely vary your speed for each quarter such as: row the first 500 at 1:44, the second 500 at 1:45, the third at 1:46, and the final part at 1:45. Using this tactic, you are prepared for the reality of lactic acid build up but stay mentally focused deep in the third 500. You will work through this tough section. You then rally for the last 500 and push the speed to gain the time you aimed for. You'll also finish in seven minutes.

For some racers, watching the count down of the meters is deadly; creating unwanted anxiety that interferes with performing. A way to stay focused on rowing each stroke well, and not on the numbers, is to work by time bites. Set a goal for each minute of the piece such as: the first minute is the start and establishing a rhythm. Minute two is for staying on your target split with a technical focus on leg drive, for minute three you shift back to feeling your rhythm combined with power. In minute four, the lactic acid is building up so you break it into five-stroke pieces to chip away at the seconds. Minute five is a mental test to hold the pace so address each stroke to get your target split. If the numbers creep up, use the next stroke to bring it down but take single strokes. When you get to the sixth minute check your monitor's meters to go, you should be in the home stretch and can push to finish strong.

Determine a plan and write it down in your logbook. No matter how detailed or general it may be practice it, physically and mentally through visualization, until you can execute it. Apply the elements of your plan in your training weeks ahead of your event. You will learn the best way to approach your race on the erg.

CHAPTER 9

COACH BOAT

VIDEO. DOCK TALK. SHAPING. PHILOSOPHY. IGOR.

DEVELOPING YOUR COACHING PHILOSOPHY

Changing your role from a rower to a coach is an exciting transition in your rowing career. Making the decision to give back to the sport and share your knowledge represents your desire to help others enjoy the aspects of rowing that have been rewarding to you. My first experience instructing was in a summer recreational rowing program at Boston University in 1982 right after my freshman year. I had a few years of sweep rowing experience, no prior coaching experience, but was eager to spread my enthusiasm about rowing. From the beginning I viewed coaching as the application of knowledge to the human endeavor and an educational process. You are a teacher as well as a trainer. My enjoyment of coaching continues to be fueled by working with athletes who are motivated and whose goal is personal improvement whatever their level of skill. At the beginning of your coaching career spend some time thinking about why you want to be a coach and what type of approach you want to take. Developing a coaching philosophy is important, as it becomes the foundation upon which you will build your program and personal style. It will guide you, your staff, and your athletes through the training process. Your coaching ideals should come natural to you and must reflect your own values. They are the ones that you will feel most at ease with teaching to your rowers and practicing on a daily basis. Your philosophy evolves throughout your career; continuing education, working with a variety of rowers, and learning from the experiences of other coaches contributes to the development of your approach and will help you refine your style.

Coaching has different purposes for rowers at various stages of their lives. You need to be aware of who your rowers are, what stage of learning they are at, and tailor your coaching to their needs. Progressing from a junior to collegiate rower then sculling competitively for several years after university, I had the opportunity to work with many coaches. Though the coaching I received at the junior level took a more hard line approach, I learned a strong work ethic, which carried through my competitive years and then into my professional life. In college, my coaches not only focused on training and winning but also shared a great deal about rowing as a lifestyle. With more experience, the dynamic with my coaches became more collective and interactive. For young athletes, coaches are an important influence on their life in terms of learning how to communicate, perform, and in building self-esteem. For those who enter the sport at a later age as competitive or recreational rowers, a coach has influence over the experiences of those they instruct. To be effective, your coaching role needs to consider the population you are working with, circumstances surrounding their lives, and their goals. In fact, changing the types of athletes you work with from time to time will broaden your skills, as you will have to adjust to a new set of goals or mindset. Regardless of the population of athletes that you work with, certain principles will guide you through your career. Here are some qualities to consider.

Consistency, confidence, and the openness to learn will strengthen your coaching and allow rowers, parents, and co-workers to have faith in your abilities. The confidence with which you approach your coaching and your job is critical. No one knows all aspects of the sport; your willingness to improve in areas you are unfamiliar with will be noticed by those you work with. Other coaches on your staff will be more likely to take the initiative to learn new things when they are in a supportive environment. If you are uncertain about training concepts, rules, or technique your athletes will perceive this. In your daily practices and at regattas, your ability to stay calm in all situations demonstrates to your crew that you can handle all situations. Your ability to work through problems earns respect of athletes and strengthens their belief in your philosophy.

Strong coach-athlete relationships develop trust and respect. Being a good listener and a sounding board can go a long way when rowers feel they can come to you with their concerns. Trust between you and your athletes will give you better insight into what influences their behavior, failures, and successes. You will be able to better motivate your athletes to reach their goals if you understand them. A common concern among rowers is that they are being dealt with fairly, especially when it comes to seat racing or boat selection. When you are able to address the concerns of individuals and handle small issues, your rowers are more likely to feel that you respect them and have their best interests in mind. Taking interest in the well being of those you are coaching pays off in the long run with a healthy team atmosphere that builds strong boats.

Stay positive; act professional and lead by example. As a leader, your actions send a message as to how you expect your team to act. When you are affirmative, professional, dress appropriately, and are punctual your conduct will be noticed. An athlete's inability to be on time can have a negative impact on your boat especially if it means being late to a regatta or even worse late to the start line. By setting an example you have a better platform to deal with such issues as they arise. Believe in your own rules and they will be easy to follow and enforce.

Set clear goals. Communicating your objectives, whether team-oriented, seasonal, or individualized, increases the likelihood of achieving them. Objectives can be part of your daily workouts, defined for specific races, or developed through the season. With every season and every new group of rowers you will have to decide what the direction of your program will take based on the circumstances.

Be organized and establish your routine. Because you will wear many hats, staying organized is essential to running your program. Your duties can include recruiting, preparing daily workouts, developing the competition schedule, making travel arrangements, assigning responsibilities to your assistant coaches, and managing all the aspects of your team's needs on regatta day. Before the beginning of each season give yourself some time to sketch out the way your program will be structured. During the season have a plan in writing that outlines what you need to accomplish daily or weekly. Include tasks that you can delegate to others. Once you get into a routine, stick to it and you will be able to make sure that even small details are taken care of. Assistant coaches or team captains are valuable resources. Delegating tasks to them can save you time and provide them with learning experiences. Take time to meet weekly with your athletes and your assistants. Short meetings keep the lines of communication open and allow sharing of any concerns that are relevant to your squad.

Help manage stress. Your coaching approach influences the way that you help your athletes cope with stress. Athletes often deal with a lot of stress in their rowing and non-rowing lives. You must also stay positive under the pressure of being effective, efficient, meeting a wide range of needs, and producing a winning team. Adults and students alike are meeting demands of work, relatives, teachers, coaches, and friends in addition to their rowing. Your willingness to provide athletes with support and your openness to their concerns can help them work through problems that might otherwise affect their performance on the team. Your ability to demonstrate staying cool and controlling your anxiety in critical situations paves the way for your squad to have great races.

Coaching is a gratifying profession, one that puts you in a position to continually develop your expertise with regard to your technical skill, level of confidence, ability to build relationships, goal setting, and constructing your own system.

You take part in the personal growth of each individual you instruct and they, in turn, are part of your growth too. Whatever the achievement level, the fact that you were instrumental in providing the opportunity for your rowers to do their best and reach the top result they were capable of is the really at the core of what we do. The habits of pursuing personal excellence carry far beyond what happens in the boat.

DOCK TALK: SCULLING INTRO

Developing the level of skill that you need to scull competitively requires a great deal of time devoted to improving stability, stroke length, acceleration, and maintaining your technique under full pressure in all water conditions. No matter how many seasons you have sculled, you will continually refine your technique making new discoveries about the stroke and how to move the boat better. The stroke is simple in concept yet often illusive. It is the wish to feel another stroke in flow and our own bodies engaged in moving the boat that keeps us dedicated to sculling for decades. We are addicts of the perfect stroke.

My coaching career started in 1982 at Boston University's Summer Recreational Rowing Program. Then continued at Middlesex School for a couple of seasons in the mid-1980s before starting to coach sculling in 1986. For the past twenty years my coaching has been predominantly at sculling camps, Craftsbury Sculling Center in Vermont and the Florida Rowing Center, in addition to giving clinics. Over the course of two decades there have been thousands of first-time scullers that I have had the opportunity to work with. Giving the dock talk introducing sculling is one of my favorite parts of any camp. Seeing how quickly one can to introduce a newcomer to the basics and getting them out in a boat to start taking strokes is something I constantly try to refine. Give the novice enough information to have a successful outing, but not overwhelming information. In a weekend camp, it is remarkably common to see someone, who was in a boat for the first time on a Friday afternoon, by Sunday morning, capture the basic motions and be ready to start practicing on their own once they return home. What is key to the initial session on the water is helping your students understand how the system of the body, oars, boat, and water interact. Rather than trying to do something to the boat, the student must become aware of how to work with the boat and learn its reactions. For those of you who will teach novice scullers or take part in a learn-to-row activity at your club here are some of the points to help guide your students through their first session.

Review how to carry the boat and handle the oars. Then go over the equipment naming all parts of the boat and the oars. Call special attention to the design of the sleeve of the oar, the shape of the blades, and the flat surfaces of the oarlocks with regard to feathering and squaring. To give them an appreciation of the power of the grip of the water on the blade, while standing on the dock take an oar. With the blade in the square position place it in the water-just let the water support the blade. Then ask each student to hold the end of the handle and try to move the blade. They will immediately feel how the water sandwiches the blade and takes hold. This small demonstration can be very helpful for the novice to gain confidence in the ability of the water to support their blades once they get into the boat. Show how to get in and out of the boat. Butting the end of the handles together towards the stern and keeping the collars against the oarlocks will hold the very boat stable. Each student should practice getting in and out a few times. Often this can be difficult if the student has poor flexibility. How much support you need to give them will depend on their general fitness level. Show how to check the footstretcher position so the oarhandles are a fist-width apart and in front of the torso about a thumb-length. Once you are in the boat push off the dock.

Orient the novices to a position of stability and make them aware of where the surface of the water is. Sit with your legs down and let the blades go flat on the water, holding the handles together at the crossover you can rock side to side to show how stable the position is. Describe the basic parts of the stroke and the position of the hands at the crossover. Row some full strokes to demonstrate the rhythm of the drive and

recovery. The real task of the first outing is to assist the sculler
to take a few successful strokes-even with just arms and body
only-and to learn how their strokes affect the boat. Review
posture, how to sit in the boat, then the points of the boat that
they are in contact with-seat, footstretchers, handles-and the
pressure against the oarlock-that will help them feel the boat
better. Encourage them to just feel what it is like to sit quietly
in the boat and know when the blades are on the water. Have
the sculler sit with their legs flat and oars feathered on the water
in the crossover position. Keeping subtle outward pressure just
square the blades and let them sit at their natural depth in the
water. Let the student see how the well the oars are designed
and that they will rest in a natural position so one doesn't have
to hold the blades in place. The water will support the blades.
Then show the student feathering the blades and then gliding
them back and forth over the surface of the water to get a sense
of the plane of the handle level.

Demonstrating how you can keep the hands light and start
taking easy strokes can be shown by rowing just arms-body,
placing the blade in the water, lean the weight of the upper
body, and drawing the handles through level with just the thumb
and index finger for two-finger rowing. When a student feels
the ease with which this can be done they will often be able to
maintain a more relaxed hold on the handles from the start and
be more careful about feeling the water. Encourage them to go
slow. Once they place all fingers on the handle you want them to
feel the handle pressing in the hook of their fingers as they relax
their bodyweight to move the boat versus trying to pull the
oars. Aim for them to feel the water support the blade giving
resistance to work against. Once the sculler can feel this rowing
arms-body only you can progress to adding the slide making the
stroke longer.

A boat familiarization exercises where the handles are lifted
and lowered on alternate sides teaches the boat's reaction to
handling the sculls. Show rowing in circles with one oar at a time

so the sculler learns to turn the boat. Keeping one oar braced against the body with blade flat on the water for stability while using the other oar, so the sculler can watch the blade of the oar they are rowing with to make sure the blade is fully squared or feathered. The sculler should practice rowing circles in both directions several times before starting to use both oars. Basic steering should be introduced, as well as, when to look over the shoulder to check in front of the boat.

This first outing is meant to provide a foundation for understanding how the equipment works, the basic stroke cycle, blade depth, posture, and fundamental maneuvering. As the sculler practices they will learn the finer points of the release and blade placement while lengthening their stroke. Eventually power application will start to be developed. Facilitating an atmosphere of enjoyment, experimentation, and a sense of adventure from doing something new will aide the progress of your sculler to start their own search for the perfect stroke.

FALL TRAINING: ONE FOOT IN

September is the velvet season, the beginning of a new annual cycle for scholastic crews. Over the next nine months, their training will progress from general preparation to specific preparation to competition, ending with championship events. Each phase has distinct physical abilities, technical skills, physiological factors, and tactics to be developed. In, *Be a Coach: FISA Coaching Development Programme Handbook-Level 2*, the general preparation period is defined as the, "longest period of the year with a high quantity of work and a gradual increase in the quality of work. Emphasis is on general aerobic endurance and improvements in mobility and strength. Specific exercises are introduced." The technical focus is on, "improvement of fundamental rowing skills with a conscious effort by the athlete to become aware of the movement pattern to be maintained and improved." It is the time for, "establishment of communication between the athlete and coach for a clear understanding of specific training objectives." This is an important point for coaches who are integrating new members into their varsity squads or working with fresh crews. Head racing performances give a coach valuable insights into the character of a new team and prove to be a good testing ground for determining the work that needs to be done during the winter months to get ready for spring.

When the autumn school docks are buzzing with curious walk-ons, you will coach good rowing skills right from the start by having a curriculum to guide you. In his collected articles, *The Slide World*, Jim Joy presents a 16-lesson plan ending with a head race. It addresses: defining terms, launching and landing, shell handling, posture, drills for balance, control, ease of motion, and group timing, concentration, plus introduces some hard work. Here is a summary of Joy's *Fall Training for Novices: High School and Universities.*

During the first five lessons all terms are defined relating to the boat, oars, and parts of the stroke. Athletes are taught to handle the equipment to and from the dock, how to enter the shell, and how to clean the shells. Launching procedures are introduced, as well as, landing by fours. Technique starts with the handgrip and the body position at the release. There is an emphasis on posture, lateral pressure, moving the blade under control, and one continuous motion at one speed. Bladework is focused on the squaring and the release action. Crews are trained how to "touch it up" with arms only progressing from pairs to all eight, then with coordination between the back and arms. Rowers are directed to feel water on the blade during the pull-through maintaining control and a steady pull. Body positions at various points on the slide: one-quarter, half, three-quarter, and full slide, are introduced with a straight back and head erect. The one-stroke-pull-through exercise from full slide is to work on constant pressure on the blade, a continuous motion at one speed, and a fluid draw with the arms flexing in a natural motion. The coach should check the oarsman's body position, hand, and head level.

The teaching of recovery timing begins from no slide then adds in the motion of the arms, the shoulders, and the seat. The relationship between the torso, the seat, and the legs should be explained. Initially, the crew works at no slide then from release to entry without a pull-through. Single-stroke rowing at one-quarter slide can then be used for practicing timing of the release and recovery.

In lessons six through ten, review movements at the entry and the release. A recommended drill is: a) no slide, blades covered-on command release the blade and extend the arms, b) no slide to half slide-on command, c) no slide to full slide-on command, d) entry-start at three-quarter slide, move forward and set the blade in one continuous two-handed motion, and e) one-stroke runs from one-quarter slide for a complete stroke cycle and body discipline. Instruct balance using hand levels then by concentration on body position and lateral pressure. Practice drills for timing: a) no slide release, b) no slide to entry, c) three-quarter slide to full for the entry, d) entry to entry for the pull-through, and e) one-quarter and half slide one-stroke rows. For bladework and balance, row by sixes and eights carrying the blades about two inches off the water, emphasize posture and lateral pressure. To start adding power, a crew rows 10 strokes firm without stopping by sixes then by eights building to 15 strokes. Then go to all eight, 20 strokes hard/ 20 strokes off x 15, attending to stroke length at each end. Work up to two 1,500-meter pieces.

The final lessons reiterate the mechanics of the entry and the release, level pull-through, timing, balance, posture, and eyes forward. Discuss the use of the legs to provide a longer stroke and power. Concentration drills for all eight include one minute each for the entry, release, pull-through, recovery, and all together repeated up to six times. Initial workouts are 20 hard strokes/ 20 light strokes x 20 sets, stressing concentration when rowing light and fartlek: 10 strokes no slide/ 10 strokes light/ 10 strokes firm/ 10 strokes hard. Build up to a long paddle. Discuss how to row a head race, row easy over the course, clean and check the shell. Be concise and clear with the race plan and race day responsibilities. Conclude the program with a head race.

The novice's first encounter with rowing is a formative one. A positive experience filled with learning and enjoyment often leads to years of participation in the sport. For upper classmen, the start of a new season is exciting and motivating. Coaches can devote time to technical work and getting reacquainted with their athletes, as well as, construct a positive competitive atmosphere. A fun exercise is to let seniors pick their crews for weekly inter-squad races and rotate who picks their crews each week. Fall festivities and good rows will prepare you for the training you need to do during the deep winter months.

SHAPING SKILLS

Steve Fairbairn is regarded as the most inspiring and innovative rowing coach of the last 150 years. His glory days were in the 1920s when he coached Jesus College, Cambridge and Thames and London Rowing to an extraordinary succession of regatta victories. Fairbairn's disciples raised standards of performance to great heights. Fairbairn, who lived from 1862 until 1938, is called the father of modern rowing. At the December 2007 USRowing Conference held in Miami, Florida, coach John Bancheri of Grand Valley State University, brought Fairbairn's spirit and important principles to a large audience of young coaches. Here are some of the main points from Bancheri's presentation, *Periodization of Technique: Shaping Exercises*, dovetailing Fairbairn's approach to coaching rowing with the process of skill development.

Fairbairn's principles for shaping rowing technique focused on the major muscle groups (legs, back, and arms), contact points (feet/legs, hips/seat, and shoulders/hands), the drive with all muscle groups overlapping to finish together, and the recovery, "fluid, relaxed, the hands pull the shoulders followed by the slide- the catch is a part of the recovery." Emphasis was on coach and athlete focusing on the blade rather than the body. Fairbairn said it was OK to look at the blade to develop the quality of the "visual rower" and felt that an oarsman learns to coach himself, "The best coach is the rower in the boat who is able to coach his own blade to perfection." Fairbairn used very visual cues. Bancheri theatrically reviewed Steve's popular prompts such as: "lateral pressure-rounded releases-strike to the balance-high feather- balance on the sill- gather and poise on the footstretcher for the entry- strike from the balance-feather down- and make the water boil!"

According to Steve, "All sports are dynamic. All successful athletes require posture, timing, control, balance, and touch." He structured the sequence of his coaching in such a way. Posture meant sitting tall as posture provides power. Timing could only be obtained by relaxing and taking your time as rushing is fatal. Control implied keeping the body braced firmly, taut, all the time against the footstretcher and the oarhandle. Balance involved keeping the boat level and keeping an even controlled weight on the oarhandle. Delicacy and cleverness in every act with clean, sharp bladework developed touch.

Bancheri says the purpose of coaching is to improve athletic performance. Practices should be designed for maximum participation because, "the more they do the more they learn," Bancheri adds, "athletes remember 10 percent of what they hear, 60 percent of what they see, and 90 percent of what they do." To prepare his crew in advance for each practice, Bancheri e-mails the daily plan including the technical focus reinforced by Fairbairn's principles, drills, and the workout of the day.

Successful coaches of beginners are masters of shaping in their sport. The novice coach is the most important coach because teaching correct neuromuscular functioning increases the chances of success. A rested athlete learns more in the first 45 minutes of practice and is best when removed from the disturbances of distractions, exhaustion, negative attitude; misunderstanding is avoided. Eliminate the word *don't* and coach in an affirmative style, "Tom, keep the blade buried." Catch the athlete performing the skill right and end on a positive note. Initially, reinforce all successes then gradually decrease the reinforcements.

The sequencing of technical drills during the shaping process includes shaping, targeting, modeling-mimicry, manipulation, and whole-part-part-whole method. Repetition is the key to establishing a skill. Shaping includes reinforcing progressive approximations of a skill. Have the same coach teach the athlete through the shaping process. Set a desired standard and establish criteria for each standard. Raise the requirements of reinforcement slowly praising small improvements. Shape only one behavior at a time, such as the release. As the athlete moves to the next step relax the previous step, for example, going from square to the feather. Use a variety of approaches such as seeing, hearing, and doing. Expect some resistance and frustration but make the shaping session your priority. If performance deteriorates, take a break, and start over.

Targeting draws the athlete's attention to the skill or focus point. An example of targeting is having an athlete focus on the release and isolating the hands. The coach then talks about focusing only on the hands, then the hands and elbows but stays focused on one skill at a time. Modeling and mimicry is demonstrating what you want the athlete to do. You can demonstrate on the erg, use video, or have experienced athletes demonstrate to others on land or on water. For example, one athlete follows another experienced athlete on the erg or two crews row side by side by four's having the non-rowing group watch the other boat while the coach points out the correct motion. Manipulation is the final aid in the shaping process. You physically move the athlete through the skill. It is done in a stationary setting or by using an athlete sitting behind another in the boat.

Getting athletes involved in behavior modification is key to success. Team rewards are the best giving athletes a sense of ownership and control, which keeps them involved and builds the system of team support. Peer rewards are more valuable than coach rewards. Coach Bancheri presented seven steps of behavior modification techniques for coaches to use during the shaping process. Step one: Define the desired skill you are teaching. Step two: Assess the current skill. Step three: Structure the situation for teaching and controlling the desired behavior. Step four: Determine methods of reinforcement. Step five: Initiate the program using immediate reinforcement gradually moving to delayed or variable reinforcement. Step six: Evaluate the program and progress. Step seven: Modify the program as necessary.

Using drills incorporates the whole-part-part-whole theory of teaching. Use stationary drills or progressive pause drills. Instruct the movement then repeat until the movement is observed to be correct. Work on one thing at a time and allow for mistakes. End each session on a positive note.

DRILLS TO SHAPE SWEEP SKILLS

In *Shaping Skills*, I reviewed the theoretical points of John Bancheri's presentation, *Periodization of Technique: Shaping Exercises* from the 2007 USRowing Conference. This part describes Bancheri's method of application.

Bancheri recommends the following guidelines for using drills in the skill shaping process. Employ the whole-part-part-whole theory of teaching Use quiet, relaxed drills such as stationary drills. Utilize progressive pause drills. Drills broken down into phases are very effective for teaching complex skills. Begin with large movements and then break the movements down into the component parts. Instruct the movement in sequence and repeat until the rowers are observed executing the motion correctly then move on to the next step. Raise the requirements of reinforcement gradually. It is important to work on one point at a time; as the athlete progresses allow for mistakes. Apply a variety of approaches that instruct the athlete to get feedback from seeing, feeling, and hearing. As new drills are incorporated the coach needs to stay focused on the goal of the session and avoid getting sidetracked. Make the early part of a practice the time for skills, ideally, the first 45 minutes. If the coach notices that the athletes' performance is deteriorating due to stress or fatigue it is necessary to repeat steps. End each session on a positive note.

Fairbairn's principles of posture, timing, control, balance, and touch are at the core of Bancheri's warm-up, drills, and workouts. Posture means sitting tall to provide power. Timing is obtained by relaxation and taking your time. Control implies keeping the body braced firmly against the footstretchers and the oarhandle. Balance involves keeping the boat level and keeping even weight on the oarhandle. Touch comes from delicacy and clean bladework. The following warm-up and drills were presented.

The "posture-timing-control-balance-touch" warm-up sequence is done by pairs, fours, and sixes. There are five components and Fairbairn's quotes are included in the instructions. First, perform the swing pick on the square with the back and arms, "The shoulders swing until the blade leaves the water." Focus on posture, 30 degrees arc, shoulder swing, and hands making circles at the release. Sit tall, "The taller you are the stronger you are, posture provides power." Take care not to perform this element too fast or the drill becomes counterproductive; maintain four to one or three to one ratio. The second step progresses to half slide on the square. Keeping the swing and adding the slide, "Slide starts when the wrist passes over the knees." Focus on body angle, early body preparation, and timing, "The hallmark of a good oarsman is a smooth relaxed recovery." Third, full slide on the square keeping the body swing, length, and catch/release angles. Control full body angle by half slide, sitting tall into the entry with shins almost vertical, butt up to the top of the slide, chest against the thighs, and chin over the inside knee with a long outside arm. Control means keeping the body taut like a rope throughout the drive and the recovery. The fourth stage of the warm-up sequence is full slide with the feather keeping all the previous steps and adding the action of bladework. Strive for uniform bladework; vertical release, feathering toward the bow, high carry over the water, early squaring, vertical entry by unweighting the hands into the entry. Balance the blade in the air on the sill of the oarlock. Aim for the "Greg Louganis" entry-no backsplash, no frontsplash, but a V-splash. Finally, move to full slide all eight or four with the feather putting all the components of the stroke together. Pay attention to a relaxed rhythm and ratio with no rush to the next stroke. The crew should row with touch-breathing and relaxing with the rhythm of the boat.

Drill sequences for posture and timing are done by partial- or whole-boat, oars squared or feathered. Double pause: pause at release hands away, coxswain says, "shoulders" pause at body angle, coxswain says, "slide" come up slide to take the stroke and pause at release hands away. Single pause: pause at release hands away, coxswain says, "shoulders" take the stroke and pause. Single pause: one-quarter slide, coxswain says, "slide" then go to half slide pause. The focus is on the posture and sequencing of body angles.

A timing-control drill is the progressive pause drill done by pairs, fours, sixes, or all eight. Sit at the release. Focus on posture, hands, and elbows, a vertical release and drop for five bobs. Repeat the same but add the feather. Then feathering the inside hand away, swinging shoulders out of the bow, pausing with the handle over the knees, blade held a blade-width over the water. Add body angle. Add one-quarter slide; begin squaring with the rolling of the wheels. Add half slide; blades squared to 45 degrees. Add three-quarter slide; blades fully squared. Another timing-control exercise is the full slide placement drill done by pairs, fours, or all eight working on a direct entry, length, and a fluid recovery.

For practicing control, have one pair stabilize the boat. Sit up at the entry, drop the blade in the water and repeat bobbing to the coaches or coxswain's cadence. Go to the Russian drill. Row the top six inches of the slide, no back, straight arms. Imagine pushing the blade with the feet. Go to full legs then full legs plus back. Shoulders swing against the leg drive, finally add in arms. All muscle groups overlapping and finishing together.

Posture development drills include exercises that emphasize positioning and keeping the outside shoulder slightly higher than the inside shoulder with a rotation around the pin: square blade rowing, outside hand only, wide grip, working to both hands feathering reinforcing posture. The final drills are for touch. The complete focus is on the blade. Teach release and squaring of the blade. Row on the square watching the bottom edge of the blade release and maintain uniform height through the recovery. Add the feather and early squaring keeping uniform height of the top edge of the blade. All drills are to emphasize good, clean rowing.

FROM THE SHELL TO THE LAUNCH

My first day coaching was not quite what I had expected it to be. A June morning about 26 years ago, I had just finished my freshman year at Boston University and was signed up as a coach for the school's summer community rowing program. At that time it was the only learn-to-row program in the area. The Charles River was generally a pretty quiet place in the summers though you might see the likes of Tiff Wood, John Bigelow, or Anne Marden training in their singles. Armed with the physiology and anatomy that I had studied as a physical therapy major plus the enthusiasm of finishing our season with a collegiate national championship, I was ready for my first job. The only problem was that I thought it started on a different day of the week. Thinking the first group would come to the boathouse on Thursday, I was unpleasantly startled when the phone rang at 6 am on Wednesday and Okie O'Connor's South Buffalo voice barked at the other end, "Where are you? All the people are here." I experienced the same typical feeling of rowing panic when you realize that you've overslept and you know your whole boat is waiting for you at the dock. I jumped on my bike, crossed the bridge near MIT, and got to the boathouse in a few minutes. It was classical summer morning with warm, humid air, and a calm river.

There were more than 70 people in the boat bays and around the dock. We had a gray flat-bottom barge that could hold 16 rowers, eight on each side. All seats in the barge were full so we shoved away from the dock. I was walking up and down the centerboard trying to think of something to say-fast. We only had 45 minutes so there was hardly time to ask people's names. We started with hands only, how to feather, how to raise and lower the handle, finding where the water was. That barge sure was slow rowing arms only. I think we went 500 meters before we had to make a giant centipede turn to the Cambridge shore and head back in. Oars were not really in sync, with some clashing going on, but the rowers were thrilled with their first outing on the river, and I was too, even though it was a bit by the seat-of-the-pants. Each session got a little better and by the end of the four-week session we held a fun regatta in the basin with all the students *racing* eights.

There are as many ways to change seats from a shell to a coaching launch as there are types of rowers to coach. Getting started in coaching is an exciting time because you are at a point where you have enough athletic confidence to begin helping others learn and enjoy the sport you do but see how much there is yet to learn. As a coach, the learning process will never stop if you don't want it to. When you are ready to start coaching you should begin to review materials pertinent to coaching and certification. The *FISA Level One Coaching Manual* is a good place to start. This well-prepared manual covers the basics of rigging, rowing physiology, technique, training methodology, fitness training, and learning methodology. It can be downloaded from the FISA website, www.fisa.org. Rowing Canada Aviron, www.rowingcanada.org, offers a competency-based training program as part of their coaching education program. RCA provides education and training for coaches ranging from the Journey One level designed to address the assist an instructor meet the needs of an entry level participant who wants to try something new to three advanced technical levels. Level one is for beginning coaches who work with novice rowers that race in local races. Level two applies to an experienced club or high school coach that trains athletes on a seasonal basis and attends regional regattas. Level three is for coaches who train rowers year round and participates in national competitions. The manuals that accompany these courses are very good reference materials. In Canada, there are also national coaching institutes. USRowing currently offers a three-level coaching certification and is the only certification program recognized by the U.S. Olympic Committee and USRowing. Courses are offered at several locations throughout the year. For more information, log on to www.usrowing.org and go to the coaching education section.

Practical experience is priceless when you start coaching. Look for opportunities to shadow coaches or go out in a launch to observe how an experienced coach works. Several universities offer work/study programs and may have options to work in the boathouse. Colleges can also have intern programs where you can combine graduate studies and coaching. Craftsbury Sculling Center has a student summer internship program for students that would like to pursue a career in coaching. Attending conferences such as the USRowing Annual Convention, The Joy of Sculling Conference, or the FISA Coaching Conference are great ways to keep up with current thinking in the sport. You can start giving private lessons, teaching indoor rowing, or doing practice exercises such as writing down a step-by-step skills outline that will help you work out for yourself the progressive approach you can take to teaching the stroke.

VIDEO ANALYSIS

Over the course of the season having regular feedback about your technique is important, as it can be difficult to rely solely on how you feel or think you look. The stroke can take a long time to master. The movements are precise and requires repetition to perfect. You need to have some way of monitoring your skill level. The analysis of video footage is a good way to study your motions, identify faults, as well as, recognize improvements in your technique. Video review gives the athlete and the coach an opportunity to work together and examine details in a way that is more controlled than on the water.

Videotaping is best done from a motorboat with one person driving and another filming. From the launch you can film the crew or sculler from the either side, each individual at the level of the rigger, as well as, from the stern or a 45-degree angle. Keep the motorboat at a speed equal to the speed of the crew when filming. In a pinch, it is also possible to film from land by having a crew row by or away from the camera. Shooting a crew from a bridge to get on overhead view is another very useful vantage point especially when looking at entry angles and stroke length. Shoot footage at varying boat speeds so you can see if there are changes in technique as the stroke rate and intensity increases.

When doing a review, the slow motion and frame-by-frame features gives you exact command over the elements of the stroke you want to look at. Be systematic as you look at a videotape of a sculler or at each member of the same crew. Some key points to identify are at each stage of the stroke: entry, drive, release, and recovery, monitor the head alignment, focus of the eyes, shoulder position, hands, and posture. Look for symmetrical movements and maintenance of posture throughout the stroke.

Observe that correct hand placement is maintained on the oarhandle during the stroke cycle. Check that lower body compression is full and the leg drive is completed. Watch for signs of upper body tension or arms-tugging implying the use of bodyweight is under-utilized during the drive and the rower is failing to lever the boat along. The quality of bladework has to be evaluated carefully at each phase. This includes entry, depth during the drive, clean release from the water, and adequate height off the water on the recovery. Timing at the entry and the release are paramount as is maintaining the speed of the handle at the transition points and completing body preparation on the recovery.

The goal is to achieve horizontal run of the boat without checking or vertical movement. Maintaining acceleration of the hull during the drive and seeing the hull increase speed after the release indicates the liveliness of the hull. For crews, a group video session is a good learning opportunity for the entire boat. To see itself as a unit and to understand collectively what style points need to be improved for better performance help give more purpose to technique workouts. Group sessions also give the coach and crew the opportunity to discuss an ideal model of the rowing stroke.

Video review is another way to look at the rig of your boat and how you are positioned in the hull. It is easier to assess compression, entry angle, and blade depth on film than it is with the naked eye. You will be better able to decide what adjustments you need to make with regards to heel height, footstretcher placement, and oarlock height when you can zero in on how you are set up in your shell and what areas my be lacking. In team boats, uniformity of stroke length is key for good power application and having the ability to observe what each rower's position is will give a coach good information to work with when making rigging adjustments.

OUR MAN FROM GUANGZHOU: AN
INTERVIEW WITH IGOR GRINKO

Igor Grinko, former national team sculling coach for the Soviet Union and the United States, is now the men's head coach of the Chinese National Rowing Team. I met with him in Munich at the first rowing world cup regatta of the 2006 season to talk about his views on coaching in different cultures.

MR: How did you get connected with the Chinese national team?

IG: In the dining hall at the Athens Olympic Games, their officials came up to Kris Korzeniowski and asked who could be recommended as a coach to prepare the team for Beijing. Kris said, pointing to me sitting at the next table, "This is the man that can help you".

MR: Why did you decide to accept their proposal?

IG: It was interesting and besides that, after Sydney, I didn't agree with USRowing's idea to only have one training base in Princeton eliminating the base in Augusta, Georgia where I was coaching. I didn't want to move to Princeton. I thought it was an unhealthy situation for our goals.

MR: Where do you live in China?

IG: According to my contract I have to be with the team all the time. We move from one training base to another, so I don't need an apartment of my own. My wife resides in Augusta, Georgia where we have spent many years while working with the US national team. She comes to see me in China.

MR: When you arrived there what did you see?

IG: I started working with the team last October. I went all around the country visiting different clubs to look for the most promising athletes. Sport schools invite gifted children to train from an early age. Richer provinces buy talented children from poorer ones. I invited only those who were the best to the national camp. Some of them are now on the team.

MR: How are athletes bought?

IG: Just like that, with money. The coaches of such schools go from town to town looking for talents. They move them to their boarding schools. Within the first two to three years they are given a general physical base. Then the children are directed to different sports according to their natural inclination. Scouts from clubs come to those schools saying they need a certain numbers of boys and girls for certain activities. Then they look through the group. The principal gives a price for each student. Actually, this tradition and style of selection comes from East Germany. Maybe it is good but the problem is even some of the gifted ones don't really know why they are put in a certain sport. It all happens at an early age. For them a good point is that they know that after this athletic career they will be given a job though they don't know in what area. The age limit is around 30 years old. An average career in the elite lasts eight years. An athletes' highest goal is to win the National Games. Everything is sacrificed for the sake of these games. Rich provinces pay $30,000 to $40,000 to an athlete for a gold medal. This is an enormous sum of money there. You can say that the orientation is more to the National Games than to the Olympic Games because it is more concrete and more promising for them.

MR: What place does rowing take in the sport hierarchy?

IG: Rowing is very important because, from the point of view of success at the National Games, it can bring many medals. It is significant to note that they think about only gold medals; besides gold there is nothing. A champion becomes a national hero. Successful athletes and coaches get many promotions. Coaches that are failures disappear from the scene immediately.

MR: As a head coach, do you have any problems in your relations with the other coaches?

IG: Because of the very strong system of hierarchy there is no room for bad relations. This society is based on authority. When I ask a coach to do something he does it. There is no discussion. Maybe I don't agree with such a system but for me it is convenient. I don't know if it is good for the final results. I teach them long-term planning and general methods of training.

MR: What is the diet of an athlete; is it like what you would see on typical Red Dragon menu?

IG: Yes, a lot of vegetables and noodles. Until recently there was a lot of seafood too but I started insisting that cooks prepare more meat for my team. In the Soviet Union, the diet in our camps was coordinated with our training sessions. So when we trained for speed, strength, endurance etc. we accordingly changed the diet. We have now started doing this in our camps. Each meal there is five or six dishes to choose from; portions are unlimited. Many excellent cooks travel with the team. The authorities issued strict laws against using drugs. If one is caught he is sent home immediately without any discussion, losing everything from his career to the respect of all people. Nor can coaches or doctors afford such a risk. Everyone wants the situation before the Olympic Games to be clean and peaceful.

MR: How do your athletes rest?

IG: The Soviets had five to six days free each month to visit family, here it is not the case. My guys only go home once a year for two to three weeks after the world championships. So the camp situation is non-stop and forever. I want them to stay human, not just be machines, which is why I insist that we regularly go on excursions or to the movies. I try to entertain them psychologically. This part of preparation was not "popular" before I came to coach. There is a traditional belief that sportsmen should be disciplined in a military fashion so from time to time a group of officers come to the camps and have the boys and girls drill under their command for a few days in a row. I try to explain that this just steals time from training but no one listens to me. If you want, you can look at it as a type of entertainment.

MR: You have coached in three systems; your comparison?

IG: If I could unite the best features of all three systems that would be my ideal. In the U.S. it is hard for young athletes to have real long-term motivation or concentration because they are oriented to their profession and earning money. In China, once athletes become involved in sport they don't need to think about their future because this is their profession. It is the best money they can earn by any means. This situation is excellent for their families too because it is a great honor to have an elite athlete in your family. In the Soviet Union, the philosophy of sport was connected with the image of heroism and this image of the hero was connected to ideology. To be an athlete was not as much about money as with the prestige it brought. It was not about personal health it was about deeds for the sake of your country. The same was true in the eastern block countries. The whole society was giving moral support to athletes along with the government. Now in Russia and in some other former republics of the Soviet Union, leaders like Putin and Lukoschenko of Belorussia try to rebuild this support system.

MR: What are the weaknesses of your Asia rowers?

IG: These athletes are completely obedient and show no initiative. They are ready to be your slave and not ready to discuss anything. An American is self-conscious. An American needs explanations and proofs from a coach and only then he will execute the task. He very often wants to debate. He is, however, a more independent thinker.

MR: And the strengths?

IG: A typical Chinese rower can workout as many hours as

you want. If you tell him five hours he will do five hours; if you tell him 10 hours he will do 10 without questions or showing fatigue. That is the result of thousands of years of traditional work ethic. In Russian, Ukrainian, and other Slavic cultures, though often chaotic and undisciplined, athletes have something I would call "fire in their blood" and that is their strong point.

MR: Where will you be preparing your team for the 2008 Olympic Games?

IG: We have a main training base in Guangzhou, north of Hong Kong up the Pearl River, one in Shanghai, and many others all over the country. We use all of them. We never stay long in one place.

MR: What is your goal?

IG: Our goal is gold.

AUTHOR: MARLENE ROYLE

Marlene Royle is one of the earliest coaches in the United States dedicated to masters rowing. Marlene's career began in 1982 coaching the Boston University Summer Recreational Rowing Program, a community sweep program on the Charles River. Next, Marlene was the varsity girl's coach at Middlesex School in Concord, Massachusetts in 1986 and 1987. In 1986, she joined the coaching staff at the Craftsbury Sculling Center in Vermont, working in various levels of the program for 20 years, including associate director from 2004 until 2006. Marlene now coaches sculling at the Florida Rowing Center.

In 1999, Marlene founded Roylerow Performance Training Programs to individually train rowers. Designing workouts and providing support via e-mail; www.roylerow.com was the first online coaching service for rowing. Marlene's athletes soon started reaching the podiums of major regattas. Marlene's coaching has produced numerous world masters medalists, masters national champions, Head of the Charles winners, and personal bests. Her programs are also used by coaches, pre-elite athletes, and juniors, as well as, those training for general health, re-entering the sport after injury, or just starting to compete.

As a competitor, Marlene has won major titles in sculling and sweep rowing including a U.S. national championship in the elite lightweight women's quad, a collegiate national championship in the novice eight, and a Head of the Charles title. She was awarded the Melissa Hale Spencer Award at the

West Side Rowing Club of Buffalo in 1980 and the Beverly Jean Cook Award while on the Boston University Rowing Team in 1982. Royle also served as Boston University crew's varsity women's captain in 1985. In 2000, she set two world records on the Concept2 Indoor Rower. She is a registered occupational therapist, with additional education in physiology, massage therapy, and strength training. Her first rowing book *Skillful Rowing* was co-authored with Ed McNeely and published in 2002. *Tech Tips* is Marlene's column on the Craftsbury Sculling Center website and her column appears monthly in the *Get Better* section of the journal, *Rowing News*.

Coaching Philosophy

Marlene's love of coaching is fueled by working with athletes who are motivated to improve and whose primary goal is personal excellence. Marlene designs and delivers training plans that provide the knowledge to increase your performance. Giving physical, mental, and strategic coaching in combination with technical support and constructive advice, Marlene is dedicated to helping you maximize your rowing skills.

Coaching is the application of knowledge to the human endeavor; Marlene views coaching as a personal educational process. She is not simply a trainer but a teacher for her Roylerow athletes so they learn more about themselves and their physiology. Marlene's systematic methodology guides her athletes to be successful competitors and the champions they want to be.

Training for rowing and sculling is a commitment. With the time involved it is important that your training be done right. If your goal is improvement then the purpose of hiring a coach is to work with someone who considers your individual needs, ensures that you train correctly, and gives you feedback. Marlene Royle's mission is to provide quality coaching options for rowers ready to take the next step towards achieving their goals.

Marlene Royle, OTR, offers training services for rowing and sculling that range from designing individual exercise programs to one-time consultations for athletes and coaches. Your training program is the most important tool to guide you through the competitive year. Based on the principles of training and periodization, Marlene will help you establish objectives, systemize your workouts, and review your progress with you. Successfully combining her medical training, professional teaching skills, and competitive rowing experience with knowledge of physiology, nutrition, and sport psychology, Marlene works with you to develop a training plan that will help you perform better.

To contact Marlene Royle e-mail to roylerow@aol.com or go to the web site, www.roylerow.com.

ARTIST: VLADIMIR FOMIN

Front cover painting:
For Sampo to Sariola
© 1996 Vladimir Fomin
Riihimaki Art Museum, Finland.

The heroes of *Kalevala* set out in a boat to find happiness. Each of them dreams about his happiness, but the search for individual happiness leads to the heroes' unity. "We all sit in one boat," says the artist. "And, what is most interesting," he adds, "the road is not getting any shorter."
-Vladimir Fomin on *For Sampo to Sariola*

Vladimir Fomin was born in 1963 in Tomsk, Siberia, and now lives and works in the capital of Karelia, Petrozavodsk. Soon after finishing his art education in 1989, the artist began participating in art exhibitions, where he presented works in his unique style. This style is the synthesis of traditional and lubok-colorful Russian folk engraving, folk ornament, and avant-garde innovations, combined with neo-primitivism, abstract, and surrealist elements. Fomin's art immortalizes many important cultural, historical, religious, and philosophical achievements of Northern European countries, particularly in the series *Vespa* related to the beliefs of ancient Karela and Vespa tribes, *Kizhi* inspired by the wooden architecture on the Kizhi island, and *Kalevale* based on the famous Karelian-Finnish epic, among many others.

In 1995, Fomin received the Best of Europe prize at the Corel World Design Contest in Ottawa, for a computer version of his painting *The Artist*. Vladimir has had more than 21 one-man shows in Russia and abroad. About 700 works of the artist can be found today in private collections, museums, and galleries in Russia, U.S., Finland, Sweden, Norway, and Germany. During Fomin's exhibition tour in Finland, Sweden, and Norway, more than 50,000 viewers saw the *Kalevala* series. Web site: www. onego.ru/fomin.

9167319R1

Made in the USA
Lexington, KY
03 April 2011